The best word to describe Bob Stuart's book ⸻⸻⸻ is *edifying*. As an experienced pastor with a burden for shepherds and sheep, he writes to strengthen the church by strengthening its leaders. I know firsthand that he knows what he is talking about—God used him to help heal my home church after a terrible split! Bob speaks biblical and practical truth into many areas of leaders' lives. This book is not for the faint of heart; it is strong medicine written by a man of God to men of God who want to be what Christ wants them to be and to do what he wants them to do. I commend it highly to church leaders, their pastors, church planters, and believers who want to pray more intelligently for their leaders, who keep watch over their souls and will have to give an account to the Chief Shepherd.

 —**Robert A. Peterson**, Professor of Systematic Theology, Covenant Theological Seminary

Poorly thought-out leadership changes, failures of succession plans (or no plans at all), and a lack of shepherding the flock through these things to locate Christ's mission and purpose—all these have left congregation after congregation wounded and weak. This book is replete with lessons, practical advice, and biblically grounded plans for leading a congregation into a new day of hope for congregations all across America. I commend it with prayers for revival and renewal in the church today.

 —**Michael A. Milton**, Chancellor/CEO Elect, Reformed Theological Seminary

Pastor Stuart is winsome and practical, yet he pulls no punches as he instructs pastors, elders, and other church leaders to take the necessary steps in pulling their churches out of decline, by God's grace. This book provides for critical self-examination, humble piety, and inspired transformation.

 —**Elliott S. W. Pinegar**, Former Pastor, First Presbyterian Church

Failed leadership is at the heart of church conflict—a difficult summation to hear, but one that must be believed and embraced if change is ever to occur. Failed leadership resulting in church conflict—and then frequently the flight of the pastor, leaving the pulpit empty—has given rise to the need for a church doctor to examine the issues and prescribe healing to revitalize a hurting congregation. Bob Stuart is such a doctor—one who diagnoses the sickness in the church, exposes the practice of poor church leadership, and prescribes the cure. Leaders, pastors, and church planters are encouraged to read this book, which will help them become the leaders they were called to be.

  —**David V. Edling**, Author, *Redeeming Church Conflicts*

Although pastors enter ministry with high expectations that they, like the apostles, will devote themselves to "prayer and to the ministry of the word," they soon learn that there is more required of them. Something that they are often ill prepared for: leadership. And unless they learn to lead well, they will fail in ministry. And so will their churches.

  As someone who has led a company, pastored a church, and trained future pastors, I have read a number of books on leadership. Not one of those books, however, has been as practical and as full of real-life examples as Bob Stuart's. Purchase it, put it on your bedside table, read it in the morning to prepare to lead well, and review it at night to see where you went wrong.

  —**Michael W. Honeycutt**, Senior Pastor, Westminster Presbyterian Church

CHURCH
REVITALIZATION
FROM THE INSIDE OUT

CHURCH
REVITALIZATION
FROM THE INSIDE OUT

ROBERT D. STUART

P&R
PUBLISHING
P.O. BOX 817 • PHILLIPSBURG • NEW JERSEY 08865-0817

Library of Congress Cataloging-in-Publication Data

Names: Stuart, R. D., 1945-
Title: Church revitalization from the inside out / Robert D. Stuart.
Description: Phillipsburg : P&R Publishing, 2016. | Includes index.
Identifiers: LCCN 2015024862| ISBN 9781596388734 (pbk.) | ISBN 9781596388741 (epub) | ISBN 9781596388758 (mobi)
Subjects: LCSH: Christian leadership. | Pastoral theology. | Church renewal.
Classification: LCC BV652.1 .S78 2016 | DDC 253--dc23
LC record available at http://lccn.loc.gov/2015024862

To my wife, Deena,
my soul mate, my encourager, and the love of my life

Contents

Foreword

Several years ago I was on a ministry trip to one of those countries that required me to receive several "unusual" vaccinations before I could leave the United States. The flight was very long, and, once I arrived, my scheduled appointments began almost immediately. After three successive days of fulfilling numerous ministry commitments in several different cities, I was worn out and illness had overtaken me. I needed a doctor, but what I wanted was *my* doctor—the man who knew me best. I had an unsettling feeling that my worsening condition was different from the usual colds, food poisoning, or common forms of flu that can accompany foreign travel. I wanted a solid diagnosis and recovery plan, no matter how distasteful or restrictive, that not only would allow me to continue to function but would also restore me to full health and prevent an even worse long-term condition. I didn't have any confidence in the quality of medical care I might receive in this distant land, so I did nothing but press on with my schedule. That was a mistake.

Many churches needing a "doctor" due to their congregations' cultural ill health make the same mistake. The symptoms are there and are evident to almost everyone, but the risks involved in taking steps to confront the many elements of dysfunction too often delay an accurate diagnosis and the development of a meaningful recovery plan. The necessity to continue to function (to maintain a certain *status quo* of expectation), to meet the demands of those pursuing their own narrow agendas, and simply the *fear of man* and *fear of change* mean that nothing is done. And that is a mistake. I have seen too many churches wither and die because church leaders failed in one of their primary shepherding functions: leadership.

My friend Dr. Bob Stuart takes on the role of "doctor" in this book as he examines the symptoms, gives a needed diagnosis, and recommends a recovery plan to move the unhealthy church to renewed vitality. This book is truly a diagnostic manual of both the common and uncommon illnesses that our churches face today. In it he unpacks, in a practical and meaningful manner, the symptoms of the ailing church and its major disease: "failed leadership." But this is no ordinary book on church leadership. Just as I experienced during my trip, difficult choices need to be faced: whom to trust, what to do, and when to take corrective action. Drawing on the leadership experience from a lifetime of roles such as combat Marine officer, attorney, church planter, senior pastor, and intentional interim minister, Bob takes us on a very frank and often painful journey into the ailing church and its most degenerative disease. Heavily salted with illustrative stories from his own experiences of over thirty years as a pastor, with accounts of the failures and triumphs of leaders from church history, and with familiar biblical stories of the leaders of the early church, Bob's book establishes the patterns of failed leadership and then prescribes the biblical cure.

You know the people who are at the heart of church conflicts, because they are the same in every church. But few leaders respond to these difficult sheep in a manner that actually changes the outcomes. This book practically and decisively points the way. This is no ordinary book on dealing with church conflicts and difficult people, however. Rather, with trust and hope in God's sovereign leadership, Bob never forgets whose church it is that we are called to shepherd. We are continually pointed to the true Physician and to his plan for his church. You and your church have already faced—or will likely face—times of trial: conflict, confusion, ill health . . . even deadness. Preparing now for that season or recovering from it means confronting the need to draw from new perspectives about old problems. I encourage every pastor and every elder to read and study this exceedingly readable, entertaining, practical, and biblically faithful manual.

Ken Sande
Founder of Relational Wisdom 360 and Peacemaker Ministries
Author of *The Peacemaker*

Acknowledgments

I wish to thank the following people:

Robert A. Peterson, professor of systematic theology at Covenant Seminary, whose labor in editing this book was a godsend. He reshaped my thinking and exhorted me to persevere in the rewriting process.

Dave Edling, formerly of Peacemaker Ministries and coauthor with Tara Barthel of *Redeeming Church Conflicts: Turning Crisis into Compassion and Care*, who read the first draft, acknowledged the need for the book, and encouraged me to continue writing.

Rev. Elliott S. W. Pinegar, then pastor of First Presbyterian Church in Bad Axe, Michigan, who reviewed and edited some of the chapters. These insights and encouragement from a young pastor inspired me to persist in my revisions.

The dedicated pastors and leaders of Christ's church, who seek to glorify God in their ministries and desire to shepherd God's flock without much honor, recognition, or gratitude. I admire them for weathering the storms of ministry without complaint, and for doing so with a servant's heart.

INTRODUCTION

Ailing Churches

So with yourselves, since you are eager for manifestations of the Spirit, strive to excel in building up the church. (1 Cor. 14:12)

THE LEADERSHIP FACTOR

There are many wonderful and dedicated leaders within the church who have been challenged by their calling, slighted by the culture, and fatigued by their service in their congregations. The church is at war, and leaders are encouraged to pick up the sword of the Spirit and do battle with the enemy. This book is not about a particular style of leadership; it is about encouraging leaders to stay faithful and avoid the pitfalls of poor leadership. Weak leaders produce weak churches, and weak churches are ineffective in reaching a dying culture with the gospel of Christ.

Although there are churches doing mighty things for the Lord, others are languishing in a culture that seeks to make them irrelevant. Those that struggle in reaching society with the gospel have probably fallen prey to a chronic ailment—poor leadership. There are many wonderful leaders in the church, but the plethora of church quarrels and the decline in church efficacy for spreading the gospel prove that there are sundry others that need retooling and revitalization. Leaders need to know the pitfalls of their calling in order to sharpen their skills as shepherds in the church.

Throughout the book, I use the word *elder* as the term for a leader in the church, but I have every intention of including Baptist deacons,

Episcopal vestrymen, Methodist council members, and the like. When I write *session*, I also mean *elder board or leadership council*. It doesn't matter what church leadership is called; though there are many extraordinary shepherds in the church, the major illness in most denominations is the same—weak or poor leadership. My hope is that this book will encourage the faithful, refresh the tired, and reinvigorate the struggling—all with the threefold goal to shepherd sheep, to spread the gospel, and to wage war against the forces of evil.

AILING CHURCHES

Statistics do not lie; and what they tell us about the church is that God's *ecclesia* is ailing and is urgently in need of treatment. The Hartford Institute for Religion Research claims that 59 percent of all Protestant churches average between 7 and 99 attendees, and 35 percent average between 100 and 499.[1] Size, however, doesn't matter when it comes to controversy, for the American Congregations Study of 2008 reported that, steadily from 2000 to 2008, approximately 75 percent of all churches had conflict within the previous five-year period over matters of money, worship, and leadership.[2] Conflict invariably leads to disgruntled people who either leave the church or withhold their giving, resulting in ineffective ministry and damaging church vibrancy.

Ed Stetzer claims that 80 percent of North American churches are stagnant or declining.[3] Harry Reeder agrees and, in his book *From Embers to a Flame*,[4] lists the factors of regression, such as falling attendance, a drop in giving, living in the past, reliance on dominant personalities, a mentality of maintenance in keeping the status quo, a bad reputation in the community, and the lack of gospel centrality.

1. "Fast Facts about American Religion," Hartford Institute for Religion Research, accessed November 18, 2015, http://hirr.hartsem.edu/research/fastfacts/fast_facts.html, quoting the National Congregations Study done by Duke University.

2. David A. Roozen, *American Congregations 2008* (Hartford: Hartford Institute for Religion Research, 2009), 26, available online at http://faithcommunitiestoday.org/sites/faithcommunitiestoday.org/files/American_Congregations_2008.pdf.

3. Ed Stetzer, *Planting New Churches in a Postmodern Age* (Nashville: Broadman & Holman, 2003), 10.

4. Harry L. Reeder III, *From Embers to a Flame: How God Can Revitalize Your Church* (Phillipsburg, NJ: P&R Publishing, 2008), 7.

The spiritual health of the local church is directly related to the spiritual health of her leaders. When the health of leaders improves, so too does the health of the church. Ailing churches, however, have a hard time recognizing their illness. Leaders have difficulty hearing that they lead dying or stagnant churches, for it is a reflection on their leadership. Good leaders, however, confront the facts, analyze the situation, and take action to revitalize their churches.

THE BALM OF GILEAD

Leaders should not be surprised that churches at various times will need revitalization, or that it begins with them. Throughout Scripture, leaders are warned by the Lord to take their calling seriously and to heal his church when it is sickly. The Lord, through the voice of Jeremiah the prophet, asked, "Is there no balm in Gilead? Is there no physician there? Why then has the health of the daughter of my people not been restored?" (Jer. 8:22). The physician whom God had in mind was a leader like Jeremiah who would speak truth—diagnosing the disease of the people, which is sin, and prognosticating the remedy, which is repentance and reconciliation with God and with men.

According to Jeremiah, the Israelites needed a doctor to professionally apply the healing balm of Gilead. The nation had been under siege by Nebuchadnezzar and had suffered for two years before falling to the Babylonian king. Evidently, no doctor or leader surfaced to apply the treatment and encourage repentance before God. The result was captivity, which was the Lord's treatment plan of disciplining his people for their iniquities in order to draw them back to him.

Israel is portrayed as a person dying of a mortal disease because she sinned against God, provoking him to discipline the people he loves. Although Jeremiah had warned the Israelites of their sin and urged them to repent, they, along with their leaders, did not heed his advice and continued to go their own way. Jeremiah was God's physician, sent to the house of Israel, but they refused his house call.

There is a balm in Gilead, for there has never been a deficiency of God's grace or a lack of means of applying it! Of course, the head surgeon is God himself, who is ever ready to perform surgery to heal his people and apply the balm of forgiveness to bring reconciliation to his wandering sheep. Yet the Lord prefers to send his resident doctors—that is, leaders in his church—to rule and shepherd "in the grace and knowledge of our Lord and Savior Jesus Christ" (2 Peter 3:18).

Good leaders are definitely needed to rule Christ's church. Poor leaders cause congregational turmoil and foster the straying of sheep. Schism normally results, pastors resign or are asked to leave, and leaders become confused about what they should do. Rather than looking toward God for his healing balm, poor leaders tend to look inward, make decisions based on expediency, and discover they have a deeper problem than first realized. Convinced that they have their own homeopathic remedy, they apply temporary Band-Aids to deeper lesions—or, worse yet, they refuse to do anything, causing wounds to worsen. In fact, weak leaders don't want a cure for their maladies; they merely want relief from the present conflicts. They view their own illness as just a cold that will pass in time when, in fact, they have double pneumonia that may be slowly killing their people. What a local church needs is the "balm of Gilead"—God's medicine for a hurting congregation, which is found in strong and wise leaders who apply God's wisdom to the needs of the church. The church is definitely ailing, and a major disease is poor leadership.

THE BOOK

As a diagnostic manual, this book lists the symptoms of poor leadership—such as bad decisions, the guise of uniformity, gossip, sacred cows, irreconcilable attitudes, fear of change, and lack of vision. To overcome the symptoms of failure, leaders will be encouraged to look toward and emulate the leadership style of Jesus, which will foster health in leadership and vitality in the congregation.

Leaders who demonstrate faith, forgiveness, frankness, and flexibility provide incentive for sheep to follow. Trusting God is the key to good leadership,[5] but trust will not happen if leaders do not love the

---

5. "Blessed is the man who trusts in the LORD, whose trust is the LORD. He is like a tree planted by water, that sends out its roots by the stream, and does not fear when heat comes, for its leaves remain green, and is not anxious in the year of drought, for it does not cease to bear fruit" (Jer. 17:7–8).

Lord; and love will not occur if leaders do not know the God of Scripture. The more we know God, the more we come to love him; and the more we love him, the more we will trust him. And the more we trust him, the easier it is to discover his will for the church.

1

Healthy Leadership

Pay careful attention to yourselves and to all the flock, in which the Holy Spirit has made you overseers, to care for the church of God, which he obtained with his own blood. (Acts 20:28)

LEADERS TAKE CHARGE

The greatest leader in all history was Jesus Christ. In less than four years of ministry, he inspired loyalty and devotion in little-known disciples who were willing to die for him. His followers spread his gospel throughout the Roman world in the face of danger and with little recompense. And now, two thousand years after he walked the earth, Christ has followers in every nation on it, numbering more than one billion, and the organization he founded—the church—remains a powerful force throughout it.

We see Christ in Joshua 5 demonstrating his "take charge" leadership style when he encounters Joshua, Moses' handpicked replacement, whose name also means "God saves." In this Christophany—an appearance of the Son of God—Christ appeared to Joshua as the captain of the Lord's army. Joshua first saw a man whom he quickly questioned, "Are you for us, or for our adversaries?" (Josh. 5:13). Curiously, the answer of this sword-carrying man was "No!" (No what? "No, I'm not for you!" or, "No, I'm not for those who hate you!"?) He said he had come as captain of the Lord's army, which meant that Joshua was under his command. The question by leaders should never be whether God is on their side, but rather, "Are we on the side of the Lord?" It is the Lord who directs, and the duty of elders is to discern that direction according to God's Word.

This Man who confronted Joshua was the Son of God, the eternal Word, and the right hand of the Power of God. Joshua immediately understood and gave him divine honors by bowing before him in worship (Josh. 5:14). Since the Man accepted the worship, which a created and devoted angel would not have done, by instructing Joshua to take off his shoes (for he was standing on holy ground), we are assured that this captain of the Lord's army was Christ himself (Josh. 5:15).

Note that Christ had his sword drawn, which gave Joshua confidence to wage war with strength and energy. Christ's drawn sword denotes how ready he is to defend his people and to fight their enemies who seek to destroy and neutralize them. Healthy leaders recognize that the church is at war and will therefore prepare themselves for battle.

Joshua is our example of a great leader who accepted his calling and took charge to lead a nation into a land filled with enemies. The book of Joshua recounts the conquest of Canaan under the leadership of Joshua. It opens with his commissioning by the Lord to be the leader of the Israelites. As the nation's leader, Joshua was exhorted to be strong and courageous, for the Lord was with him; and since God was his companion and cohort, no one could deter his objective of securing Israel's inheritance (Josh. 1:2–7).

The one requirement for success was Joshua's faithfulness to the law of Moses. Church leaders today have the same exhortation—to be strong in the Lord and courageous to fight the spiritual battles that cause disruption to the peace of the sheep. They are to remain loyal to their instruction manual, which is the Word of God, and to show enthusiasm in serving the people of God. Godly leadership in the local church is a virtuous and "noble task" (1 Tim. 3:1), and it leads to good standing within the congregation (see 1 Tim. 3:13). Like Joshua, church leaders may experience the pleasure of seeing Christ bear spiritual fruit in and through them. They will conquer obstacles, serve as instruments of reconciliation, and receive the blessings of others as they willingly and eagerly minister to the sheep that have been placed under their care. Good leaders follow the example of Christ and, in so doing, will receive an "unfading crown of glory" from the Chief Shepherd (1 Peter 5:4).

PARITY OF LEADERSHIP

When men are set aside for the office of elder, all are equal in authority. There is no hierarchy within the body of elders, for all are called by the same Lord and led by the same Spirit. This does not mean, however, that all are equally gifted, for the Spirit determines the type of gift as well as the measure of that gift given to officers in the church (1 Cor. 12:11). Although they occupy the same office, elders are diverse in giftedness and leadership ability, for God raises up leaders among leaders. The twelve disciples of Jesus are examples of this. As apostles, the Twelve were equal in position and authority, but Peter, and eventually Paul, were considered leaders among them.

There is, however, a great temptation for leaders, for authority brings power, and power tends to corrupt. William Pitt, the British prime minister from 1766 to 1778, once said in a speech to the House of Lords in 1770, "Unlimited power is apt to corrupt the minds of those who possess it."[1] Lord Acton, the British historian and moralist, also opined on power in a letter to Bishop Mandell Creighton in 1887 in which he said, "Power tends to corrupt, and absolute power corrupts absolutely."[2] To prevent corruption, church leaders are to recognize the parity of elders—all are equal in rule and ministry. No one is greater than another, although some may have greater leadership skills, as did Peter and Paul. When one seeks to exert influence over others negatively, a split in the elder board will surface, conflict will result, and the peace and unity of the church will be disrupted.

LEADERSHIP STYLES

Churches are in constant struggles, for the enemy prowls about looking for ways to neutralize them in promoting the gospel. Leadership

---

1. Quoted in *The Speeches of the Right Honourable the Earl of Chatham in the Houses of Lords and Commons*, new ed. (London: Aylott & Jones, 1848), 94.
2. John Emerich Edward Dalberg-Acton, *Historical Essays & Studies*, ed. John Neville Figgis and Reginald Vere Laurence (London: Macmillan, 1907), 504.

is not easy, for churches are wounded from the battles. Healthy leaders, however, make healthy churches. There is a correlation between the health of a church body and the strength of godly leadership. Elders are to be taught and trained what it means to shepherd their flock. Good leaders will be patient, dedicated to the people, and humble in their interaction. Too commonly, however, men are nominated for office because they are known businessmen or friends of the pastor, or because they have substantial influence in the congregation. Some may attend leadership classes that mainly teach church doctrine and the rudimentary duties of elders. Doctrine is important, but churches are also encouraged to train leaders as shepherds who demonstrate love, care, and discipline.

There are three primary management styles seen in church elders: the "cattleman," the "drover," and the "shepherd." Only the shepherd is a healthy style, while the other two represent corpulent and anorexic conditions, respectively. Cattlemen symbolize obesity because they over-indulge in their self-importance. They have a dominant managerial style that drives people to the place they want them to be. They make backroom decisions, think more in terms of the negative, and are critical when their goals and desires are not met. They set their own agendas, become the core elite on the elder board, and foolishly think that their decisions are best for the church, when in fact they are best for themselves or the pastor whom they blindly support.

Churches usually have cattlemen within their leadership board. I once had to confront a number of men at a church who had formed their own executive committee and ruled with an iron will. Since their talented pastor had been part of this group, they formed various minis-tries with separate boards on which they sat, made financial and ministry decisions that affected the congregation at large, and thought nothing about any conflict of interest. When confronted with the apparent conflict, they were incredulous that I would even mention it. I told them that their first calling was to shepherd the flock of their church. Being on other ministry boards was their choice; but when sitting as a church elder and representing the people, they had to abstain from any discussions and votes that would benefit another ministry of which they were a board member, even when that ministry was intricately connected to the church. Voting money and resources from the tithes of the congregation, or allowing the services of the staff to benefit another organization that elders have an interest in, is assuredly a conflict of interest. This is a violation of a church leader's fiduciary responsibilities in overseeing the tithes and gifts to the church.

Drovers represent anorexia because they are slim in importance and do not understand what a healthy church body looks like. They have a distorted self-image and fail to see that their tendency to be supportive of the cattlemen affects their own spiritual growth, keeping them undernourished in true leadership principles. Drovers normally vote with cattlemen because of the perceived influence of these cattle barons. They therefore act as hirelings to the cattlemen because they move and tend the cattle for approval from the cattlemen, not realizing that sheep are not cattle and cannot be driven. They must be led! Drovers are the nice guys who hate confrontation. They are favorably looked upon by the congregation and are easily voted onto boards and committees. They are like reeds in the wind, however, and will bend to the side that they identify as most dominant and influential. They easily fall into the pattern of being "yes men" for the cattle barons and the pastor because they are thin in courage and they go along with the status quo.

A church that I was familiar with had more than thirty elders. I would categorize them into three groups—the progressives, the peacekeepers, and the Bible-centric group. The progressives, as cattle barons, were only a handful of men but wielded the most influence, in both power and money. The peacekeepers were the drovers and numbered about fourteen, which was about the same number in the Bible-centric group, also known as the shepherds. Although the peacekeepers would have biblical views more closely aligned with the Bible-centric group, they cast votes that supported the progressives, which allowed the progressives to mold the church into their image. The writing was on the wall, for decisions made by the progressives and supported by the peacekeepers were not in line with the general character of the congregation and eventually had a detrimental effect on parishioners' ability to understand the direction of the church. The result was a scattering of the sheep, who drifted into other pastures where they found more of a Bible-centric ministry. Leaders who felt disenfranchised also left, seeking churches that were more in line with their philosophy of ministry.

Shepherds are the healthy third category of leadership and are servant-leaders who have the concern of the sheep in mind. They are pleasant and polite most of the time but are firm and steadfast when they have to be. They are seen where the sheep are found, are unobtrusive in their leadership style, and have the ability to motivate and empower others. People enjoy being with them, working for them, and supporting them in their ministerial calling. These leaders have the moral fortitude to act decisively, for they understand that their calling from Christ is to tend and care for their sheep. They use their experience to act wisely, to set proactive agendas, and to deal immediately with problematic issues.

An example of a shepherd-elder is a friend of mine who had a number of families under his oversight in a medium-sized church. One of his sheep, an employee of the church, was having problems with an assistant pastor. When she confronted the pastor with her concerns, tensions escalated. She was subsequently summoned to his office to meet with him and a member of the personnel committee who had a reputation for austerity and inflexibility. Needing an advocate, she asked this elder friend to attend the conference and give her support as her shepherd.

This he did. Although the meeting was unfruitful, with no issues being resolved, my friend stood in the gap, defended his sheep, and reprimanded the two men for the way they were treating a young woman. Sheep need help and intervention in times of need and discouragement. The shepherd-elder is called to provide this comfort and defense, if needed, against those who would seek to disturb God's flock.

Sheep are not to be driven; they are to be led! Making board decisions without legitimate concern for the sheep is like negotiating cattle deals in the back room of a saloon, then hiring cowhands (pastors and staff) to move the sheep in the direction of the vision (that is, a cattle drive). Such decisions eventually lead to conflict in the church because the sheep feel abandoned, run over, and not cared for. And then comes the war between the cattlemen and the shepherds, for cattlemen dislike sheep crowding their pastures!

TROUBLE IN THE CHURCH

During the 1880s and 1890s, controversy in the West between American cattle ranchers and unwanted sheepmen led to the death of many a cattleman and shepherd. Range wars were fought over land, water rights, and the issue of sheep overgrazing grasslands. These range wars still occur in the church, for cattlemen and shepherds still vie for territory called "the congregation." Leadership splits cause great controversy in the church, leading to discouragement and the eventual scattering of the sheep, who seek more peaceful pastures.

I have also found in some churches deflated leaders who were once excited about ministry, but who have become uninterested in their roles as overseers and shepherds of the people. These leaders experienced conflict, suffered innuendo and gossip, and were attacked for being uninvolved with or uncaring of the sheep. Although the assaults for the most part were unwarranted, constant harping tends to take its toll, and wisdom for governing the church suffers. If Scripture insists that the wise are strong and that wisdom and understanding build the house (Prov. 24:3–5), why then is God's church mired in stagnancy and becoming more irrelevant in a post-Christian culture? The answer is poor leadership—the major illness in today's church!

Not all leaders are poor and ineffective, but statistics over the past fifteen to twenty years demonstrate that American churches are either stagnant or in decline. Ed Stetzer, writing in 2003, stated that 80 percent of churches were trending downward.[3] With the closing of between four thousand and seven thousand churches each year, the percent of decline has not decreased since his book was written, and may in fact have increased.[4] Richard Krejcir states that every year 2.7 million people

---

3. Ed Stetzer, *Planting New Churches in a Postmodern Age* (Nashville: Broadman & Holman, 2003), 10.

4. Steve McSwain, "Why Nobody Wants to Go to Church Anymore," Huffington Post, *Religion* (blog), October 14, 2013, http://www.huffingtonpost.com/steve-mcswain/why-nobody-wants-to-go-to_b_4086016.html.

fall into inactivity, which translates to a church exodus. He found that people leave because of hurt, disillusionment, or neglect.[5]

Many reasons can be found for dead and dying churches, but much of the blame falls on leadership. The problem is magnified because of the blindness or unwillingness of some leaders to recognize the decline of their own church. Elders must ask themselves this question: "Do we believe that our church has plateaued and is now actually in decline?" An affirmative answer is the first step toward renewal and revitalization. Pride and an unteachable spirit blind us to the symptoms of decline. Healthy churches are vibrant, community oriented, and growing numerically and/or spiritually.

The second question that elders should ask themselves is this: "If we believe that our church is in decline, are we willing to make the necessary changes to reverse the trend?" *Change* is a fearful word, especially to leaders who are entrenched in traditionalism and the status quo. Without realizing that God is engineering change, leaders will not discover his will for their church and will so continue the slide into obscurity.

Some obstreperous elders in a church I once consulted with refused to accept the fact they were in decline, even though the symptoms were blatantly obvious. Blinded by their pride and obstinacy, they informed me that the church was perfect the way it was and therefore needed no changing. Such thoughts from leadership demonstrate foolishness and hardness of heart. Rejecting counsel, especially from unbiased consultants who are hired to express their opinions, is the way of fools (see Prov. 12:15). The abovementioned church is still "perfect"—perfectly deteriorating into irrelevancy. Leaders must ask themselves, "If our church ceased today, would the community care?" Another soul-searching query is, "If our church ceased to exist, what would it be remembered for?"

The third question that is proposed to elders who realize that their church must change naturally flows from the first two. "If we believe that change is needed, when are we willing to initiate change?" Strong leaders are not afraid of proper change, for they realize that God has

---

5. Richard J. Krejcir, "Statistics and Reasons for Church Decline," The Francis A. Schaeffer Institute of Church Leadership Development, last updated 2007, http://www.churchleadership.org/apps/articles/default.asp?articleid=42346&columnid=4545.

called them to be courageous and has promised to be with them in the transitions (Josh. 1:9). Refusal to change is a mark of poor leadership, for good leaders understand the needs of those within their flock and know that change may be required to provide the sheep with refreshing water and nourishing pastures.

Change is not the enemy, for change is an ongoing certainty. Wisdom dictates knowing what to change, when to change, and how to change. Fortitude garners the courage to make changes. Leaders are to remember that change is the essence of life, for God is the author of both life and change. They must therefore be willing to surrender what the church is today for what the church could become tomorrow.

The problem remains, however, that many leaders are unwilling to admit that their church needs revitalization. They want to hold on to the past, and therefore they make decisions that continue the church's ineffectiveness. A declining church is indicative of the great disease that is attacking the church today—poor leadership.

THE CURE FOR POOR LEADERSHIP

Church leaders normally take vows to uphold the Word of God, to receive and adopt their church's confessions of faith, to rule in accordance with their church government, to perform their duties faithfully as servants to the people, to set a worthy example as an officer of Christ, to submit to their brother officers in the Lord, and to strive for the purity, peace, unity, and edification of the church. Choosing men who will take their vows seriously and execute them with integrity is a cure for poor leadership. Training elders to be shepherds, therefore, is of utmost importance, for without it cattle barons will emerge with drovers quickly acquiescing to them.

Most pastors and elders say they are good leaders. Yet of the congregations surveyed by the National Congregations Study in 2006–07, 12 percent reported conflict arising from lay leadership, and a full 35 percent reported conflict centered around their clergy.[6] Paul understood

---

6. "American Congregations at the Beginning of the 21st Century," National Congregations Study, Duke University, June 2009, http://www.soc.duke.edu/natcong/Docs/NCSII _report_final.pdf.

the result of visionless leaders and warned the elders at Ephesus to watch out for themselves and for the flock entrusted to them by God (Acts 20:28). Though elected by the people, elders are actually selected by God to shepherd his sheep. Understanding this awesome responsibility should motivate leaders to become better shepherds.

The apostle John applauded a Christian named Gaius for modeling the gospel to brothers and strangers (3 John 1–6). In the same letter, however, he condemned Diotrephes, a selfish church leader who not only refused hospitality to itinerant missionaries but also slandered the apostles and opposed their teachings (3 John 9–10). Diotrephes is an example of a prideful leader who causes conflict in a church. His leadership style was that of a cattle baron who wanted nothing to do with true shepherds.

Overcoming toxic leadership starts with selecting godly men, training them in their calling, and reminding them that they are shepherds, not cattlemen or drovers. As shepherds of God's flock, they will be held responsible for the care and protection of the sheep. Paul iterated that, after his departure, wolves would appear among the leaders to draw the sheep away from the truth, not sparing them or caring for their needs (Acts 20:29–30). Wolves acting as leaders are seriously detrimental to the spiritual health of the flock. A leader of a wolf pack insists that his views are right, teaches contrary to Scripture, and shows little concern for the well-being of the sheep!

Timothy Laniak of Gordon-Conwell Seminary in North Carolina took a one-year sabbatical to investigate shepherding in the Middle East. Upon his return, he wrote the book *While Shepherds Watch Their Flocks*. A common question that he asked the shepherds of Jordan, Israel, and the Sinai was, "What does it take to be a shepherd?" Some said, "You must grow up with it." Others said, "You must learn by hanging around true shepherds." The most striking and affecting answer came from a Jordanian Bedouin named Abu-Jamal: "You must first have a heart for it."[7] A leader with no heart for people is not a true shepherd.

---

7. Timothy S. Laniak, *While Shepherds Watch Their Flocks: Rediscovering Biblical Leadership* (Matthews, NC: Shepherd Leader Publications, 2007), 29.

The apostle Peter agreed with this principle of having a shepherd's heart when, in his first epistle, he described what good leaders look like. He exhorted the elders to shepherd the flock of God voluntarily, purposefully, eagerly, lovingly, and in an exemplary manner (1 Peter 5:1–3). The first qualification for becoming an elder, therefore, is to aspire to the office (1 Tim. 3:1). An elder candidate wants to be an elder. He realizes that he serves voluntarily, which means that he must have the proper heart for service. If he doesn't like people and has trouble relating to others, then he doesn't truly aspire to being a shepherd. He may want to rule, but governance in Christ's church includes shepherding the flock.

Peter, as a brother elder, understood heart motivation. He remembered what Christ had told him after the resurrection. "If you love me, Simon, *feed my lambs*. If you love me Simon, *tend my sheep*. If you love me Simon, *feed my sheep*" (see John 21:15–17). Christ, in addressing his fallen disciple, used Peter's birth name, not his spiritual name. The Savior was reclaiming Peter from his previous denials of knowing Jesus, which he had committed in the weakness of his flesh. "Simon, if you really love me, then become the shepherd I have called you to be!" The heart of a shepherd is seen in Peter, for he loved Christ and was willing and able to feed and care for the people entrusted to him. He was not under compulsion to serve, because his heart was attuned to the heart of Christ.

Not only are elders (or pastors) to shepherd voluntarily, but they are to do so purposefully—that is, in accordance with the will of God (1 Peter 5:2). Shepherding, therefore, must be in line with the dictates of Scripture, which is God's will. Ignorance is no excuse for only poorly tending the sheep of Christ. As teachers will be held to a stricter accountability for what they teach (James 3:1), leaders will also give account for managing the church and shepherding the flock (Heb. 13:17). Paul, like Peter, connects the activity of shepherding with leadership. He clearly identified to the elders at Ephesus that shepherding was leadership, for he admonished them to be careful about their position as overseers of the people (Acts 20:28). Poor shepherds make poor leaders, and they will contend with God for feeding themselves at the expense of the flock, for not caring for the sick, and for not seeking the lost (Ezek. 34:2–5).

Good elders follow the dictates of Scripture and tend the flock according to the will of Christ.

Elders, according to Peter, are also to shepherd eagerly (1 Peter 5:2), not for financial gain or increased reputation. Shepherding is not a chore, for it is to be done enthusiastically. It is not for the faint of heart or for those who feel that serving God's people is merely a mundane task. Those who desire only to govern the church, and who have no heart for involving themselves in the lives of people, should not consider themselves called to pastoral work. But if elders love people, then they should be so filled with Jesus that their sheep see the Savior in them. These men who will shepherd earnestly will also rule well and, therefore, will be worthy of double honor (1 Tim. 5:17).

Governing well includes loving people in such a fashion that the office of elder is not denigrated. Leaders who love sheep do not flaunt their position as being superior to the very people whom they are called to shepherd. The decisions they make are hopefully judgments for the betterment of the people. Being dictatorial is not the calling of a servant-leader. When his disciples were squabbling over hierarchy in the kingdom, Jesus reminded them that unbelieving rulers lord their authority over the Gentiles. This is not to be the case for leaders in Christ's kingdom, for whoever desires to be great must first be a servant to others; and anyone wishing to be first among brothers must be a slave to others. The model is that of Christ, who came not to be served but rather to serve his followers and to give his life for them (Mark 10:35–45).

The final trait of an elder of God's people, according to Peter, is that of being an example to the flock (1 Peter 5:3). Leaders are to be model citizens, people to be emulated, and teachers to be admired. A bad reputation in the church or in the community disqualifies men from church leadership. Peter said that elders are to shepherd in an exemplary way, and a tarnished character precludes such service. Modeling virtue, courage, love, and care will cause the sheep to easily hear the voice of their shepherds and to follow their lead unhesitatingly.

Choosing and training godly leaders who are scripturally qualified is the cure for poor leadership. Since it is the congregation who nominate their leaders, the body of Christ must be taught what good, biblical leadership looks like. Anyone who is nominated should be asked if he truly aspires to the office of elder or deacon. An important question proposed to a candidate should be, "Why do you want to be an officer in Christ's church?" If his answer is vague and his desire to serve Christ is not enthusiastic, I would kindly ask him to decline the nomination and to prayerfully consider what it means to be a servant to the people of Christ's church.

I cannot overly stress that a church officer is called to represent Christ as a shepherd to his people. Although he will serve on a board and make decisions with his fellow elders, he is encouraged to find the will of Christ and discuss this among his brothers. A board of elders should be led by the Spirit to discover God's will for the local church. Decisions should have the best interests of the sheep in mind, as well as the spreading of the gospel to the local community.

THE SYMPTOMS OF POOR LEADERSHIP

There are many godly leaders in God's church today. This book is a refresher course that commends them for avoiding the pitfalls of leadership. For others, this book will serve as a tool to train them in becoming shepherd leaders by encouraging them to adopt the leadership traits of Jesus and to avoid the nine pitfalls that are inherent in weak leaders. In the following chapters, I will review the leadership qualities of Jesus that will help to overcome the common faults of weak leaders. After looking at the symptoms of poor leadership, I will suggest treatments to eradicate them in order to help to conform our character to that of the captain of the Lord's army. If the church of Christ is to grow in vitality, its leaders are to grow as Joshua did in courage, righteousness, wisdom, and perseverance.

2

Making Tough Decisions

Give me now wisdom and knowledge to go out and come in
before this people, for who can govern this people of yours,
which is so great? (2 Chron. 1:10)

DECISION TIME

Upon learning of the illness of Lazarus, Jesus said to his disciples,
"Let us go to Judea again" (John 11: 7). This shocked his followers, for
they knew that the Jews were seeking to stone him if he reappeared
in the holy city (John 11:8). He made the decision anyway—to raise
Lazarus from the dead even though his safety could be compromised.
It was from that time forward that the Jewish leadership made plans
to kill him (John 11:53). When the days drew near for Jesus to face the
cross and be taken up to heaven (Luke 9:51), he set his face toward Jerusalem. In other words, Jesus chose to enter the lions' den, which would
lead to his murder. This was a difficult decision, but it had to be made.

Church leaders will find themselves faced with challenging and
arduous decisions. These tough decisions are not for the weak of heart.
In warfare, strong decisions have to be made. Jesus, by choosing death,
disrupted Satan's strategy and put an end to the sting of death. Good
leaders make good decisions under pressure; poor leaders make bad
decisions, which is a symptom of poor leadership.

SYMPTOM #1 OF POOR LEADERSHIP: BAD DECISIONS

Leaders, by their position, are decision-makers and are not to shirk this responsibility. When not in God's Word—the gymnasium for strengthening spiritual muscles—their mental capacity for righteous decision-making deteriorates. Without scriptural nourishment, poor judgment arises and leaders will act as a board of directors rather than representatives of Christ. The result is that business decisions are made that sometimes harm the sheep. Harry Reeder believes that the church is on the brink of a self-inflicted death spiral because leaders have adopted worldly boardroom principles of decision-making that promote greed and self-centeredness.[1] Decisions about shepherding the flock become less important, causing sheep to stray and controversy to arise. Hence, a symptom of the disease of poor leadership is bad decisions.

An elder board once gave approval for their pastor to serve another institution that desperately needed his services. He was to remain as pastor to the church and to continue to preach and minister to the people as best he could. Although it was recognized that he would not be able to fully serve the sheep of his congregation, the board consented to the pastor's request in light of his explanation that he could do both jobs, especially if the staff picked up many of his pastoral responsibilities. Some elders expressed opposition to this decision but were rebuffed as malcontents for not supporting the majority.

The decision proved highly beneficial to the other institution but caused disgruntlement among some leaders of the local church. Was the decision the right decision? Was it a decision based on Christ's will for the congregation? Was the decision fully thought out?

One question from a dissenting elder was, "How can a person serve two masters?" Jesus, when speaking about an individual's treasure, said that it is impossible to do so, for where one's treasure is found, there will one's heart be as well (Matt. 6:19–24). It is difficult to serve two institutions with different boards of directors, for it is human nature to enjoy one job more than the other. One master will be ill served

---

1. Harry L. Reeder III, *The Leadership Dynamic: A Biblical Model for Raising Effective Leaders* (Wheaton, IL: Crossway, 2008), 12.

because the servant's heart will not be fully involved with the required responsibilities.

The rejoinder made by the supporting elders was that they thought the pastor, being remarkably gifted, could do both jobs, and do them well. Indeed, there was no doubt that the pastor was an extraordinarily gifted man. He seemed to have boundless energy and worked many hours during the day. The question still remained, however. Because pastors and elders are called first to serve the flock, was this decision actually beneficial to Christ's sheep?

Another oft-forgotten question to ask is, "What would the long-term consequences of this decision be?" In this instance, what would happen to the pastoral function of the senior minister? Knowing that the pastor would not be readily available to the congregation, not to mention the staff, the elder board should have asked themselves, "How would care for the sheep be accomplished?" Did the church have a staff person who could readily fill the void and be accepted in place of the respected senior pastor? Furthermore, did the church have a staff person who could manage and minister to other employees in the absence of the senior pastor's leadership? The elder board thought that the entire staff could fill in the gaps, and they appointed the associate pastor as executive pastor to manage the staff. That was an ill-advised decision, for the associate did not have the management skills to do so or the support and respect of other staff members.

The elders should have known their staff, their personalities, and their skills before making an important decision about allowing the senior pastor to take on the additional responsibilities of another job. If they really knew the staff, they would have realized that they needed to call a gifted executive pastor—assuming that they had the finances to do so—who could lead the staff and serve the congregation as the primary care shepherd.

In addition to reviewing staff gifts and possibly hiring another pastor, the elders should have discussed consequences that were likely to affect the congregation. In this day and age, group perception is reality, and the congregation felt that their pastor was abandoning them to help another organization. One of the main reasons for people's leaving churches is a perceived lack of care. These sheep interpreted the board's decision as indifference. The decision of the leaders made them appear aloof and out of touch with the flock. It is not difficult to foresee annoyed congregants expressing dismay, disagreement, and displeasure. The inaccessibility of their pastor eventually caused an uproar and multiplied problems for the elders. In this sense, the elders did a disservice to the pastor by putting him in a situation that would cause discord among the flock and denigration to the office of pastor.

FEAR OF MAKING TOUGH DECISIONS

Too many men, although they've been elected to represent the congregation, dread making difficult decisions that may offend the pastor, upset a major donor, or lose a certain ministry leader. Making no decision because of trepidation is still making a bad decision. Spiritual leadership is a calling from God, not simply filling a vacancy on a board. If a person doesn't want to debate, discuss, and make difficult decisions, I doubt that he truly aspires to the office of elder, for courage is a prerequisite for shepherding the flock of God.

A young pastor in a church in a southern state was asked by a staff member not to preach on Romans 9, because it would offend some people in the church who had not fully grasped the Reformed faith. The pastor had been preaching through Romans and had prepared three sermons for chapter 9. He was faced with the dilemma of whether to offend people and lose staff over preaching a tough chapter of Scripture that mentioned God's hating Esau, giving mercy to some and not to others, and making vessels of honor and vessels prepared for destruction from the one lump of clay. The pastor had a difficult decision, but pleasing God was more important. He preached his three sermons and lost his music leader and one of the church counselors.

Leaders will, at times, be forced to make unpopular decisions that are righteous nonetheless. Some sheep may not understand and may even disagree with the decision at the moment, but in the long run will experience the benefits. Elders and pastors take their orders from Christ, whose message is, "Love my sheep and tend to their needs" (see John 21:15–17). Loving sheep includes making hard decisions.

An elder board decided to refrain from forming a pastoral search committee until they resolved conflict within the church and revisited their vision and philosophy of ministry. Two businessmen within the church thought that this was a bad decision and spoke against the leadership, telling others that the elders could not make a decision. To them, hiring an interim and not immediately searching for a new pastor was a process fraught with futility. They were strong personalities who demanded immediate action. In fact, the elders were acting—just not according to the wishes of these two men. They believed that the Lord wanted them to get their house in order before looking for a pastor.

At the risk of driving these two men away from the church—they were generous givers—the elders confronted them. That was another hard but right decision. The men did not repent and eventually left the church. The elders stood firm, made a good decision to delay the search committee, and reformulated the church's vision and philosophy of ministry. Once done, they instructed the search committee to find the pastor who would best fit the profile of the church.

Another difficult decision for shepherds is the institution of church discipline. Confronting sin and exhorting repentance is not a pleasant experience. I once asked an elder who accused other elders of being schismatic why charges were not brought against the alleged troublemakers. His answer was that his brother elders and the pastor would never do such a distasteful thing. I reminded him that redemptive and curative church discipline is biblical and gives an accused party opportunity for self-defense, as allegations against a leader may be no more than biased opinion.

Being a troublemaker or a malcontent is sinful, but refusing to indict such a person is also wrong, for it violates the command of Jesus, who laid out the procedure for confronting sin (Matt. 18:15–17). If disagreements are sinful, then a brother must go to the sinner and reprove him in private. If he listens, then the brother has been won over. If he doesn't listen, then one or two more are to accompany the accuser so that there will be witnesses to confirm the facts. If the person still doesn't listen and repent, then the church, through its elder board, is to become involved, and that may eventually result in a trial and censure if guilt is proven.

Although elders are nominated and elected by the congregation, their ordination is from Christ, mediated by the Holy Spirit (Acts 20:28), and so they will answer to the Great Shepherd for the care and maintenance of the local flock (Heb.13:17). They are to realize that the church does not belong to them or the pastor, or to any one particular person or family of influence. The church is Christ's, and he commands elders to be involved with his sheep, feeding them properly, ministering to their needs, and executing discipline when needed.

Leaders called of God should know the right thing to do. The hard part is finding the courage to do it. Biblical leaders are officers in Christ's army and are therefore commissioned to make tough calls. General Norman Schwarzkopf once said, "Do what is right, not what you think the high headquarters wants or what you think will make you look good."[2] Bucking the trend and going against the grain is not easy. But if it is right, then leaders must do it!

TREATMENT FOR BAD DECISIONS

Ill-advised and fearful decisions are sinful in that they miss the mark of determining the will of Christ. In the Presbyterian system of government, the elder board is called a *session*, which indicates sitting in council together to formulate right decisions based on the knowledge of Christ. "My people are destroyed for lack of knowledge," cried Hosea (Hos. 4:6). In fact, the Israelites had rejected the knowledge of God, leading to a misunderstanding of his character and the inability to discern his will. God's character and will are revealed in Scripture, and, since he is always at work to accomplish his will (Isa. 46:10; Eph. 1:11), it behooves elders and leaders to ground themselves in the knowledge of God in order to determine his desires for the local church.

My mother was once diagnosed with an insufficiency of Vitamin B_{12}, which caused equilibrium problems and a lack of clarity in judgment. In an analogous way, a dose of Vitamin B_{12} is what many leaders need. B_{12} is required for normal functioning of the brain and nervous

---

2. Norman Schwarzkopf, quoted in *The Military Quotation Book, Revised and Expanded*, ed. James Charlton (New York: Thomas Dunne, 2002), 60.

system. Church leadership is, as it were, the brain of the congregation and, as such, affects the nervous system of the body. Arrested development in leaders will produce unhealthy sheep. As B_{12} is involved in the metabolism of each cell in the human body, leaders must be intimately involved with individual sheep—that is, the cells of the congregation—and must help them to produce the energy needed to become all that Christ desires. B_{12}, therefore, is the wisdom of God, which elders are commanded to seek.

The beginning of wisdom, however, is the fear of the Lord (Prov. 1:7; 9:10). And if elders truly fear God, they will want to please him by discerning his will for the people. As the lack of B_{12} affects the equilibrium of the body, the lack of godly wisdom among leaders will cause frustration and agitation among the flock. Solomon asked for wisdom—not wealth—and God rewarded him by granting his request and also by giving him riches and honor (2 Chron. 1:11–12). Wisdom is a great asset and should be at the top of all prayer requests of leaders. If elders are righteous, then their mouths will utter wisdom and justice, for the law of God is set in their hearts (Ps. 37:30–31). The key, however, is uprightness; and no one is blameless without the righteousness of Christ being imputed to him.[3] If they are in Christ, then elders should seek the mind of Christ, which gives them the wisdom promised[4] to serve the flock entrusted to them.

Two elders in a midsized church believed that wisdom came after spending time with God. Twice each year they would retreat to a place where they could be alone with God for two to three days. During that time, they prayed, read Scripture, reviewed issues in their church, and determined how they could better minister to their pastor and their sheep. They removed the distractions of everyday life in order to seek the mind of Christ. Not everyone has the luxury of being able to do this, but the principle remains. *Set aside time to be alone with God, and our minds will become bathed in the things of God.*

---

3. "For our sake he made him to be sin who knew no sin, so that in him we might become the righteousness of God" (2 Cor. 5:21).

4. "And because of him you are in Christ Jesus, who became to us wisdom from God, righteousness and sanctification and redemption" (1 Cor. 1:30).

CONSENSUS VOTING

Consensus voting is a remedy for bad decision-making, for it stresses unity and eliminates discord among brothers. Most elder boards espouse majority vote but fail to question whether such a procedure follows the will of Christ. If elders are called by God to serve his church, then it is reasonable to assume that the Holy Spirit will lead a group of elders in the same direction. Disorder and confusion are not from God (1 Cor. 14:33).

The root of the word *consensus* is *consent*, which means that those who voted in the minority are to support the decision to move forward. The apostle Paul encouraged this attitude when he wrote to the Romans and prayed that they would be of the same mind with one another according to Christ and that with one accord they would glorify God (Rom. 15:5–6). Consensus appeals to those who voted in the negative to submit to the decision of the majority without disgruntlement. In other words, elders, led by the Spirit of God, will have the intellectual integrity to support a decision because submission requires it, even though they voted against it. After everyone has expressed his opinion and a vote is taken, those in the minority should be asked by the moderator whether they could support the decision. Nonsupport means that the person has a conscience issue that will not allow him to submit. If he thinks that making the decision is sinful, he should demonstrate why he believes so. If the person is not a troublemaker or a double-minded man, and if he expresses his scriptural concerns, then the moderator should not certify the vote but should postpone enactment and call for prayer. The same issue should be placed on a future agenda, to determine whether minds have changed after prayer and contemplation.

A pastor once told me how this consensus vote worked in his church. There was a vote of ten elders in favor of a decision and one against it. The negative elder explained that he was very uncomfortable with the decision and thought that it was made hastily without counting the cost of what it would mean for the future. The pastor wisely deferred enactment of the vote and called for a season of prayer. They would revisit the issue in a month's time. Meanwhile, he encouraged his brothers to meet individually with the elder who had voted in the negative and try to resolve his concerns. A month later discussion ensued, a motion for reconsideration was made, and a new vote taken. This time the vote was unanimous—the ten in the previous majority joining the one negative because they had been convinced that he was right in the first place.

If, however, those in the minority are not convicted that the majority are biblically wrong, then the vote should be certified with all the elders supporting the pronouncement. When they leave the session or board-room, consensus states that all are unified as brothers in the resolution. Those who were in the minority are not to speak against the vote or to share their concerns with any congregant. This is what submission to each other means: it is not necessarily agreement, but voluntarily placing one's will under another's when one's own preference would have been otherwise. What the congregation should see is a unified board that seeks the mind of Christ.

Another pastor whom I know never implements a decision by the elder board if brother elders are adamantly against it. He does not believe in forcing a vote upon a vocal and disturbed minority, but he works behind the scenes, meets with people who object, discovers their reasons for their declarations, prays with them, and brings up their concerns at the next meeting if they remain adamant against the decision. Upon further discussion, if a consensus cannot be reached, then enactment of the decision is tabled. For this pastor, unity is what a Spirit-filled decision represents, and harmony is found with consensus voting.

QUESTIONS THAT ELDERS IN THE MINORITY MUST ASK THEMSELVES

A brother in the minority on a particular vote must ask himself two questions. First, "Is this decision that my brothers are making sinful?" In other words, does it violate portions of Scripture or push the limits of integrity? A frank discussion should follow to determine if the decision is righteous and beneficial for the sheep and does not violate precepts and principles of Scripture.

The second question is this: "Does this vote bind my conscience in a way that I believe will make it hard for me to support?" Like Martin Luther's, our consciences are to be held captive by Scripture or by logical inferences drawn from it. If a session decision seems to be testing the limits of Scripture, then we must express our concerns and have dialogue with the other elders on why our conscience is struggling with the decision and why our dissatisfaction is not only a matter of preference.

To "bind" is to secure the conscience to an action that imposes necessity upon it. For instance, the elder board may decide to hire an orchestral string quartet to play during a Sunday morning worship service. A dissenting elder takes issue with the decision, for he sincerely believes that hiring professionals to participate in a Sunday service is to promote performance in worship. He feels that the vote of the majority is binding his conscience, for he earnestly thinks that those hired, especially those who are unbelievers, should have no part in leading God's people in worship. After further discussion and debate, he remains unconvinced that hiring professionals is proper and in good conscience cannot support the decision. In such a case, the motion to hire professionals should not be enforced; otherwise the majority is requiring a brother to walk continually with a stone in his shoe, which is what a bound conscience feels like.

A similar issue faced another church that struggled with whether to hire singers as choir section leaders. The music director who presented his request to have four people audition and be hired for the parts of lead tenor, bass, alto, and soprano felt that the choir needed these voices to help them maintain a superior level of singing. The vote to approve the music director's request was equally split among those in favor of hiring, those against such action, and those who abstained. The pastor, as moderator, was forced to break the tie, and he did so by siding with his choir director. The number of those abstaining, together with those voting against the action, meant that a majority of elders was actually unconvinced about hiring section leaders. Consensus voting would have the moderator not break a tie but instead explore the reasons for abstentions and determine if there were indeed conscience issues involved.

If those in opposition to the main vote do not believe that the decision violates Scripture and binds their conscience, then in good conscience they are to submit to their brothers and support the decision, believing that it is God's will. This attitude preserves the peace and unity among brothers. Wise leaders realize that consensus voting is one method for discovering the will of Christ for the congregation. Wisdom is also required in implementing board decisions and leading sheep to accept and follow pronouncements.

THE WILL OF GOD

The will of God is what is good, acceptable, and perfect, and it does not conform to the world (Rom. 12:2). Paul prayed that by God's will he could convey joy to others and be refreshed in their company (Rom. 15:32). Joy, peace, and rest come from the Lord. This doesn't mean that people won't suffer, but it does mean that God has promised repose to his people. Decisions that cause unrest and schism are not of the Lord, for God desires brothers to dwell in unity (Ps. 133:1). God's will, therefore, is for peace, and each leader is to strive to be at peace with all people (Rom. 12:18). Elders therefore ought to promote tranquility within the congregation by being peacemakers, not peacekeepers.

God's will is for his shepherds to lead his sheep to green pastures, having them lie down in security beside quiet waters (Ps. 23). Shepherds have the responsibility to provide a harmonious atmosphere and safe environment, encouraging people to love one another and to enjoy one another's company. Any decision contrary to the peace of Christ is not according to the will of God.

The will of God may also produce godly sorrow, which leads to repentance without regret (2 Cor. 7:10–11). Tough decisions confront people in their sin and call them to repent—to turn from their contemptible and immoral ways. God's will is for his people to be sanctified in righteous living through the gospel being preached, lived, and shared with others. Church discipline does produce sorrow, for it is not pleasant. Paul confirms this by telling us to mourn when we discover sin within the congregation. Leaders who mourn over sin are to take action to remove the cancer by judging the sinner and removing him from the assembly. Why do we do this? So that the man may suffer in his expulsion in hopes of saving him in the day of the final judgment (1 Cor. 5:1–5)! Decisions to institute church discipline are difficult indeed, but they must be made to sanctify the church body.

The will of God is for his people's sanctification, which includes abstaining from sexual immorality (1 Thess. 4:3). This cannot be clearer. This admonition also means that elders, when they hear of any sin in the church, must confront it and institute corrective discipline. Elders and leaders who refuse to do so should not be in leadership positions, for they take lightly Jesus' command to confront a wayward brother and to bring the issue to the church if necessary. Leaders are to do what is right, even under adverse circumstances. Doing this eventually brings peace and unity to the church and silences the ignorance of foolish men (1 Peter 2:15).

Since the will of God is for brothers and sisters to love and sacrificially serve one another (John 15:12–13), leaders are to model such love by selflessly caring for their sheep, not by giving lip service or by putting on a front to please people, but by genuine dedication (Eph. 6:6–8). They demonstrate love among themselves by building brotherhood, exhibiting hospitality, and providing opportunities for sheep to experience their care. By being present with the sheep at various church functions and events, elders express their concern and love for them. When leaders refrain from events or evening services, they convey aloofness and unconcern to observant sheep.

Finally, the apostle Paul reminds us that the will of God is to pray without ceasing (1 Thess. 5:17). Leaders especially are to be of sound judgment and sober spirit for the purpose of prayer (1 Peter 4:7). They should be holding their congregants up to the Lord in prayer consistently. Time at session meetings should be set apart to pray for the sheep. Prayer is a necessity for leaders in finding the will of God, in ministering to their sheep, and in building the foundation for a powerful church that will push against the gates of hell.

The apostle Paul realized the importance of prayer, which is to accompany the spiritual armor that Christians are to don. We are at war with the Devil, and so Paul reminds us to pray constantly in the Spirit and to make supplication for all the saints (Eph. 6:18). He especially asks that the saints pray for him to deliver God's Word boldly (see Eph. 6:19). As Charles Spurgeon had people praying for him while he was preaching, leaders who pray for their pastor are surrounding him with protection in the battle for the spiritual health of the sheep. I was much impressed with a number of churches I visited whose leaders met early Sunday morning to pray with and for their pastor. They took seriously the admonition of Paul to pray for the one who speaks the gospel, for the pulpit is the parapet of orthodoxy and the canon of truth.

There is no secret in objectively finding God's moral will, for the Word of God is his will. It is somewhat harder to determine God's subjective will, but since he is active, never sleeps, and is accomplishing his good pleasure, his will is present. It is up to elders to verify that will for their congregation. To do so is to look around and see what God is already doing in the church and then to motivate the people to join in. There is no need to start huge programs if God is already at work discipling his people and promoting his gospel. He has in the congregation those whom he has called, with their gifts endowed of the Spirit, their personal talents, and their motivational aspirations. Elders have the responsibility to discern those gifts, promote those talents, and encourage those aspirations.

Too many churches try to be all things to all people. This is impossible, especially for the smaller churches, which do not have sufficient financial or personnel resources. No matter what size a church is, God is still at work to do his will. Leaders are responsible for discovering what God is doing in their churches. If a church seems stagnant and dying, then it needs reviving, first by ensuring that the gospel is preached, and second by having the elders disciple those whom the Lord has entrusted to their care. God's will for churches in decline is revival—not stagnation. Elders in declining churches are therefore charged with finding help to move their churches from the ash heap to a place characterized by people with hearts on fire for Christ.[5]

CALLED OF GOD

Decision-making is about Christ—what he wants for the local church. His will is discovered through the discussion and collaboration

---

5. "From Embers to a Flame" Ministry specializes in revitalizing churches. See www .emberstoaflame.org.

of elders called by his Spirit to rule the local church. A leader represents the Savior's mind, his thinking, and his purposes for his sheep. Paul admonished followers to conduct themselves in a manner worthy of the gospel of Christ so that they stood firm in one spirit, with one mind striving together for the faith of the gospel (Phil. 1:27). Elders, called of God to shepherd his sheep, should be of one mind in doing so. Since all believing leaders have access in one Spirit to the Father (Eph. 2:18), it seems logical that God will lead them in a similar direction to discover his will for the local sheep. We were all made to drink of one Spirit (1 Cor. 12:13); therefore, our judgments should be representative of the one Spirit. Unity of leadership is important and will be discussed in the next chapter.

3

Unity, Not Uniformity

And above all these put on love, which binds everything
together in perfect harmony. (Col. 3:14)

A HOUSE DIVIDED

After healing a demon-possessed man who was blind and mute,
Jesus was accused of doing so by the power of Satan. His response to
the Pharisees was that a kingdom divided could not stand. If he, by
the power of Satan, was casting out the demons of Satan, then Satan's
kingdom was already fractured (Matt. 12:23–26). The kingdom of
Christ is to be unified under the direction of the King himself. Wise
leaders, submitted to Christ, will stress unity, promote harmony, and
build consensus among the brothers.

When leaders put their personal preferences above unity, schism
results in the body. The congregation becomes polarized and the seeds
of discontent take root. They germinate and spring up as noxious weeds,
causing conflict in the body and fracturing any unity that was present.
The result is a house divided, leading to church splits and tarnishing the
name of Christ. Good leaders promote unity in Christ. Paul stressed this
principle when he said that leaders, shepherds, and teachers were given
to the church to equip the saints in the building of the body of Christ
until all reach the unity of faith as mature believers (Eph. 4:11–13). Peter
emphasized unity among believers by exhorting all to be of one mind as

they demonstrated sympathy, brotherly love, a tender heart, and humility, which would keep them from returning evil for evil (1 Peter 3:8–9).

UNIFORMITY

Unity, however, is not uniformity. An associate pastor once informed me that elders who could not support the senior pastor should resign, for they demonstrated disunity among the leadership. His definition of unity was conformity to the majority's will on the elder board, which basically was controlled by the pastor's inner circle of "yes men." This is not unity, but rather a demand for uniformity, which is to conform in overall sameness, ideas, and homogeneity. This assistant believed that those who went against the pastor's desires were divisive and should be removed from leadership. He quoted Titus 3:10, which says that we are to reject factious men.[1]

The context of the verse had to do with avoiding foolish controversies and ridiculous disputes about the Law (Titus 3:9). Discussions at board meetings, especially about ministry ideas, are not silly and thoughtless arguments. Furthermore, if men are factious, they are to be given a warning as the Scripture in Titus instructs. To label a leader factious because he disagrees at a board meeting is akin to accusing him of sin. If the assistant pastor truly believed it was sin to express contrary ideas and opinions, then he should have followed Scripture and his denominational procedures for charging an elder with sin. Although drastic, such action gives a naysayer his day in court. He would then be allowed to defend his integrity or be found guilty of sinful action.

God calls us not to uniformity but rather to unity in mission, vision, and purpose for the sake of Christ and his gospel. Paul entreated the Ephesians to walk in a manner worthy of their calling as he urged them to demonstrate humility, gentleness, patience, and forbearance of one another in love (Eph. 4:1–3). Doing so would lead to the preservation of unity in the Spirit, which is illustrated in practice when there is peace among brothers. Unity is oneness based in the Spirit of God (Eph. 4:4–5),

---

1. "As for a person who stirs up division, after warning him once and then twice, have nothing more to do with him, knowing that such a person is warped and sinful; he is self-condemned" (Titus 3:10–11).

for there is but one body, one faith, and one Lord. Leaders are called to become one in the Spirit to equip people for the work of service, which in turn builds up the members of the congregation so that they may attain unity of the faith (Eph. 4:11–13). And it is this unity of faith that causes individuals to grow in the knowledge of Christ, maturing and protecting them from bad doctrine and deceitful scheming by those who would seek to lead even the elect astray (Mark 13:22). Uniformity is not the quest, but unity of faith is.

SYMPTOM #2 OF POOR LEADERSHIP: THE PRETEXT OF UNIFORMITY

Uniformity is a symptom of poor leadership because it discourages the free exchange of ideas and frustrates leaders who desire open dialogue and frank discussion. Although the pastor may be first among equals, the parity of eldership means that each elder is accorded the same privilege as any other leader to express his views freely without being denigrated for views contrary to those of the senior pastor. Uniformity says, "Get on board with the pastor, or leave for being a hindrance to his vision." Unity says, "Let's trust one another by collaborating to promote the gospel and to enhance the kingdom of Christ in our local community." Trust is built among leaders when attentive listening is exercised, when the benefit of doubt is given, when loyalty is chosen over personal demands, and when agreement is made to pursue a common vision.

Vision is to be established by the church leadership. If a church is without a senior pastor, the vision should not remain in limbo but should be continued or reestablished by the lay leadership, for it is the elders and deacons who stay with the flock while pastors come and go. The elders and deacons have the primary responsibility of outlining the structure of what Christ wants the church to be in the local community for the purpose of accomplishing the mission of making disciples. Any pastor presently on staff will, of course, be part of the process for establishing vision and the philosophy of ministry for carrying it out. A newly called pastor will enhance an already established vision by massaging it with his ideas and suggestions. He then implements it through his staff with the help of his elders and deacons.

The church is Christ's; therefore, the vision is his, but leaders in cooperation with each other define that vision for the local community. Where there is no vision the people cast off restraint (see Prov. 29:18). In other words, people will wander in every direction, demanding what they desire the church to be, with the result of suffocating the gospel. Programs will be established to meet perceived needs, but they may never achieve the task of making disciples. Common goals on a common path are products of harmony in leadership, not forced compliance to demonstrate uniformity.

TREATMENT FOR UNIFORMITY

When the human body dries out and rough skin appears, we apply lotions and aloe-based products—such as Aveeno, Noxema, and Gold Bond—to soothe and comfort our skin. Aveeno, for instance, is a moisturizer that applies easily, is not greasy, and softens sensitive skin. The church needs such a product, especially at the leadership level, to ease sensitivity among brothers when issues and personalities cause abrasions. Spiritual Aveeno is *unity*, which is the cure for uniformity that causes abrasive rashes on the body of Christ and especially among leaders. Unity pleases God (Ps. 133:1) and is the spiritual ointment provided to soften the rough and irritating skin. This is especially so where it may occur among leaders.

Elders in the Presbyterian church take vows to seek the peace, purity, and unity of the church. Unity, however, doesn't necessarily mean agreement, but it does imply the pursuit of peace. Although free expression must be fostered at elder meetings, to avoid irritation and harsh interchanges, no report—whether written or oral—should be received or discussed if it contains intemperate language. Scripture tells us to speak the truth in love (see Eph. 4:15), and so our words must be chosen carefully, for death and life are in the power of the tongue (Prov. 18:21). To apply spiritual Aveeno is to promote oneness among the elders, helping them to become a "band of brothers." This soothes ruffled feathers, leads to unity, and displaces uniformity. Shakespeare first used the term *band of brothers* in a motivational speech delivered by Henry V on St. Crispin's feast day before going into battle.

And Crispin Crispian shall ne'er go by,
From this day to the ending of the world,
But we in it shall be remembered—
We few, we happy few, we band of brothers;
For he to-day that sheds his blood with me
Shall be my brother.[2]

In order to be such a band of brothers, elders are to put aside self and to commit themselves to Christ at all costs, not to any particular personality. Understanding this, they boldly stand together as shepherds of the sheep through good times and difficult ones, encouraging one another to do the right thing, displaying humility in their calling, and committing themselves to harmony in leadership. They will therefore seek peace with one another to reconcile differences and will aid one another in carrying out their duties as overseers of the flock.

Christ, in his High Priestly Prayer, petitioned the Father that his disciples be one, even as he and the Father are (John 17:20–21). A band of brothers is one unit whose individuals stick up for each other in the midst of controversy, fighting alongside each other to pursue the vision of Christ and standing firm on truth when weaker men might compromise. Unity easily results when men have bonded as a cohesive group, but even if the elders are not a band of brothers, they can have unity if their purposes, goals, and minds are aligned with the will of Christ. Without true unity, a forced uniformity may occur to bring those of lesser influence into the voting bloc of the stronger.

How do you build a band of brothers? The same way that the military does it! It is by compelled relationship, which is a forced association of blending men together into one cohesive fighting unit! Stephen Ambrose, in his book *Band of Brothers*,[3] chronicles the training, fighting, and devotion of men in Easy Company, 506th regiment, 101st Airborne division of the US army during World War II. Although the unit experienced 150

2. William Shakespeare, *Henry V*, ed. G. Blakemore Evans et al. (Boston: Houghton Mifflin, 1997), 4.3.57–62. References are to act, scene, and line.

3. Stephen Ambrose, *Band of Brothers* (New York: Simon & Schuster, 1992).

percent casualties[4] from the invasion of Normandy through the Battle of the Bulge to taking Hitler's "Eagle's Nest" in Austria, they remained faithful to each other, giving their lives if necessary for their brothers who fought beside them. These men had a common cause: defeating Hitler and stopping the spread of Nazism. They had a common vision: to survive by helping one another through the perilous encounters. And they had a common pledge: to remain strong in battle when retreat was the easier course, even if it meant death. Though many in it died, the unit persevered and became one of the most decorated military units in the US armed services.

If elders are to be a band of brothers, they must form close relationships with one another, ones that increase trust and foster peace and unity. Suggestions for "compelled relationships" are numerous, but some are listed below.

Require a leadership-training program for all elders—for those nominated and those already serving. Even though a sitting elder may have already been through the course, he should be required to attend, not just for a refresher course but to act as a mentor to those who may be elders in the future. He should meet with a candidate in the ensuing weeks, reviewing material that was learned and answering questions that arise. The training program should include what true shepherding is and why it's important to establish relationships among elders.

Schedule two overnight elder retreats per year—one for vision and program review, and the other as a study retreat. The program review should be frank and honest to determine whether objectives were accomplished, especially in achieving the mission of making disciples. The study retreat is to strengthen each elder's walk with Christ. A book could be assigned to be read beforehand, and then at the retreat each elder could provide a summary of a chapter and lead a discussion about it. Sample

---

4. This means that the unit kept losing men even after being replenished with new recruits. If a company consisted of 100 men and 50 were killed, then another 50 joined only to experience another 50 killed along the way, to be replenished with 50 more with another 50 killed in the ensuing battle, that would yield 150 percent casualties.

topics for books include leadership, understanding women, mentoring, or biographies of great Christians.

Many churches schedule elder retreats on a Saturday at the church. It may save money, but it does not cultivate relationships, for such a meeting is not a retreat but an added business meeting. Overnight events force men to dine together, to talk with each other, to share what may be on their hearts, and to have fun together. Conservative churches must put the "fun" back into the word *fundamentalism* without belittling the "mental" part of the word. Men who play and recreate together build fondness for one another, which deepens relationships and fosters unity.

Go to a restaurant, pub, or coffee house after an elder meeting. Socializing after a meeting helps to debrief and adds to relational bonding. In order to do this at a reasonable hour, meetings should always have a docketed end time—sometime no later than 9:00 or 9:30 p.m. Too many elder meetings lag into the late hours, and decisions made when men are weary will often be bad decisions. Agendas should not be overly crowded and should be set by the moderator (or council chairman) and sent out a week before the meeting. Elders who want to put items on the agenda are to present them to the moderator with their reasons for inclusion at least a week or ten days before the meeting. Reports should be included with the agenda that is sent out.

The length of discussion times for various items should be set and a vote taken to extend the discussion after the time has elapsed to talk about an issue. No new business should be allowed at the meeting, because others have not had sufficient time to consider it. A person may bring up something new only in order to have it docketed for the next meeting. To further shorten the meeting time, electronic voting should be adopted for items of lesser importance that could be decided between formal meetings. The email vote may then be confirmed at the next stated meeting and recorded in the minutes. Long meetings do not build brotherhood. In fact, the opposite occurs, for upon completion of the meeting men rush home to prepare for their next day's activities and jobs. When business takes precedence, relationships suffer; and when relationships suffer, unity will not be enhanced.

Schedule social gatherings for elders and their wives. Hospitality is a result of being devoted one to another in brotherly love (see Rom. 12:10–13). An old Jewish proverb says, "Food is love." When we break bread together, we rejoice with one another and draw closer together. Social get-togethers should be planned at least once a quarter. Whoever hosts the party should have ice breakers—such as questions to be answered by the attendees that reveal some facet about who they are, what they like, and how they would respond to various situations.

Establish an accountability network. One of the problems in the church is a failure of significant accountability. Without it, church discipline will never be effective. Elders are answerable to God, who called them as shepherds, and they will be judged accordingly. It therefore behooves leaders to establish meaningful accountability among themselves. Two or three elders should meet frequently (weekly or biweekly) over breakfast or lunch and should hold each other responsible for their growth in Christ and for their shepherding of the flock.[5] The pastor should also be required to participate in an accountability group. If the church has a large number of elders or council members, then each year the accountability groups should be realigned with different elders. If the church has active and inactive elders, then the inactive should also be included in groups.[6]

5. Questions that could be addressed in accountability meetings include:
- What struggles did you have this week?
- Does anything in your Bible reading concern you, or was anything difficult to understand?
- What sheep have you had problems ministering to? May I help you in this regard?
- In what way did you fail in your witness for Christ?
- Are you wrestling with any serious sin? Has pornography been an issue with you?
- Is there anyone whom you have a hard time forgiving? How have you attempted reconciliation?
- Are you angry with anyone? Is bitterness toward anyone stored in your heart?
- Are you okay with the board's decision that you voted "no" on?
- Have you just lied to us in answering any of the above questions?
- How can I pray for you this week?

6. I do not like the term *inactive*—for once an elder, always an elder, and the duty of shepherding doesn't cease with inactive status.

Support consensus voting, which promotes both brotherly submission and the peace and unity of the church. Unity among elders doesn't mean unanimity, but it does mean harmony and concord. A person doesn't have to agree with decisions, but he does have to support them without coming across as disgruntled or dissatisfied. Consensus voting avoids controversial decisions that engender discord by asking those who voted in the negative if their "no" vote was a conscience issue based on a scriptural premise. In other words, if a person truly believes that the vote is unbiblical and attempts to bind his conscience, then the implementation of the vote should be postponed. The matter should be tabled, prayed over, and brought again for discussion at a future meeting.

Most elders who cast votes that place them in the minority do not have a biblical objection for their negative vote. In such cases, they should be reminded that when they leave the session room, they are in solidarity with their brothers. The elder board is to be unified in the eyes of the congregation. They are not to talk about their negative vote or to gossip about the decision. This is what submission to one another is about. The church should see the elders together, not split over a matter. Peace and unity among the leaders is what the Lord desires, for sitting together in conference is how the elders come to an understanding of God's will for the entire congregation.

Adopt the Five V's of relationship building as guidelines for developing closer affiliations. The first *v* is *view of self.* Understanding that we are sinners saved by grace through faith and that faith is a gift from God (see Eph. 2:8) should make us forever thankful. We are sinners with logs in our eyes and therefore should not act as if we are better than anyone else. We are to treat each other with deference, for we are brothers and sisters in Christ. The second *v* is *vacuous* (empty), which reminds us to empty ourselves of pride. Being full of oneself is a formula for pushing others away from us. We are to do nothing from selfish ambition or conceit, but in humility we are to count others more significant than ourselves (Phil. 2:3).

The third *v* is *vulnerable.* As Jonathan risked his life in defending David from Jonathan's father Saul (1 Sam. 20:30–33), we must be vulnerable at times to improve our relationship with others. For instance, we should be easily approachable so that people may feel free to speak to us or to confront us with our own sin. Furthermore, we are to be willing to speak about our own hurts in order to comfort those who have suffered affliction, because God first comforted us in our affliction (see 2 Cor. 1:3–4). The fourth *v* is *vocal*. Talking with one another and sharing our likes, our hurts, our disappointments, and our concerns is absolutely necessary in building relationships. "A word fitly spoken is like apples of gold in a setting of silver" (Prov. 25:11). And words spoken are to be truthful and given in love (see Eph. 4:15). Remaining quiet and seemingly aloof will repel others from us, not draw them closer.

The fifth *v* is *visible*. If we desire relationships, we must be visible; we need to attend and participate in church-sponsored events. Relational people are noticeable and are readily available to help and serve others. The gospel has called us to freedom. We are not to concentrate on self but to serve others in love, for we are called to love our neighbors as ourselves (see Gal. 5:13–14 and Matt. 22:37–39). Loving neighbors implies involvement with them, and involvement entails the building of relationships.

IMPORTANCE OF RELATIONSHIPS

Jesus built relationships with twelve men from different backgrounds and with varying personalities. Many of us have difficulty socializing with people of diverse backgrounds, distinctive temperaments, and disparate behaviors. Yet, if God has brought leaders together in one place, one church, and one mission—to shepherd God's people and to rule his local church—then leaders should be eager to foster deeper relationships among themselves. Jesus called fishermen, tax collectors, zealots, and skeptics; he spent time with them and molded them into a cohesive group of evangelists, caregivers, and pastors. Although the disciples came from dissimilar backgrounds, they were compelled to relate to Jesus and to one another because of their calling. A zealot who hated tax collectors and saw them as Roman sympathizers had to forgive, socialize with, and work with one. Rome's internal revenue agent had to share offerings with smelly fishermen. And fishmongers had to put up with skeptics who would rather dine on fish in a town's café than gut them, fillet them, and prepare them for market.

What all these men had in common was Jesus! What church leaders have in common is Jesus! Relationships are therefore built around the person, work, and will of Christ, which brings unity rather than uniformity. Establishing solid relationships among leaders is of utmost importance. Although personalities and temperaments are unquestionably different, leaders must see beyond the differences to build the brotherhood into a team that understands that Christ is the ultimate leader who has the best interests of his sheep in mind. As relationships are built, personal idols are razed and harmony follows. And good relationships produce needed resources in the church—both in leadership assets as well as in material necessities.

The next chapter calls us to put away personal idols. Idolatry has always been a problem among the people of God, and leaders are not immune to setting up altars to their personal ideas, whims, and desires. When leaders refuse to slay their own idols, relationships are negatively affected. The good news is that loving Christ and sacrificially serving his sheep prevent idols from hijacking our hearts.

4

Know Thyself

Therefore, my beloved, flee from idolatry. (1 Cor. 10:14)

LEADERS UNDERSTAND THEMSELVES

The maxim "Know Thyself," often attributed to Socrates, was written at the entrance to the Temple of Apollo at Delphi. Legend conveys that seven sages of ancient Greece gathered in Delphi to inscribe these words at the entry to the sacred oracle. The adage has become the hallmark of Western philosophers who encourage people to understand themselves, their limits, and their capacities. Leaders must know themselves, their strengths, their weaknesses, their mission, and their capabilities.

Jesus not only knew his mission—to do his Father's will—but he knew himself. When he told the paralytic that his sins were forgiven, he was accused of blasphemy, for only God could forgive sins (Luke 5:20–21). He then asked his detractors, "Which is easier, to say, 'Your sins are forgiven you,' or to say, 'Rise and walk'?" Then, to prove that he had the authority to forgive sins—which was an assertion of his divinity—he healed the paralytic and told him to pick up his pallet and go home (see Luke 5:22–25).

Jesus never questioned his identity. In fact, he asked his disciples who they believed that he was. Though others thought Jesus to be John the Baptist, Elijah, or Jeremiah, Simon Peter confessed him as the Christ, the Son of the living God (Matt. 16:13–17). As a leader, Jesus wanted his followers to know exactly who he was, for his identity defined his mission. Satan tried to deter Jesus from his purpose to satisfy God's justice by tempting him with earthly authority if he would worship the Enemy of God. Jesus' reply was, "You shall worship the Lord your God, and him only shall you serve" (Luke 4:5–8). Church leaders who truly know themselves will guard against distractions and idols that become obstacles to their mission, which is to serve Christ and his sheep.

SACRED COWS

Knowing oneself is to realize one's tendency to introduce personal predilections and ideals into the church. If blind spots are not revealed and repented of, then they might easily become sacred cows, which are notions, concepts, and tastes that become so highly regarded that they are closed to criticism and immune to disparagement or inquiry.

A sacred cow, of course, is nothing more than an idol that receives special prominence. The Israelites, when they fashioned the golden calf in the wilderness, called it their god who had brought them out of the land of Egypt (Ex. 32:4). They thought that making a molten idol was not that offensive as long as they called it the God of Israel. Worshipping the idol made them happy and gave them a great sense of fellowship. What could be so wrong with this enormously successful and emotionally moving worship service? The people were adulating, they were dancing and singing, and most of all they were directing their worship to the god who had delivered them out of Egypt (see Ex. 32:18–19). But God would have none of it. Even though the celebration was called "a feast to the LORD" (Ex. 32:5), it was not a rite prescribed by God or one that could be inferred from his instructions. Erecting a golden calf and regarding it as a form of true worship was, in fact, counterfeit reverence. God will not share his glory, and so he executed justice on those who had fashioned their own god and created their own foreign rules of worship.

Leaders are to be aware of their own tendency to fashion sacred cows, as this would disrupt ruling the church with integrity and godliness. Elders are to love one another in such a way that their brotherhood allows them to challenge one another when dictatorial or unbending ideas are presented for adoption. A sacred cow could be a preference, a penchant, or a creative idea that is elevated to the status of "Do not touch" or "Do not question." Ideas and opinions among leaders are to be encouraged, but if one becomes nondebatable or not open to criticism, then it must be lovingly confronted and the blind spot must be pointed out. If pride surfaces to defend a sacred cow, then disunity among leaders may lead to conflict in the church.

SYMPTOM #3 OF POOR LEADERSHIP: IDOLS OF THE HEART

When elders approached Ezekiel to seek God's advice, the Lord appeared incredulous and spoke frankly to his prophet: "Son of man, these men have taken their idols into their hearts, and set the stumbling block of their iniquity before their faces. Should I indeed let myself be consulted by them?" (Ezek. 14:3). Iniquity was right before the elders; yet their blindness prevented them from seeing the idols of their hearts. Since these leaders were determined to continue ruling Israel, they thought it best to consult God's Word through his prophet Ezekiel. Yet to confer with the Lord without first slaying idols was the height of presumption.

Idols of the heart are stumbling blocks that cause estrangement from God (Ezek. 14:4–5) and become impediments in seeking his will for the church. To sit in session as leaders is to exchange ideas and debate proposals in order to truly determine the will of God. Maintaining idols blinds us to the desires of Christ for his church. It is difficult for most of us as leaders to admit that we have idols that block the vitality of the church. Good leaders, like watchmen on the wall, are vigilant for idols that may creep into their hearts. We will examine six such idols.

Self-importance

One idol that sneaks into the heart of leaders is *self-importance*. Thinking too highly of oneself clouds judgment (Rom. 12:3). Diotrephes, a first-century church leader, had the flaw of self-aggrandizement and was accused by John the apostle of putting himself first—that is, above others (3 John 1:9). Diotrephes displayed haughtiness in disrespect toward John, demonstrated a lack of hospitality toward missionaries, and asserted his own authority.

Self-importance puffs a person up to the point of deceiving oneself into believing that he or she has more influence than others. Diotrephes dared to talk wickedly about one of Christ's personal disciples, deluding himself into believing that he was superior to John. Elders, too, must be wary about their own importance, which could lead them to form cliques with others and to speak ill of those who oppose them.

An elite faction within leadership easily surfaces among those close to the pastor. This inner group begins to act as an executive committee with the pastor, formulating the vision of the church and creating the agenda to accomplish it. Discussion at the stated meetings becomes more like explanation and fine-tuning of what has already been decided by the smaller group. These men become the power brokers in the church, normally believe that they are called to make these decisions, and unknowingly turn the elder group into an oligarchy. Leaders are servants, not oligarchs; they are equal among brothers and are cautioned not to form inner circles that could disenfranchise other leaders.

An example of this is a church that formed a governance committee of five elders to include the pastor. They formulated the vision, made decisions on what was best for the congregation, and directed the ministry of the staff. This committee was a *de facto* commission formed to protect the insecurity of the pastor who was being criticized by some staff and congregants for his lack of shepherding. The men on the committee were his friends, had benefited from his ministry, and desired to protect his position in the church. The other twenty elders felt disenfranchised because they had no direct access to the pastor or influence when it came to congregational decisions. Discontent, which was already brewing, became an issue in leadership as well as in the congregation. The result was the exodus of many leaders and congregants to the point where the pastor finally resigned.

The opposite of self-importance is humility. An elder in a large church demonstrated his submission to his brethren by never complaining about a vote with which he disagreed. Even though he and the pastor did not see eye-to-eye on numerous issues, he believed that the collective body of elders was more important than he as an individual. He therefore would not criticize in public any decision that was contrary to his particular assessment. He was first and foremost a "churchman" who believed in unity and in the mission of the church. He spoke his opinions at elder meetings and never conveyed to others his disenchantment when voted against.

A large church with more than fifty elders may need a group of men as a governance committee to set the direction and agenda for the church because of the sheer size of the leadership. To act as a committee of the whole with numerous elders is cumbersome, inefficient, and unmanageable. Yet most churches are not large and do not have a great number of elders. To form an executive committee around the pastor of a smaller church creates the possibility of factions among elders, leading to jealousy and distrust. The pastor will spend more time with certain leaders than ministering to the whole group, which tends to fracture the brotherhood and erode parity among elders. Paul appealed to the brothers at Corinth that they form no divisions, but that they all agree, being united in mind and judgment (1 Cor. 1:10).

Paul, in his letter to the Philippians, stressed the importance of leaders being of the same mindset. He wrote,

> So if there is any encouragement in Christ, any comfort from love, any participation in the Spirit, any affection and sympathy, complete my joy by being of the same mind, having the same love, being in full accord and of one mind. (Phil. 2:1–2)

Because the leaders were of one accord, Paul appealed to them to intervene in the disagreement between Euodia and Syntyche—two women who had once served with Paul but were now at odds with each other (Phil. 4:2–3). Solidarity in leadership makes peacemaking among discontented congregants more palpable and more authoritative.

Doctrinal Fixation

Another idol that confronts leadership is *doctrinal fixation*. Leaders are to be theologically sound and able to convey truth to others, but they must take care that dogma doesn't become their lifeblood. If theology becomes our god in that we become preoccupied with doctrine to the neglect of people, then we become deadly orthodox and self-centered.

To outsiders, we are obnoxious, ingrown, and not interested in reaching the community for Christ. The unchurched, as well as newly born Christians, are more concerned with survival in the everyday world than with an inflexible theology. They do not know doctrine or particularly care about it, for they live in the trenches of life and are won through relationships, not religious studies. Jesus is the truth and the life (John 14:6) (life implying a relationship), a combination that is not to be bifurcated. Moreover, it was his disciples' relationship with him that led them to learn true doctrine. Churches that stress "truth and nothing but the truth" are perceived by the local community as dogmatic, unloving, and impersonal. Of course, this may not be the case at all, but perception in this post-Christian society becomes reality to the less informed.

I'm an example of one who promoted truth above relationships when I was first converted and still practicing law. People had to know the truth, for only the truth could set them free from whatever sinful bondage they were in. I was so obtrusive with my theology that I witnessed to the senior partner of a law firm on a drive from Washington, D.C., to view a real estate project in Annapolis, Maryland. He was a captive audience and "needed to hear the truth and nothing but the truth," or so I thought. I told him that Scripture was God's revelation to us, but he had no interest. I could sense that he was uncomfortable, but I continued with my obnoxious discord anyway.

I was more concerned with pelting him with truth than with building a relationship. But theology is best taught in the context of a relationship; otherwise, it is lecturing someone who is not interested in theological discourse. This lawyer wanted nothing to do with me after that drive to Annapolis. For him it was a "ride to hell" and back. Whenever I had to work with him, he would do it through a third party. He did not want to spend time with a doctrinal fruitcake and Jesus nut. Leaders that preach doctrine to the exclusion of building relationships with the flock will come across as dispassionate about real life situations with which their sheep struggle.

Personal Preferences

The third idol prevalent among leaders is that of *personal preferences*. Some leaders have difficulty entertaining ideas from others or suggestions that may upset long-standing tradition. Yet Scripture warns us not to be taken captive by philosophy or human tradition (see Col. 2:8). Convention in worship and the rigidity of an order of service fall into the category of sacred cows. When people don't want to deviate from them or entertain new ideas in worship, this can have the effect of elevating these preferences to the status of idols.

An elder in a Presbyterian church once lobbied his fellow leaders to sing only from the *Trinity Hymnal*, which was his sacred cow. He believed that no other music should be allowed, especially anything modern, which included "modern expressions of the traditional"—songs like "In Christ Alone" and the "Power of the Cross" by Stuart Townend and Keith Getty. Although many contemporary songs may eventually find their way into the *Trinity Hymnal*, this elder believed that if the tune and/or the words had not originated a hundred or more years ago, they were not fit to be used in worship. Music preferences, then, can easily become idols and cause controversy in the church.

Tradition, though it may be considered a separate sacred cow, is an extension of the idol of *personal preference*. An interim pastor once asked if he could tweak the order of service to reflect individual confession of sin rather than corporate reading. His desire was to have a verse of Scripture printed in the bulletin and then to read it and explain how the people may have violated it during the previous week. He would encourage the congregation to take a silent moment to confess the sins that he had just enumerated. Two elders in the church thought that this change was demeaning to the prior pastor who had instituted the form of worship. Such insistence on one form of liturgy is controlled idolatry. This is not to say that churches that prefer a more traditional liturgy are idol worshipping. Rather, the idol is rigidity or inflexibility within any form of worship, traditional or otherwise. The issue becomes idolatrous if leaders elevate the form of worship above the substance or object of worship—namely, God himself.

A church I visited in Hawaii immediately held my attention. The pastor was about sixty years old, and his congregation comprised mostly gray heads. The worship team, however, was young, and they sang songs that were mostly contemporary. The instruments that they played included a guitar, flutes, and drums. I was a bit surprised when I looked around and saw the older generation smiling and singing along with them. After the service I asked the pastor if he had lost a number of older people when the younger generation began leading the worship service. He smiled and told me that his congregation loves to see the young people participating in worship. He went on to say that the older generation preferred having the young with them and would not allow their preferences and traditions to become a wedge between them. They believed that music, no matter the form, still led them to worship Christ. The people of the church would not allow the style of worship to cause schism, and therefore they encouraged the young to participate, which had the effect of retaining them rather than driving them to other churches.

When Jesus accused the Jews of setting aside God's Word in order to make excuses not to care for their parents by saying that their money went to religious causes, he pointed out that they were breaking the commandment of God for the sake of their tradition (Matt. 15:3–7). Custom and tradition can easily become law when enforced on others. Leaders are to encourage their sheep to focus on the main things of God, not to make traditions out of secondary matters. The Hawaiian pastor understood this and refused to allow tradition to become a barrier between the younger generation and the older people who might otherwise have been more bound by convention.

The Pastor

A fourth idol that affects leaders is their *pastor*. Some leaders view their spiritual leader as God's gift to the church who can do no wrong. They put him on a pedestal and cater to his every whim. When congregants take issue or complain about his lack of shepherding, these leaders defend him and automatically believe that the complaining sheep are sinful. Their blindness to any faults in the pastor prevents frank discussion among leadership and eventually inflames conflict. A misplaced allegiance to a pastor is another form of idolatry.

Blind loyalty to a pastor becomes idolatrous if it colors the judgment of leaders. In one church, a few elders, devoted to their former pastor, placed themselves in the minority on many board decisions. Their constant negative spirit put them at odds with their brothers who desired change in the church. When confronted with their continued dedication to the former pastor, they disagreed with the assessment. They were told that their first allegiance was to the flock over which Christ had made them overseers, not to a pastor who was no longer in the church. They were encouraged to discuss issues with the benefit of the sheep in mind, not the legacy of the departed pastor.

Elders are to be forward-looking and are to try to determine if their decision today will be detrimental for the sheep tomorrow. Such foresight can occur only if the leadership is united, working together to discover God's will, and concerned about how decisions will affect their sheep. Leaders are not to issue judgments that seriously undermine the care of the sheep while pragmatically benefiting the pastor. When board pronouncements cause congregants to respond negatively, the elders with blind loyalty to a pastor often conclude that the sheep are at fault, not they themselves.

At the other extreme are leaders who view the pastor as the problem in the church so that their fixation on his faults becomes an idol. They blame him for lack of church growth, for being remiss in his care of the flock, and for segregating himself behind office doors. They might also accuse him of being more intellectual than relational or vice versa. They are never happy with his management and constantly criticize his leadership. Such a negative obsession is, in its own way, idolatrous.

What occurs more frequently, however, is division among leaders. Some support the pastor and others disdain him, causing a split in leadership and a schism in the congregation. In either case, idolatry is at the root—expressed either as blind loyalty or as determined opposition. Disagreement within churches usually arises from one of three sources: the pastor's lack of leadership, a disgruntled assistant pastor, or a disenfranchised ruling elder or other church leader. All leaders have followings, easily causing factions to form with each side firmly planted in support of their own person or idea. Such uncompromising positions are idols in need of toppling.

The Tribal Leader

A fifth idol among leaders is the *tribal leader* whom weaker elders revere and dare not contradict. The tribal leader is a cattle baron who wields great power in the church through finances or personal influence. He is widely known in the local community and usually holds positions of note. He has surrounded himself with family members who think the world of him and with people who desire to walk in his social circles. He may have been a founder of the church. Since he is highly persuasive and most influential, some leaders are afraid to offend him. They dread his leaving the church and taking his money with him. Such fear amounts to idolatry, for it places a man above God. Like the apostle Paul, we are not to seek the favor of men or strive to please them, but rather we should endeavor to please God, for true faith motivates us to live as bondservants of Christ (see Gal. 1:10), not as slaves to men.

Tribal leaders think that the church is their personal possession. They direct most ministries in ways that please them or fit their philosophy. One such tribal leader told a friend of mine that when he became an elder he ceased representing the congregation. My friend commented, "I thought an elder, elected by the congregation, represented the congregation." He was informed otherwise. Evidently, that was not the policy in this church, for, once elected, the elder became part of a ruling body governing the church rather than shepherding the people.

What people thought was not that important! They were cattle to be driven, not listened to. They had no say in how the church was ruled, even though church documents provided the means of removing an undesirable elder. The form of government practiced by this tribal leader in a Presbyterian church was not Presbyterianism; it was nothing other than an oligarchy. His church was ruled by the privileged few that formulated policy according to their own preferences.

Unrepentant Sin

A sixth idol found in leaders is *unrepentant sin*. Many men struggle with pride, greed, egocentricity, pornography, and a lack of consistency in spiritual leadership at home, rationalizing these sins as idiosyncrasies that do not need repentance. Other leaders fail to see their insistence that the church follow their ideas and preferences as sin, and they hardly ever think that their corresponding stubbornness is sin, either. Refusing to repent from known sin and failing to change for the sake of Christ are both tantamount to idolatry. To do so is to place our sin above God, disobeying his Word and abusing his grace. When others point out our sin, we are to acknowledge it, ask for forgiveness, and repent. Failing to do so is obstinacy, and obstinacy is another form of idolatry, for it says, "I am right and others are wrong, including God."

Leaders will constantly struggle with their flesh, as did the apostle Paul. As long as we are in this body, we will war against our sinful nature. As sinners, we will not walk perfectly with Christ—we will sin. Our response after realizing our iniquity will make us either better leaders or worse! If we are humble and ask for forgiveness and repent from our sin, then we are good shepherds, understanding what our sheep go through. If we fail to acknowledge and repent of our sin, then we are poor shepherds who will lose credibility with the sheep.

TREATMENT FOR IDOLS

To know ourselves is to know that we will battle our own idols, which are little gods that preoccupy our attention and assume the place in our hearts that belongs to God alone. Idols cause spiritual heartburn and discomfort, keeping our focus on self. Heartburn medications such as spiritual Pepcid, Rolaids, or Zantac are needed to overcome the idol-burning sensation within us. Antacids are thus needed to neutralize the idols of the heart.

Spiritual Rolaids spells relief through the letters "R&R"—that is, *recognition* and *repentance* of idols. Because it is not easy to identify our own idols, we normally need others to point out our blind spots, our irritating character flaws, and our sacred cows. A wife, close friends, mentors, and accountability partners should have permission to point out our flaws and idols. True relief comes not just when we are remorseful for our sin, but when we actually repent and abruptly change to go in the direction of Christ's righteousness. When we do confess, God is faithful and just to forgive our sin and cleanse us from all unrighteousness (1 John

1:9). The Lord is our divine cleanser, for he scrubs away our idols and gives us a new heart and spirit (see Ezek. 36:25–26).

The Lord will confront the idols of his people (Ezek. 14:4), for he will have no false gods before him (Ex. 20:3; Deut. 5:7). As with the Israelites before us, God usually deals with idols through his Word, people, or Spirit. The Holy Spirit awakens us to idolatrous preferences through the illumination of Scripture, confrontation by others, or provocation by the still small voice within us.

The cure for idol worship is repentance. "Therefore say to the house of Israel, Thus says the Lord GOD: Repent and turn away from your idols, and turn away your faces from all your abominations" (Ezek. 14:6). Failure to do so leads to unpleasant consequences, for the Lord will set his face against idolaters and will cut them off from the people (Ezek. 14:8). Unrepentant leaders will become problems in the church and centers of conflict that embroil a congregation in divisive disputes.

What keeps us from repentance? Pride, self-righteousness, weakness of character, fear of others, and rationalization that our idols are not sinful! If leaders refuse to repent, God's will for the church may remain undiscovered, and the sheep will suffer for lack of guidance and direction. Leaders therefore must crucify their pride, admit their iniquity, and change their attitude to stop the sheep from straying to other congregations (see Ezek. 14:10–11).

Admitting sin may be difficult because we don't realize the depth of our transgressions. The Old Testament's description of five basic sins of the Israelites still has much to teach us today. Recognizing the various sins and their nuances will hopefully bring us to repentance, making our walk with Christ more authentic and vibrant.

The most common definition for sin is "missing the mark."[1] The word picture that illustrates this sin is an arrow missing a bull's eye, which is God's law, will, or directive. Leaders may commit this sin at home by not loving their wives as Scripture commands, at work by not

---

1. In Eccl. 5:6, "Let not your mouth lead you into sin," the word for "sin" is *chattah*, which means "to miss the mark or bull's eye" (see James Strong, *The New Strong's Exhaustive Concordance of the Bible* [Nashville: Thomas Nelson, 2003], Strong's number 2398).

treating bosses or employees with kindness and respect, and at church by failing to shepherd the flock as outlined in God's Word.

An interim pastor, visiting with the woman in charge of payroll, was told that he was the first senior pastor who had ever said "Good morning" to her. He was flabbergasted that a pastor would not visit his support staff to encourage them in their ministry and thank them for their service. The previous pastor had missed the mark in ministering to people who poured their lives into serving God with the talents and gifts he provided them.

A second sin explained in the Old Testament is "overstepping a boundary."[2] The picture is that of stepping outside one's circle of influence and authority. Leaders commit this transgression by usurping the authority of another, by dominating or manipulating a discussion or a relationship, or by forcing their will upon another. Demanding that others accept their ideas for vision and planning falls within the province of this sin. Insisting that their worship preferences be instituted is overstepping a boundary, for it forces their will and desires upon others.

An elder once confronted a young assistant pastor for not wearing a tie to the service. He told him that he was not dressed to please God in worship. However, this was not the prerogative of this elder. He overstepped his authority. If a dress code were to be applied to pastors who were attending but not participating in the service, then it would be for the session to decide—not an individual elder.

A third sin is to "lean rather than to stand straight."[3] The picture is that of a plumb line being misaligned—not being flush against the

2. In Jer. 7:24, "But they did not obey or incline their ear, but walked in their own counsels and in the stubbornness of their evil hearts, and went backward and not forward," the word for "incline" is *natah*, which comes from a primitive root meaning "to stretch or spread out or turn from the path" and here means "to extend or spread beyond the bounds morally" (see ibid., Strong's number 5186).

3. In Isa. 5:18, "Woe to those who draw iniquity with cords of falsehood, who draw sin as with cart ropes," the word for "iniquity" is *avon*, which is a derivative of *avah*, which means "to bend, twist, or cause distortion." Literally, it means "crooked" or "failing to measure up" (see ibid., Strong's number 5753). In Greek the word is *skolios*, from which scoliosis of the spine comes. In Acts 13:10, Paul admonished Elymas the magician when he said, "You son of the devil, you enemy of all righteousness, full of all deceit and villainy, will you not stop making crooked the straight paths of the Lord?"

wall. It is being just a little bit crooked, but crooked nonetheless. Many believe that closeness to the plumb line is all that the Lord requires. But being even mostly correct is unacceptable, because God says that we are to be holy, for he is holy (Lev. 11:44; 1 Peter 1:16). Leaders fail to stand straight when they tell "little white lies" and exhibit dishonesty when they are not forthright with the congregation.

A woman tried to see her pastor on numerous occasions in order to talk about her concerns. She had been quite vocal about him being a poor shepherd and sought a face-to-face meeting. Not many pastors like to be told how lousy they are at ministering to the flock and will therefore do what they can to avoid the confrontation. This pastor went too far by instructing his secretary not to schedule any appointments with the woman and to say that he was unavailable when she called. This was dishonest, for he was leaning rather than standing straight by not telling the truth and meeting with one of his sheep.

A fourth sin is "diminishing that which should be rendered in full."[4] The word picture is that of a glass of soda pop being only three-quarters full rather than topped off. It is not being entirely fair or just, for it is giving less than equity requires. It is not giving one's all and, in so doing, defrauding another of his or her just due. When we work haphazardly and slack off, we are cheating our employer from the 100 percent effort for which we are being paid. When we fail to keep our entire word, we have not rendered in full the promise we have made. Leaders who cursorily study an issue or who give lip service to caring for people are diminishing the office of elder, for they are not rendering in full the vow they have taken to rule the church well and to shepherd God's people. When they promise to strive for the peace and unity of the church but refuse to be reconciled with people and to seek harmony within the congregation, they are not living up to their calling as elders.

A young pastor was promised a raise upon completing his ordination trials. He spent a year studying for the exams while ministering

---

4. In Deut. 25:16, "For all who do such things, all who act dishonestly, are an abomination to the LORD your God," the word for "dishonestly" is *avel*, which implies an unfair judgment (see ibid., Strong's number 5766). It is giving less than what is required by equity. It is cheating, not giving one's all, and in so doing dealing unjustly with others.

in the church as pastor to students and as a worship leader. He passed his exams and was ordained to the ministry, but his paycheck remained the same. The elders failed to live up to their word by diminishing that which they had promised in full.

The fifth sin disclosed in the Old Testament is "ignorance."[5] This may seem harsh, but, as the saying goes, ignorance of the law is no excuse. The sin of ignorance is the sin of error and inadvertence. Leaders, in assuming the office of elder, claim to know Scripture and God's way for loving their wives, ruling the church, caring for the people, and worshipping the Savior. Tim Witmer of Westminster Theological Seminary agrees that many elders governing God's churches are ignorant of shepherding duties. In his book *The Shepherd Leader,* he describes attending a denominational conference on leadership and being utterly surprised when the seminar leader failed to include in his biblical metaphors for leadership the word *shepherd.* Witmer concluded, "With the concept of shepherding so conspicuously absent from meetings such as this one, it should be no surprise that the ministry of shepherding leaders is so conspicuously absent in many of our churches today."[6]

Teaching leaders to be shepherds lessens the sin of ignorance. A leadership training course that teaches men how to shepherd the sheep of God is the solution required to overcome such shepherding illiteracy. Doctrine is important and should be included in this training, but learning how to care for people is the work of an elder and is therefore more essential than reciting the Larger and Shorter Catechisms. Learning how to shepherd is the will of Christ, for he is the Good Shepherd who models the care of his sheep.

As mentioned, relief from sin is spelled "R&R": recognition and repentance. And repentance means to intentionally change and go in the opposite direction from which we are going. If we are missing the mark, then we must go toward the mark. If we have been overstepping

5. In Num. 15:27, "If one person sins unintentionally, he shall offer a female goat a year old for a sin offering," the word for "unintentionally" is *shagagah,* which is the sin of error or inadvertence (ibid., Strong's number 7684). In other words, it is sinning through ignorance.

6. Timothy Z. Witmer, *The Shepherd Leader: Achieving Effective Shepherding in Your Church* (Phillipsburg, NJ: P&R Publishing, 2010), 2.

a boundary, we need to stop forcing our wills upon another. If we have been a little bit crooked, we need to confess our dishonesty and speak truth without equivocating. If we have not been giving our full attention or service, we need to admit our lethargy and start giving our all in whatever we do. If we have been sinning in ignorance, we need to seek the knowledge necessary to make us better leaders. "Knowing ourselves" is to be aware of our tendency to sin but to appreciate that God intimately leads us to repentance.

QUARRELS OVER PREFERENCES

The apostle James tells us that the source of our quarrels and conflicts is rooted in the pleasures of our hearts (see James 4:1–8). We want what we want when we want it. Our sacred cows are the heart's pleasures, and one of the biggest partialities of the heart that causes conflict in the church is music. Leaders must understand that music—whether traditional or contemporary—becomes emotional in two ways. First, music causes emotional responses in people. God created us with the capacity for emotional response; therefore emotions in and of themselves are good, not evil. Yet one definition of sin is to misuse, abuse, or pervert anything good. Second, the issue of music causes emotional reactions in people when it is considered with respect to worship settings. Since emotions are easily influenced, caution must be exercised when emotional topics, such as preferences for music in worship, are considered and debated.

Insistence on having a certain style of music as the law of worship elevates our desire and preference to the level of a sacred cow, for it becomes the center of our belief and devotion. Requiring the congregation to worship in our preferred way may be overstepping a boundary by restricting the freedom of others. Our freedom to clap, to sing praises, to laugh, and to feel good should not be restricted by another's conscience (see 1 Cor. 10:27). To condemn someone for clapping or raising hands during a service is to render judgment on that person or persons. We do not know the intent of the person's heart and should not jump to the conclusion that, just because a song from the choir or praise group elicited an emotional response, it was entertainment rather than worship. People may be clapping in appreciation to the Lord for providing gifts and talents that help them to worship him.

In some churches with traditional values, contemporary songs are frowned upon and clapping is seen as approval of entertainment. In fact, singing any contemporary song, especially if accompanied by guitars, saxophones, or drums, is viewed as amusement. But such a view is a personal judgment! A string quartet playing classical music may also be entertainment; yet, to the person who has difficulties with contemporary songs, classical renditions are considered worshipful.

Shouldn't leaders decide the type of worship to be followed by the congregation? Of course, for God calls men to lead his church and to oversee worship! They are free to structure a service based on what they believe Scripture allows and what they believe the will of God is for the local congregation in worship. If they have a greater love for the traditional, then the church should be more traditional. Having said that, I believe that shepherds are to know their sheep and the mindset that the Lord has given them for worship.

Understanding that God is the Creator of all personality types, leaders should realize that people are drawn by God to worship him with different musical preferences precisely because they were created differently. Although we are called to worship God in spirit and in truth (John 4:23–24), we are not required to worship him in only one dimension with the same music. One short-term mission trip to another culture should convince even the most ardent skeptic that it is possible for the Lord to be honored by diverse styles of worship.

Since God the Creator has enabled people to develop many different musical instruments, a variety of sounds may well please him in worship. Diverse personality styles worship God differently. Requiring one type of music may create a one-dimensional church that encourages similar types of worshippers while discouraging other types. If the elders decide that a certain musical style is God's will to worship him in their congregation, then establishing that form is perfectly sensible.

Elders have the responsibility to oversee worship, but not to stifle it. If there are varying personalities attending a local church, then the structure of worship should not be so inflexible as to repress some in worship. Rather, it should be flexible enough to encourage all the people to adore the Lord in worship. Some churches follow the regulative principle, which states that worship is to be governed only by those elements that are instituted, commanded, or deduced by good and necessary consequence from Scripture. Yet there is flexibility even within the order of "regulated" worship. Others follow the normative principle, which asserts that whatever is not prohibited in Scripture is allowed in worship, as long as it is agreeable to the peace and unity of the church.

God has placed elders in particular churches not only to oversee the sheep but also to arrange how they worship him. Although worship styles may vary, leaders are to implement the form and style of worship that they believe is most suitable for their congregation. Elders should be in agreement with whatever form of liturgy is selected. Idolatry surfaces when one or two elders become adamant in having their way in worship. Stubbornly refusing to submit to other elders who desire a change in the order or style of worship is to elevate idols above the will of God.

NO PROFIT IN IDOLS

Habakkuk asks, "What profit is an idol when its maker has shaped it, a metal image, a teacher of lies?" (Hab. 2:18). In other words, idols that we personally make are foolish propositions, for trusting in something concocted from our own imagination is the height of ignorance, so there is no lasting benefit—only temporary appeal. If we think that our preferences are beneficial for the congregation, this may be presumptuous and may cause more disharmony than unity within the body.

Leaders of a large Presbyterian church struggled with their own sacred cows. Some had held fervently to their own musical preferences in worship but realized that change was needed to complement the younger generation. The pastor also desired to reach out to the unchurched generation, whose musical tastes were much different from those of the presently churched. The elders were confronted with the challenge of ministering to those inclined to traditional worship who liked the status quo, while at the same time listening to the younger generation who were drifting into other churches that had a contemporary style of worship.

Although the traditional service was a blend of hymns and modern choruses, it was not contemporary enough for many of the younger generation. The elders decided that the early service would remain traditional, but they adopted a new approach for the later service. Contrary to the tastes of some elders, the music for the later service was to become more receptive to the younger generation. Putting aside their own preferences, the leaders hired a new worship leader to lead the more contemporized service.

To avoid great controversy, however, the leaders began the change gradually. About two years before the change, they instituted a measured use of PowerPoint slides in both morning services. Only the words of modern hymns and choruses were projected on the screens. When a hymn was to be sung, only the number in the hymnal appeared. After a year, the outline of the pastor's sermon was shown on the screen, and the words of the hymns were also projected. People now could sing from the hymnal or from the screen.

With these modifications, people were slowly adapting to the use of modern technology, which would make it easier to approve a complete change in worship for one of the services. The elders also gave a six-month notice of when the change would commence. During the intervening months, informal meetings were held by the elders to explain their reasoning for modifying the style to a contemporary service, and members of the congregation were given opportunities to ask questions and express concern. A couple of months before instituting the change, the worship leader for the contemporary service led a song or two in the normal service to give the congregation a taste of what the contemporary service would be like. When the change was finally inaugurated, there were not as many disgruntled people as had been first anticipated. Communication and gentle change produced a congenial result.

Elders in a smaller church also learned to adapt in order to make Sunday worship meaningful and relevant to the younger generation. The worship service that they enjoyed was very traditional. They also thought that only the organ and piano were appropriate for accompanying hymn singing. They had a number of talented young folk who were leaving to attend other churches because of the music. After prayer and discussion, the elders came to the conclusion that their own preference for style of worship and keyboard choice was close to idol worship. In their deliberations and research, they discovered that the organ, when first introduced in worship, was considered by earlier generations to be the Devil's instrument. Upon learning this, they came to the realization that music throughout history had been controversial and had become the object of battles that split churches.

Every generation seems to have musical tastes that become ensconced in tradition. When an unbiased study of musical instruments in Scripture is pursued, we discover a number of types of instruments that are apparently pleasing to the Lord. The elders of this particular church realized that to obstinately promote one or two instruments for the accompanying of worship was an idol in need of slaying.

These elders had previously defined "sacred music" to be solemn, melodic, and pleasing to the Lord. Ancient hymns and organ music fit their definition of worship. However, they came to realize that their definition was a personal preference, and they relented in their ruling on the use of instruments in worship and on the types of spiritual songs that could be sung. They then approached some of their young people and asked them to participate in the worship service by singing and playing their musical instruments. Liturgy did not change, but the musical offerings did, in that a blended service that comprised both hymns and modern songs was instituted. The older generation accepted the change and was delighted to see the young adults involved with leading worship on Sunday mornings. The younger people were appreciative and excited to be included in worship. Because the leaders slew their "sacred cow" of particularized worship music, the young now felt involved in worship and remained in the church.

Another idol toppled by a church elder from a midsized Presbyterian church was the high regard in which he held the pastor. He believed that the pastor was literally God's anointed and could do no wrong. Anyone who differed from the pastor's views or wishes was considered an antagonist and in sin. At a session meeting of elders, he confronted one of the pastor's adversaries and told him that he was out of accord for bringing up negative things, even though he was reporting what people in his shepherding group were saying. The meeting turned sour and the accused elder resigned and left the church.

A friend of the accusing elder lovingly confronted him and pointed out that his esteem for the pastor amounted to idolatry. He reminded his friend that a session is a council of elders that discusses, debates, and determines Christ's will for the church. Elders are all called of God to serve as shepherds. It is through the collective will of ordained men that the will of Christ is determined for the church. Otherwise, a small group of elders becomes an oligarchy in which power rests, and they dictate what is to be done and call it the will of God.

Being in agreement with the pastor may be God's will in most cases, but it is not to stifle debate. Disallowing contrary views and labeling them adversarial is not what ordained elders are to do. The elder who was confronted realized that he had made his pastor an idol. He was truly convicted of his own inappropriate behavior, asked forgiveness from the elder who had resigned membership, and became more involved with shepherding his sheep and encouraging the church staff.

When we continue to prop up our idols by promoting our preferences, our tongues will wag in defense of them. Gossip will creep into the church and discontent will spread. The next chapter will deal with taming the tongue and putting out the flames of gossip.

5

Tamed Tongues

For "whoever desires to love life and see good days, let him keep his tongue from evil and his lips from speaking deceit." (1 Peter 3:10)

WORDS SPEAK FOR THEMSELVES

Jesus, in warning his disciples to be wary of false oaths, said, "Let what you say be simply 'Yes' or 'No'; anything more than this comes from evil" (Matt. 5:37). In other words, "Let your words speak for themselves." Godly men need not swear to things in daily conversation; they need only to affirm or deny statements as they relate to truth, which thereby renders oaths unnecessary. Jesus spoke truth, and his followers could rely on the veracity of his spoken word.

Jesus communicated truth even when it was to his own detriment. In answering Caiaphas, who demanded to know if he was the Christ, Jesus answered, "You have said so. But I tell you, from now on you will see the Son of Man seated at the right hand of Power and coming on the clouds of heaven" (Matt. 26:64). Caiaphas used the words of Jesus to condemn him and summarily asked for the death penalty (Matt. 26:65). Before Pilate, Jesus affirmed his kingship (John 18:37), which would guarantee the death sentence. He said that he had come into the world to bear witness to truth, for he is the truth. His disciples, therefore, should follow his example, proclaiming truth and attacking falsehood. Leaders will speak truth and not inflame half-truths or promote exaggerations.

POWER OF WORDS

Encouraging words from a dedicated leader, a faithful parent, a devoted teacher, or an interested coach can change the course of a young life. My dad was my biggest supporter. As strict as he could be, he had words that lifted me in my times of distress. As a ballplayer, I had my moments of discouragement and defeat, but no matter my performance, I was a winner in his eyes. He never belittled me or made me feel incapable.

When I became a coach, I employed much of what I had learned from my father. And the biggest reward for pouring your energy into others is hearing, "Coach, thank you for all you have done for me. You changed my life and motivated me to pursue excellence." Words are very important, for they either build up or tear down. "A word fitly spoken is like apples of gold in a setting of silver" (Prov. 25:11). To the contrary, unprofitable and empty words bring displeasure to God (see Eph. 5:6).

YENTA

The Yiddish word *yenta* normally denotes a woman who loves to meddle in the affairs of others. She's an intrusive gossipmonger who spreads tales and causes suspicion within the community. Yentas, however, are not confined to being female or Jewish; they are quite present in the Christian church. Human nature loves to pry into the affairs of others, relating it to third parties. Being meddlesome is offensive, but spreading innuendo through gossip is categorically sinful.

At a meeting of church leaders to discuss a building program, a pastor was confronted by an elder on the matter of a young man who was leaving the church. The pastor asked the elder how he knew that the man was leaving. His answer was that his wife had spoken to another elder's wife who had spoken to the young man's wife who had related the contents of a private letter to her husband reminding him of his church vows. The letter, sent by the youth pastor, evidently offended the wife, who then told a friend about it and the possibility of their family leaving the church.

The elder should have cautioned his wife about gossip, which spreads like wildfire and hurts the people involved. Neither he nor his wife should have entertained derogatory remarks about another. They should have directed the gossiper to stop spreading innuendoes and to confront the person they thought had committed sin.

There are yentas in the church who promote gossip under the pretext of news. Of course, news quickly changes into editorial comment and hurtful accusations. Those of us who, like the psalmist of old, wish to abide in the Lord's tent, on his holy hill, must walk in integrity, speaking truth without slander, bridling our tongues, and not picking up the offense of others (see Ps. 15:1–3).

SYMPTOM #4 OF POOR LEADERSHIP: GOSSIP

Gossip is not only a sickness in the church; it is a symptom of poor leadership. Some leaders turn a deaf ear to gossip because confrontation is uninviting; others have difficulty stopping it because their tongue is as loose as others' are. When rumor and innuendo run rampant, it takes a toll on the peace and unity of the flock. It is sinful to wag one's tongue, using disparaging language about others and causing turmoil among the sheep. Gossip stirs up dissension and causes schism among friends (see Prov. 16:28). Gossip and disunity are therefore closely linked, for a loose tongue hardly knows the truth behind a situation and then continues to spread falsehood, causing discord and disarray among the flock.

When we entertain gossip, our human tendency is to believe the one who has spread the rumor. The elder mentioned above assumed that the writer of the letter was wrong and was interfering. The truth of the matter was that the young man had asked his friend, the youth pastor, to compose a letter detailing the meaning of the term *covenant*. Furthermore, the elder did not know that the pastor was meeting regularly with this young man, who was a friend of the pastor's children, having grown up with them. And finally, the pastor was committed to discipling him, a fact unknown to all the people who were spreading rumors.

People have an innate desire to know the sordid details that rumors convey, and human nature loves to spread what was heard in the form of half-truths, uncharitable presumptions, and outright lies, which can greatly harm the person and the church body. We are exhorted to keep a civil tongue and not speak deceit, but rather to do good by pursuing peace among us (Ps. 34:12–14). Good speech and peace in the body of believers go hand in hand.

Gossip is hearsay, the spreading of which assures displeasure and disharmony among congregants. When leaders participate in this sin, dissonance is magnified and strife among the leadership is sown. The Lord lists seven things in Proverbs 6 that are an abomination to him, and one of them is the sowing of discord among brothers (Prov. 6:16–19). The apostle Paul, anticipating his return to the Corinthian church, said that he feared he would discover strife, jealousy, angry tempers, disputes, slanders, gossip, arrogance, and disturbances among them upon his arrival (2 Cor. 12:20). What happened in the first century reappears in every generation of the church, because people still war with their flesh and repeatedly succumb to their fallen natures. Rather than striving for peace and unity, they spread rumors and take sides in controversies.

An interim pastor missed a session meeting due to weather problems while he was traveling. An elder introduced a motion that would effectively let his contract expire without renewal. A new senior pastor had been selected, but was yet to be approved by the presbytery and could not assume duties until three months after the end of the current interim's contract. The reason for not renewing the contract, according to the resolution, was that the pastor had offended a number of people in the congregation, thereby causing discord and schism. The motion was tabled until the pastor's return and until the pulpit committee could ask the newly elected pastor about his preferences. His desire was to renew the interim pastor's contract up to a month after his arrival in order to have a smooth transition into his new position.

At the next meeting of elders, the pastor confronted the presenter of the motion and asked whom it was that he had offended, for he certainly needed to apologize. The elder would not produce names, but insisted that there were lots of people. The pastor admonished him that if he knew these people and had talked with them, then his duty was not to entertain gossip but to instruct the affronted ones to come to him and tell him how he had offended them. Listening thoughtlessly to complaints may be harboring gossip, which could eventually cause strife among leaders. This elder and one other on the session tried to split the unity of the leadership, which favored continuance of the interim. Not getting the motion he wanted, the dissatisfied elder and one other shortly resigned from the elder board, claiming that they could not submit to the decision of their fellow elders in renewing the contract of the interim pastor.

There was no schism in the church, only dissatisfied elders who felt disenfranchised because they did not get their way. The gossip was among a few families in leadership who did not like what the interim pastor was doing in preparing the church for their new pastor. When leaders spread scandal, the church may be greatly affected if proper action is not taken immediately.

TREATMENT FOR GOSSIP

Without wood, a fire goes out, and without gossip, contention dies down (see Prov. 26:20). How, then, is gossip dealt with? What the church needs is a good mouthwash! Listerine or Scope kills germs in the mouth and leaves a refreshing aftertaste. Scriptural mouth cleansing is summed up with three *S*'s.

The first *s* in mouth cleansing is *safeguarding* one's mouth. We are instructed to guard our ways that we may not sin with our tongues (Ps. 39:1). To do so, we must place an invisible muzzle over our mouths, which will in turn guard our souls from trouble (Prov. 21:23). Applying the THINK acronym in Ephesians 4:29 is that muzzle! We are to let no unwholesome word proceed from our mouths except that which edifies for the need of the moment and gives grace to the one who hears.

The *T* in THINK is for *Truth*. What we say must be true; otherwise it is slander, deceit, and gossip. And when we speak truth, it must be in love (Eph. 4:15); otherwise, it should not be spoken. The *H* in THINK is for *Honorable*. What we say must be principled, wholesome, and respectable. If not, then don't say it! The *I* in THINK is for *Intent*. What is our intent behind saying what is on our minds? Is it to edify? Or is it to hurt? Furthermore, just because we have something true to say doesn't mean that it should be vocalized at that moment. The *N* in

THINK is for *Need*. Is there a real need to say what we want to verbalize at the present time? Some of us like to hear ourselves speak and are too impatient to wait to say something at the right time. We have this inner urge to spill the beans and tell others what we know. The THINK test exhorts us to have self-control and to postpone telling what we know until an appropriate time, if ever. Finally, the *K* in THINK is for *Kindness*. Assuming that what we say is true and there is a need for saying it now, the delivery of our words is to be kind to the person who hears. In other words, will our speech be gracious to the hearer and to the one whom we may be talking about? If we cannot convey truth graciously, we should not speak at all.

The THINK test is also helpful in teaching husbands and wives how to rightly communicate with each other. Too many times spouses feel tension and allow their tongues to be controlled by their emotions. "Think before you speak" is an admonition to all spouses.

Leaders are also exhorted to think before they express contrary opinions concerning controversial subjects, and especially when defending their personal sentiments. If we allow our speech to be tamed by our thoughtfulness, our relationships will improve and will have opportunity to thrive.

The second *s* in mouth cleansing is a *soothing* tongue—one that speaks encouragement, not hurt. A person who loves to chat is vulnerable to a loose tongue, which easily falls to or augments deceit (see Ps. 50:19). If we are to speak well of people, then we should speak comforting words, for death and life are in the power of the tongue (Prov. 18:21). Deadly words are those that cut like a knife, stabbing and destroying the personal worth of another. Lifelike words are uplifting, like fresh water given to one who is wandering in a desert of discouragement (see Prov. 12:25; 18:4). Timely words are those that are chosen carefully in order to minister truth and sincerity to the receiver. Words spoken carefully and judiciously are precious, for they can rekindle hope when all seems lost, give comfort and warmth to a cold and lonely life, convey acceptance when our significance has been shattered, and renew confidence when failure grips us. Words, then, are the keys to encouragement, for like "apples of gold," they are priceless.

The third *s* in mouth cleansing is *stopping up* the ears—we should not listen to hearsay. If we refuse to entertain gossip, we will have no trouble with our mouths repeating it. We therefore need to plug our ears when people say that they want to tell us something about another person or something negative about the church or its leaders. Sinners will speak rashly, but those of us who caution others about gossip will bring healing to the situation (Prov. 12:18). Those who listen to gossip are as wrong as the one who is speaking it (see Prov. 17:4).

Preventing the spreading of gossip is fairly simple. When a person starts to speak ill of another in our presence, we are to stop him at that moment and say, "I don't want to hear this. You need to speak to the person involved about your hurt or your concerns, as Jesus has instructed us to do." If the person says he is afraid to go to the one he is angry with or has concerns about, then offer to go with him to see the person. If the speaker refuses to do so, then a gentle rebuke is in order, followed by an exhortation to submit to the dictates of Scripture. The question should be asked, "Whom do you live to please—Jesus or yourself?" To please Christ is to act in faith and obey his commands to be reconciled with other believers.

Yet the heart is deceptively wicked (Jer. 17:9), and the tongue is an extension of the heart, for it can become a deadly arrow, speaking peace from one side while slaying with deceit from the other (see Jer. 9:8). The tongue, as small as it is, can spark a huge wildfire within the church; like a serpent, it dispenses deadly poison along the way (see James 3:5–8). It must therefore be put out quickly and not fanned with the flames of discontent and curious ears. If the person cannot accept reproof and continues to speak ill of others, his religion is worthless (James 1:26). Then formal discipline should be initiated.

CONFIDENTIALITY

To avoid gossip among leaders, elders should embrace strict confidentiality. What is said in elder meetings is to remain in those meetings. A Peacemaker Ministry friend of mine once told me that the biggest offender of confidentiality is often the pastor. When his ideas are rebuffed, he takes it personally and then wags his tongue to others who are close to him. Not liking his leadership challenged, he knowingly or unwittingly reveals his disenchantment to others.

Leaders, however, must agree on the scope of confidentiality. Failure to do so fosters the breeding ground for rumor and innuendo. Leadership is not easy, and decisions will not always be graciously received. To prevent gossip, elders must decide on the breadth of their confidentiality—that is, whom may leaders tell about what was discussed at elder meetings? Whoever is present during leadership discussions must be instructed about the confidentiality rules of the board. Even though an item may not be a sensitive issue, sometimes the content of the discussion may concern personalities in the church.

Elders must decide whether wives are to be included in the scope of confidentiality and therefore may be told of discussions. I realize that many elder boards refuse to include spouses in their debriefing after meetings by instructing their members not to disclose what went on at their meetings. If dialogue was not in an executive session or closed meeting, then I see no problem with including wives in discussing what occurred at session meetings. It is well-nigh impossible for a man not to speak about his business to his wife. The two have been made one by union, and what one says in the privacy of the home is to stay in the home and not to be spread among congregants. Since God has made the two one flesh (Gen. 2:24; Mark 10:8), then spouses should be included in each other's affairs. Furthermore, wives are to submit to their husbands (Eph. 5:23). In placing their wills under their husbands, who are duly called to the eldership, wives are to agree to the rule of confidentiality and are not to publicize what husbands tell them in private.

The problem, of course, is gossiping wives. If a leader is known to have a wife who finds it difficult to keep quiet about sessional matters, then she should be confronted with her loose tongue and should not be entrusted with such information in future. If she has the reputation of a yenta, her husband is to lovingly confront her. A qualification for office is for an elder to properly manage his household (1 Tim. 3:4) and for his wife to be dignified without being a gossipmonger (see 1 Tim. 3:11).

The rule of confidentiality also means that, even though a vote may have been taken in an open meeting (that is, not in an executive session), elders agree not to discuss the reasoning behind their vote or to reveal the final vote tally to members of the congregation. Once a decision is made, it is the elder board's decision, and each elder is to present a unified front. This especially applies to anyone who is voting in the negative. If elders mention to congregants the reasons behind their votes, it may unwittingly cause discord among the flock.

I admired an old elder friend of mine, who is now with the Lord, for his feistiness in debate at the session level. Many times he was in the minority, but after the vote and in public, he spoke only of the board's decision as if all elders were unanimous. He never spoke contrary to the majority decision and neither did he discuss his reasons for voting against it. He truly believed in the vow he had taken in submitting to his brothers, and so he placed his will under the majority even though it was difficult for him to do so. He therefore promoted a united front and showed no dissatisfaction with the vote taken.

THE IMPORTANCE OF HEARING CORRECTLY

Gossip may also be the result of hearing incorrectly. We are to be quick to hear and slow to speak (James 1:19). In other words, we are to be attentive listeners, getting our facts straight and not spreading what we thought we heard, which could surely cause hurt to others. Too many of us like to speak before hearing and therefore act as yentas without knowing it. The rule is to listen before we speak; and when we do convey information, we do so without disparagement and without revealing a confidence (which is a breach of trust).

Eli, my grandson, sat next to me on a loveseat in the sun porch when he was five years old. His other grandfather was sitting across from us on a matching sofa. We were both asking him questions, and he was answering with extraordinary clarity and using words like "actually." I then asked him, "Eli, are you smarter than me?" He looked up at me with his soft blue eyes and said, "No, Grampa, I'm not smarter than you"—then, with a slight pause—"but I am smarter than Uncle Jeff." Well, his other grandfather and I almost fell off our seats with laughter. Once I got my composure back, I asked Eli why he thought he was smarter than his uncle Jeff. His poignant reply: "Uncle Jeff thinks Spiderman carries a shovel!" Again, we had trouble containing our laughter.

Shortly thereafter, I phoned Jeff, my daughter's husband, and told him what Eli had said. Jeff chuckled and told me that, when the whole family was at Lake Tahoe the previous summer, he was in the hot tub telling stories to Eli and some of my other grandchildren. One of the stories he made up was a story about Spaderman, a super hero who carried a spade or shovel. Eli evidently heard incorrectly and confused Spaderman with Spiderman, and everyone knows that Spiderman doesn't carry a shovel.

What Eli heard was not what Jeff had said! Beware of "hot tub" stories that cannot be clearly heard because of the din of the crowd or nearby clamor. Eli was a child and can be excused for misinterpreting a story due to noise disturbance. Yet distractions are no excuse for adults' not listening intently in order to hear the facts. Interpretation of those facts is another issue. The more attentively we listen, however, the better chance we have of understanding the original meaning of the speaker.

Words are important, and listening is even more critical. Many disturbing issues in a church result from miscommunication, which leads to gossip and the escalation of conflict. Julia,[1] an elder's wife, called the other wives to invite them to pray for their husbands during the elder meetings. Of the nine or so wives who had been invited, only one other joined the organizing wife. She then called others whom she knew as prayer warriors to join her. As the elders met, the prayer group prayed for the ruling body of the church to be led by the Spirit to make wise and godly decisions. After a couple of meetings, Josephine, a friend of Julia's who was absent from the other prayer sessions, asked to join the group and was enthusiastically welcomed. At the next prayer session, Julia prayed for the senior pastor's wisdom, direction, and energy to pastor the church and also to wisely direct another nonchurch ministry that had previously been approved by the session.

Josephine heard something different in the prayer and interpreted it to mean that Julia was praying against the senior pastor and hoping

1. Names in this account are not the actual names of the parties involved.

that he would leave the church and concentrate on another ministry. Because the elders had been questioned by a number of parishioners about the feasibility of the pastor performing what they thought were two full-time jobs, and because Julia's husband was one elder who questioned the wisdom in the session's decision, Josephine wrongly assumed that Julia was against the pastor and drew a false conclusion from the prayer.

Rather than following the biblical procedure of confronting Julia with what she thought was sin, Josephine committed her own sin of gossip by telling a friend and close confidant of the senior pastor her interpretation of Julia's prayer. Camilla, the pastor's trusted friend and wife of another elder, assumed that Josephine's interpretation was correct rather than clarifying the incident. Jumping to an improper conclusion leads to further gossip and hurtful consequences. Scripture tells us that the first version of a story seems plausible until one comes forth to examine it (Prov. 18:17). In other words, we are not to form a conclusion before investigation and clarification. Otherwise, we make fools of ourselves,[2] and a fool delights only in revealing his own mind rather than in understanding the complete picture (see Prov. 18:2).

Camilla received the gossip without further investigation, passed on false information, and caused additional conflict not only in the church but also within the elder board. Julia, who had been a friend of Camilla's, was now estranged, and her husband was seen as a negative influence on the elder board. Although Josephine eventually apologized to Julia, the damage was done, and peace among elders was fractured. Camilla remained recalcitrant and unforgiving. Her refusal to apologize and be reconciled caused further hurt among wives of leaders and added strife within the leadership. To seek peace and refrain from strife is honorable, the refusal of which leads to quarrels and turmoil, making the perpetrators fools (see Prov. 20:3). Fools believe they are right, but the wise listen to godly counsel (see Prov. 12:15) and make amends when shown their wrong. Elders have a high calling and are to be wise peacemakers, reconciling relationships and bringing tranquility to the flock.

---

2. "The way of a fool is right in his own eyes, but a wise man listens to advice" (Prov. 12:15).

EARS

God created us with two ears and one mouth, which in a way indicates that listening is twice as important as speaking. Gossips, however, put the emphasis on the mouth and normally hear from only one side of their head. We should therefore avoid overly inquisitive people, for what they hear from us will surely end up in the gossip mill.

An antidote to gossip is humility, for unpretentiousness places the importance of others above self. And when self is harnessed, the feelings of others are considered, which in turn restrains gossip. The next chapter will explore the virtue of humility in which selflessness conquers selfishness.

6

The Virtue of Humility

And the haughtiness of man shall be humbled, and the lofty pride of men shall be brought low, and the LORD alone will be exalted in that day. (Isa. 2:17)

HUMILITY

The dust from his overalls bounced and scattered on the ground as he walked into the local bank. His appearance was a bit disheveled, and the bank teller who had to wait on him was disconcerted, even refusing to cash a check until some identification could be produced, for a man with a stubbly beard and unkempt hair hardly engendered a sense of trustworthiness. The man had no identification on him, yet he expected service anyway. Once the manager was called, the man in bibbed overalls was quickly paid and given a profuse apology for the actions of the uninformed teller.

C. P. Washburn was one of the richest men in Middleboro, Massachusetts. He owned the grain mill built in 1899, which was added to the National Historic Register in 1980. The mill was known primarily for producing animal feed, which was important for local agriculture, especially the poultry farming business that flourished in the early 1900s.

Dusty old Washburn wasn't too proud to work his own mill. He refused to be something other than what he was—an industrious but humble laborer. He may not have made great first impressions, but his work ethic was impressive. He certainly did not think more highly of himself than he ought.

SERVANT LEADERSHIP

Servant-leaders personify humility, which is a virtue that Scripture extols. It is a state of mind that pleases God (Col. 3:12) and provides gladness to the heart (Ps. 69:32). Christ, of course, is the model of humility that all leaders should follow. Although he was God, he left his heavenly abode and became a lowly man (Phil. 2:7–8). Christ's lowering himself to become man is a great incentive for church leaders to empty themselves in order to serve their sheep. The hallmark of a church leader is servanthood. Jesus, in quelling the controversy that arose after the mother of James and John had asked that her sons sit on Jesus' right and left hand in the kingdom to come, said to his disciples,

> You know that the rulers of the Gentiles lord it over them, and their great ones exercise authority over them. It shall not be so among you. But whoever would be great among you must be your servant, and whoever would be first among you must be your slave, even as the Son of Man came not to be served but to serve, and to give his life as a ransom for many. (Matt. 20:25–28)

Jesus is the epitome of servant leadership, which is what pastors and elders are called to model. They are not to look for honors and rewards, nor are they to be served. Church leaders are to serve the sheep who are entrusted to them. To be like Jesus, leaders are to follow Paul's admonition in Philippians and to do nothing from selfishness or empty conceit, but with humility to treat those whom they serve as more important than themselves (see Phil. 2:3). Being a servant-leader in the church reduces conflict, helps the operation of God's ecclesia to run more efficiently, and sets the example for sheep to follow. A humble leader avoids the pitfall of pride, which is the opposite of humility and another symptom of poor leadership.

SYMPTOM #5 OF POOR LEADERSHIP: PRIDE

Pride and Prejudice, a novel by Jane Austen, is a classic study in the haughtiness of man. In 1995, the British Broadcasting Corporation created a miniseries from the book that starred Colin Firth and Jennifer Ehle. In one scene, Mr. Bingley confronts his friend Mr. Darcy about seeing Jane Bennet in London and unabashedly asks, "You tell me now that she was in London all those months, and you concealed it from me?" Darcy's reply: "Yes; I can offer no justification. It was an arrogant presumption based on a failure to recognize your true feelings. And Miss Bennet's!"[1]

Arrogant presumption is opinionated egotism, which is the opposite of humility. It becomes an issue in some churches when leaders think too highly of themselves and of their church. Arrogant leaders assume that they lead strong and influential churches, when in reality their churches may be stuffy and self-absorbed. They allow their history to bloat their own importance. They reside in the past, resting on ancient laurels rather than being what God desires them to be in the present.

Pride was one of the eight evil thoughts first devised as an inventory of human frailties by Evagrius Ponticus, a fourth-century monk. In AD 590, Pope Gregory reformulated the list into seven deadly sins. The Roman Catholic Church called these sins *capital vices* or *cardinal sins* and included them in catechizing exercises for the purpose of instructing followers about the dangers of fallen humanity's vices. Such a formulation seems superfluous, since Jesus himself warned of personal arrogance when he said that pride is one of thirteen sins that emanate from the heart and defile people.[2]

Pride surfaces in leaders who seek to control the mind and direction of the church to which they have belonged for so many years. In the 1947 movie *The Bishop's Wife*, starring David Niven, Cary Grant, and Loretta Young, there is a confrontation between the bishop and a

---

1. "Mr. Bingley Returns," *Pride and Prejudice: The Special Edition*, vol. 2, directed by Simon Langton (1995; New York: A&E Home Video, 2001), DVD.

2. "For from within, out of the heart of man, come evil thoughts, sexual immorality, theft, murder, adultery, coveting, wickedness, deceit, sensuality, envy, slander, pride, foolishness. All these evil things come from within, and they defile a person" (Mark 7:21–23).

Mrs. Agnes Hamilton, who has pledged over a million dollars to build a new cathedral. She wants it built in a certain way, with a memorial chapel dedicated to her deceased husband. Upon leaving the meeting, she emphatically threatens the bishop by saying, "You will build that cathedral as I want it, or you will not build it at all."[3]

THE CHURCH AT LAODICEA

The church at Laodicea is a biblical example of the prideful church. The people were rich in material goods and were so wealthy that they had need of nothing, although spiritually they were wretched, pitiable, poor, blind, and naked (Rev. 3:17). Laodicea was a prosperous banking center. It was so proud of its wealth that it refused Roman disaster relief after the earthquake of AD 60 and was therefore rebuilt from its own resources. It was also known for its textiles (especially wool), its medical school, and its production of ear medicine and the highly regarded Phrygian eye salve.

The church, though wealthy, became complacent in the spread of the gospel. Its members thought they needed nothing and didn't realize that their spiritual condition was one of misery and poverty. Whatever we have, as individuals or as a church, really belongs to the Lord. What we do with it belongs to us. The problem is that we have the tendency to hoard our capital and keep it for a rainy day. Ironically, being a wealthy church may be a deterrent to spreading the true gospel, for it keeps our focus on the earthly rather than on the heavenly. For instance, during the 1980s there was a push toward promoting the mega church. Bigger churches had the money, the people, the programs, and the reputation. They concentrated on technique and expansion and acted like the gurus of the "here and now" church growth movement. Pastors of some smaller churches became envious of those who had huge churches. But then such small churches, too, became overly stodgy because of their worldly desires that enticed them to be bigger and greater. Money can't buy love, particularly the love of Christ. In fact, riches can easily be

---

3. "Cathedral Committee," *The Bishop's Wife*, directed by Henry Koster (1947; Santa Monica, CA: MGM Home Entertainment, 2001), DVD.

detrimental to spiritual growth, especially if we claim that the Lord has blessed us with it but then fail to use part of it for the enhancement of his kingdom on earth.

When we don't grow spiritually, we become lukewarm, just like the Laodiceans. Christ knew their deeds as he knows ours. The Laodiceans were neither cold nor hot, for either condition would have been more pleasing to the Lord (see Rev. 3:15). Laodicea was located on the Lycus River in the same province as Hierapolis and Colossae. Hierapolis contained hot springs to the north of Laodicea. Colossae was to the south, but at a higher elevation than Laodicea, and from it flowed fresh, pure water. The hot water from Hierapolis met the cold water from Colossae at Laodicea on the Lycus River, and there the mixture became lukewarm.

In this metaphor, to be hot would be to have the properties of hot springs, healing waters for those who were hurting; to be cold may be likened to bringing cool refreshment to people in need of encouragement. Jesus commended both conditions, but to be lukewarm meant that the Laodiceans were tepid in their spiritual life and thought more highly of themselves than they should have. So, because they were neither hot—acting as healing balm—nor cold—spreading the refreshing taste of the gospel—Jesus would spew them from his mouth (Rev. 3:16).

A Laodicean church today is one that stands on its past record and continues to be rich through the legacies left by appreciating donors or by money bestowed by present influential benefactors. It may have magnificent edifices and little by way of financial worries, but its leaders allow the membership to live on past reputations. They fool themselves into thinking that they are still relevant in their community. Poor leaders have caused them to become prideful in their own self-importance, for they have ceased being pertinent with the gospel years before.

A church that is full of its past is lethargic when it comes to ministering the gospel to the local community! When we are overly consumed with self-importance, it is hard to be flexible and adaptable to the changing times. What is the major sin? Arrogant presumption characterized by self-righteousness! Poor leadership is most often characterized by pride and haughtiness, which eventually leads to dishonor (Prov. 11:2) and destruction (Prov. 16:18).

THE LEADERSHIP CHURCH

A pastor was adamant in explaining that his church was a leader-ship church. He and a few of his supporting elders prided themselves on the fact that their church had formed many ministries and was highly influential in the area. What is a leadership church? Does it mean the church is setting a trend that other churches quickly follow? Or does it mean that the church is so progressive that other churches have looked toward it for direction? This pastor's church had many fine qualities, but it was far from a "leadership church." In fact, the elders were in a state of conflict in vision and direction and didn't have their finger on the pulse of the true needs of the sheep, who had started wandering to other pastures. The truth was that church had been in decline for five or six years after its high point, and the leadership refused to recognize the degeneration.

Arrogance makes us concentrate on "me," and when we do, we forget that the church is not ours but Christ's. How soon we forget that the church is an assembly of professing Christians who come together to worship Christ, obey his Word, and promote his gospel (see, for example, Rom. 16:5; Col. 4:15)! As a people of Christ, we are the body of the redeemed, for we are part of all the elect given to Christ by the Father (John 10:29). The church belongs to Christ, for he is the Good Shepherd who surrendered his life for the sheep (John 10:11). And if the church is Christ's, then leaders must humble themselves and submit to the lordship of Jesus, for he is the head of the church (Eph. 5:23).

The story of Pinelands Presbyterian Church in Miami, Florida, is an example of a declining church becoming revitalized when the leaders were willing to humble themselves and become gospel-centered. Harry Reeder, in his book *From Embers to a Flame*,[4] explains how his first pastorate was an eye-opener to ministry. Asked to close the church down during his first week as pastor, and receiving a disturbing call from a former pastor saying that the church had the mark of Satan on it, Dr. Reeder had two choices: run and look for another pastorate, or

4. Harry L. Reeder III, *From Embers to a Flame: How God Can Revitalize Your Church* (Phillipsburg, NJ: P&R Publishing, 2008).

confront the declination and seek revitalization. He chose to stay the course, confront the evil, and preach the gospel. Applying principles that he gleaned from Revelation 2 and Christ's message to the church at Ephesus, Dr. Reeder exhorted his leaders to remember their past and connect with it in a positive way, to repent of their sins that had caused the church to stagnate, and to recover their first love, Christ, by centering their lives and their church on the gospel.

When members of the leadership fail to see the stages of decline in their church, they actually participate in its downfall. Wearing rose-colored glasses and seeing a wonderful church, a family church, and an active church of the past blinds leaders to the reality of the church's decline. Like the person who has cancer growing on the inside of her body and yet seems very healthy at the moment, the local church may seem fine now but have a disease eating away inside—a disease that will eventually surface, causing debilitation and possible death. That disease for the most part is pride and self-importance. Leaders are encouraged to look through the lens of Scripture and to adopt the principles of revitalization, for that is the will of Christ, who loves his church.

HOW THE HAUGHTY FALL

Scripture is replete with examples of arrogant leaders thinking more highly of themselves than they ought. Haughtiness is seen in Goliath, who mocked David's puniness. The lesson? The bigger you are, the harder you fall (1 Sam. 17). David later succumbed to arrogance when he fell into adultery with Bathsheba and had her husband killed. The result? Adulterous eyes led to malevolent intent (2 Sam. 11). Rehoboam displayed haughtiness when he listened to wrong counsel and split the nation of Israel. The result? You become like those with whom you hang out (1 Kings 12:1–20). In these cases, all three people arrogantly presumed that their authority was consummate and that they therefore deserved success.

When church leaders become haughty, they unknowingly cause their church to slip from being the vibrant and relevant institution it once was. Arrogance causes blindness to our spiritual condition, and blindness will cause us to fall into the pit of complacency. Paul Tripp says that a "spiritually blind person not only fails to recognize his blindness, he is convinced that he has excellent vision. A fundamental part of being spiritually blind is that you are blind to your blindness."[5]

Pride may manifest itself in the pursuit of greater growth. Blind to the core principles upon which the church was founded, leaders may seek expansion of programs as a remedy for decline. Programs themselves are not bad, but when they are instituted in hopes of preventing further decay, they become millstones, pulling the church further down into oblivion. The Corinthian church may be an example of overreaching, for it had become rich and famous. Using a gentle form of hyperbole, Paul mocked the Corinthians as being superior but reminded them that God had given them everything they had (1 Cor. 4:7–8). Even the Ephesian church, which was the model of early Christian vibrancy, needed revival a couple of different times after slipping into stagnancy. Jesus, in his revelation to the apostle John, said that this great church had lost its first love—him (Rev. 2:4). In other words, as great as this church was, it may have overextended itself by doing so many things that the gospel of Christ was muffled. Or maybe it was the leadership's succumbing to the idea of expansion, wanting to extend her importance but inversely causing the church's decay.

Pride at times may blind leaders to weighing the downside of a venture or a new program, so placing the vibrancy of the church at risk. Scripture is replete with men refusing to assess information that has been placed before them. Samson, for example, would not listen to his parents about taking a Philistine for a wife (Judg. 14:1–3) and shunned their advice. Rehoboam refused counsel from his father's seasoned advisors (1 Kings 12:6–8). King Ahab was not about to listen to a prophet whom he hated (see 1 Kings 22:13–29).

Prideful leaders have difficulty listening to those who have contrary opinions. Like an organization basing its decisions on inadequate or mismanaged information and suffering for it, churches will suffer if they refuse to listen to constructive criticism. Israel wanted a king,

5. Paul David Tripp, *Instruments in the Redeemer's Hands: People in Need of Change Helping People in Need of Change* (Phillipsburg, NJ: P&R Publishing, 2002), 279.

which confirmed her unhappiness as a nation with God as her head. They wanted to be like other nations, and so demanded a human king.

King Saul was the "makeover" that the people of Israel wanted. Desiring to be like other nations, Israel pleaded for a king and was given Saul, a member of a prominent family, who was tall, handsome, and well-spoken. The people were delighted with the choice, for now they could be like other nations with a king to lead them into battles. He would be their salvation (see 1 Sam. 9–10), but in fact he led them into collapse and dishonor.

The book of Judges is a history of God's people sinking into decline and servitude to other nations as a result of arrogant presumption. Each generation would experience the oppression, would moan about the situation, and would eventually cry out to God for deliverance. The Lord, taking pity on them, would raise up a judge and empower him to free the people from their oppressors. When the judge died, however, the people became complacent, returned to their wicked ways, and pompously assumed that God would continue their favored status. Their pride and sinfulness aroused the anger of the Lord, who enjoined other nations to chastise them, catapulting them back into decline and bondage (Judg. 2:18–20).

Blindness will keep leaders from seeing how irrelevant their church is. Whenever I see a "For Sale" sign on a church, I wonder if the leaders failed to recognize the signs of decay. Although churches can close for a variety of reasons, I still wonder what part leadership played in locking the doors. Did leaders surrender their core convictions and fall to worldliness or isolation? Had they missed the hidden signs of deterioration? Did they neglect their sheep who started wandering? Did they allow falsehood to creep into the pulpit? Whatever happened, a once-vibrant church is now empty, forlorn, and foreclosed.

TREATMENT FOR PRIDE

The antidote to pride is humility. It is the medicine that relieves stuffiness. It is a man's pride that brings him low, but he who is lowly in spirit will obtain honor (Prov. 29:23). Leaders are to do nothing from selfishness, but with humility of mind they are to treat others as more important than themselves (see Phil. 2:3). This type of servant-leader will shepherd the people of God according to the will of God.

A number of years ago, I heard Clebe McClary, a motivational speaker and Silver Star recipient who lost an eye and an arm during the Vietnam conflict, speak on the proper definition of *pride*. I never forgot what he said, because he used *pride* as an acronym. PRIDE—Proper Responsibility in Daily Effort! For elders, their primary responsibility is the care of their sheep according to the will of the Great Shepherd. This is a daily matter—one not to be replaced by "pie in the sky" church growth programs or extemporaneous ministries desired by the pastor or an influential member of the church. Leadership must humble itself to discern God's will for the sheep. Failure to do so may bring God's judgment upon an unsuspecting congregation (see 2 Chron. 32:24–26). This will become evident in a stagnant church that is ineffective in reaching the community with the gospel of Christ.

The Lord hates pride, arrogance, and perverted speech (Prov. 8:13). The problem with most leaders is that they don't recognize their own pride and therefore inoculate themselves against true wisdom and discernment. They think they are making right decisions, but in reality they are adding to the ineffectiveness of the church. The self-important church is the reflection of its leadership. Here there needs to be humility in order to reconcile the church to the purposes of Christ. And whoever humbles himself like a child is the one who is greatest in the kingdom of heaven (Matt. 18:4)!

MODEL OF HUMILITY

Jesus himself is the epitome of humility. The Son of God thought nothing of taking the form of man to become a servant, even to the point of death on the cross (Phil. 2:6–8). The humiliation of Christ, who condescended to enter humanity, is the example for all who are undershepherds of the Great Shepherd. Elders, by taking an oath to shepherd the flock of Christ, are called to demonstrate the love, care, and humility of the one who died for the sheep. How can any leader be arrogant when the Son of God modeled servanthood by washing the feet of his disciples (see John 13:5–17)? This washing left a great impression upon them, for their ministries were characterized by humility and their exhortations frequently promoted modesty and self-effacement.

Peter first thought that Christ's washing his feet was too demeaning for the Savior. Jesus, however, rebuked Peter and said that refusal meant that Peter would have no share in his ministry. Peter could not tolerate this thought, and so he humbly complied. In his own ministry, Peter exhorted his followers to clothe themselves with humility toward one another, stating, "God opposes the proud but gives grace to the humble" (1 Peter 5:5).

Paul, who once was proud of the fact that he was a Hebrew of Hebrews, became a servant to Christ, promoted humility toward others, especially Jews, and warned believers not to be arrogant (Rom. 11:18–20). To the Corinthians, Paul proclaimed that God had chosen the lowly and despised to confound the "high and mighty," so that none could boast in the presence of God (1 Cor. 1:28–29). He told the Galatians that he boasted only in the cross of Christ (Gal. 6:14). He urged the Ephesians to walk in a manner worthy of their calling, which is characterized by humility, gentleness, patience, and love (Eph. 4:1–2). He admonished the Philippians to do nothing out of selfish ambition or conceit, but in humility to count others more significant than themselves (Phil. 2:3). He instructed the Colossians to put on compassionate hearts, kindness, humility, meekness, and patience (Col. 3:12).

The name of Jesus is synonymous with humility and servanthood. To be his follower is to represent his character to a desperate and dying world. Humility of character in a leader, like pollen attracting bees, is a sweet allurement that sheep will follow.

CHURCH HUMILITY

A church in the Midwest is an example of being humbled before the Lord. After two major schisms that saw the exodus of hundreds of people, including part of the church leadership, the remaining elders admitted that they had failed as shepherds and were complicit, although not maliciously, in a conflict that had split the church. They wanted help and were willing to confess before their sheep their neglect and irresponsibility in trying to keep peace in the church. They were unanimous in seeking help to restore and revitalize the ministries of the church. They understood that this meant change and that the status quo would not do.

A humble church is a church that desires to redeem any internal strife and conflict for the glory of God and that therefore recognizes the need to be revitalized. This in all likelihood means change, and change can frighten leaders. It is change that God uses to rescue churches from irrelevancy and decline. The next chapter will address change as a good thing, as a new direction authored by God.

7

Christ-Centered Change

And to the angel of the church in Sardis write: "The words of him who has the seven spirits of God and the seven stars. 'I know your works. You have the reputation of being alive, but you are dead.'" (Rev. 3:1)

THE CHURCH AT WAR

"O church, arise and put your armor on"[1] is a line from a modern hymn by Keith Getty and Stuart Townend. It is a reveille to awaken the church from complacency to battle against the enemies of God. Through the lyrics of the song, Getty and Townend encourage church leaders to rally their troops, equip them with the sword of the Spirit, and train them for warfare.

Warfare against the church of Christ is constant. Leaders are called to put on their armor and lead their people into battle, realizing that they are taking orders from the Captain of the Hosts: Jesus Christ himself. Jesus said that he had not come to bring peace as the world understands it, but he had come with a sword that would divide families (Matt. 10:34–35). Although he did first appear as a teacher and shepherd to his disciples, his second coming will be as a fierce combatant. John describes

1. "O Church, Arise," by Keith Getty and Stuart Townend, Thankyou Music, 2005. Other popular compositions by Getty and/or Townend are "In Christ Alone" and "How Deep the Father's Love for Us."

this warrior-king, in Revelation 19, as a judge who makes war, has eyes of fire, and wears clothing dipped in blood. He will strike down the nations and tread the winepress of the fury of God's wrath. No one will be able to withstand his attack, and the sword coming from his mouth will destroy those who are evil (Rev. 19:11–21).

Church leaders are the lieutenants of Christ, hopefully familiar with warfare and willing to wage battle against the enemy that seeks to devour and destroy the sheep. As soldiers, leaders are called to wield the truth and become active in the culture war, living and presenting the gospel to those who think it offensive.

THE CHURCH AT SARDIS

Becoming active, however, assumes that leaders are not comatose or near death, for they are to equip and energize their congregations to fight the battles before them. Some churches, however, appear "dead as a doornail," a phrase popularized by William Shakespeare in his play *Henry VI*. The character John Cade says, "If I do not leave you all as dead as a doornail, I pray God I may never eat grass more."[2] In 1843 Charles Dickens used the expression to describe Scrooge's old partner, Marley, as being as dead as a doornail.[3]

A doornail church shows little life, yet lurking within the body is still the beating of the heart that belongs to the Captain of our souls— Jesus Christ. How sad for a church that once had vibrancy and relevance in the community to exhibit such a low pulse that barely maintains life! Her entrenched ways, uninviting atmosphere, and lack of outreach are akin to posting a sign on the door that reads "Closed Due to Death."

The church at Sardis, in Revelation 3, is an example of deadness. It protruded into the community but was bent over dead. The Lord Jesus addresses the church: "I know your works. You have the reputation of being alive, but you are dead" (Rev. 3:1). The worst thing that could be said to a church is: "You have the reputation of being alive, of being a great church, but in reality, you are dead." What leads to the

2. William Shakespeare, *Henry VI, Part II*, ed. G. Blakemore Evans et al. (Boston: Houghton Mifflin, 1997), 4.10.40–41. References are to act, scene, and line.
3. Charles Dickens, *A Christmas Carol* (London: Chapman & Hall, 1843), 1.

death of a church? Poor leadership! Leaders frequently fool themselves into thinking that their church is vibrant when, in fact, it is much like the church at Sardis.

Churches may be characterized by deadness because their leaders sleep on duty. They are called to be watchmen and shepherds, but when they fail to be vigilant in keeping the church alive for the sake of Christ, the people become lethargic, set in their ways, and centered on self and not on reaching their community with the gospel. When leaders snooze, their spiritual muscles atrophy. Like muscular dystrophy, a physical disease that progressively weakens the body's skeletal muscles, spiritual dystrophy is the progressive decay and weakening of the muscles of scriptural truth. The church becomes a mausoleum in the community, for spiritual growth ceases and deadness takes over. It is difficult to maintain the power of godliness when a universal deadness and declension prevails.

When the spirit decays within, our outward devotion becomes merely form without substance. We may look good on the outside, but inwardly we are rotten. Jesus affirmed that poor leadership leads to dead or comatose communities when he accused the Pharisees of being like whitewashed tombs (Matt. 23:27)—all dressed up and looking good on the outer surface but full of corruption, decay, and deadness on the inside. When the spirituality of leadership degenerates, the church reflects the atrophy by becoming ingrown, with the gospel becoming irrelevant to the community.

"O church, arise" was the rallying cry of Christ, who exhorted the church at Sardis to "Wake up, and strengthen what remains" (Rev. 3:2). Evidently there was some breath left that needed resuscitation. Leaders, however, must be willing to do CPR and resuscitate the life of a dying church by making necessary changes and injecting the gospel into their local ministries.

SYMPTOM #6 OF POOR LEADERSHIP: FEAR OF CHANGE

Fear of change is common, for fluctuations from the status quo upset the equilibrium of an expiring congregation. The loss of a pastor, by either retirement, conflict, immorality, or death, will bring change whether the leadership likes it or not. In fact, change is inevitable because life is not stagnant and the culture is constantly morphing. Besides, Christ is always at work extending his kingdom, which means that a believer's existence is dynamic, not static. Mausoleum churches that have been sedate in their graveyard for a number of years will have the biggest difficulty changing, even if change is small. Such churches need to learn an important lesson—that part of doing God's will is being open to Christ-centered change.

Poor leaders fear change because it may disrupt their own security. They don't know how change will affect their relationship with the pastor or with other leaders. And if a new pastor is coming or has been installed, they have no idea what type of association they will have with him. They certainly don't want to lose their influence and positions of authority in the congregation or on the leadership board. Fear is an emotion that causes people to hide from or avoid their problems. It is a core issue in human beings that has plagued them since Adam hid from God. In answer to the Lord's question, "Where are you?," Adam replied by saying that he had become afraid at the sound of God because he was naked, so he hid himself (Gen. 3:9–10). Fear causes us to retreat and to circumvent issues that should be dealt with. Dying churches certainly have many issues confronting them, so they must "wake up" from their deadness and their refusal to change!

In serving a particular church as pastor, I was confronted by a couple of elders who warned me not to make any changes, even slight ones, because change would be viewed as condescending to the prior pastor, whom they loved dearly. However, this was not the prior pastor's view, but rather just the opinion of those who had devoted themselves to his vision and ministry style. Just tweaking an order of service was, in their eyes, tampering with the "holy grail." The pastor whom I followed didn't mind me changing things. So why did the elders feel so insecure? They were unprepared for change and feared losing influence on the board. They were very close to the former pastor and were content with living in the past.

Fear of change is a definite symptom of poor leadership. What makes matters worse is when there are leaders who are possessive of a church that really belongs to Christ! "It's been this way for a long time, and we like it this way. We want no changes to our church." Such attitudes keep the church entombed to its past and make it unappealing for newcomers to stay, unless, of course, they are comfortable hanging around a cemetery.

CHANGE IS GOOD

From the beginning, in the garden of Eden, to the culmination of Scripture in Revelation, change has always been under God's purview. Why, then, do we fight against it, demanding our own wills and desiring the status quo? Change is what the Lord uses to cause us to grow spiritually, to help us understand him more fully, and to prepare us for the final and perfect change when, at the last trumpet, the dead will be raised imperishable (1 Cor. 15:52–53). Since change is part of God's sovereign will, it must be good, even when bad things happen. God uses evil situations to accomplish his purposes, which are always good. For instance, the death of Christ on the cross was the result of the evil intention of men, but it accomplished God's good purposes to save the elect.

In God's providence, he chose Esther to be taken from her family (that is, from the care of Mordecai), thereby engineering a change that would affect the course of history. Did she want to become part of the harem of a pagan king? Probably not! Did she have to learn to adapt to a life-altering situation? Of course! Did she have to trust in God's sovereign rule when evil was pressing her? By all means! Esther realized that her life was not her own—it belonged to God. Even though God is not directly mentioned in the book of Esther, his presence is felt throughout, and Esther's countrymen depended on her as God's facilitator of deliverance. When faced with a life-and-death situation, she submitted to the rule of God, believing that she lived "for such a time as this" (Esth. 4:14). Understanding the goodness of God, which propelled her to do God's will above her own, eased any inner turmoil she may have felt.

Conflict in a church pales to insignificance when compared to the conflict that Esther faced. Struggles and disagreements in a church may force change, but any upheaval is to be seen as occurring within God's providence. And if God is at work in us, willing and working for his good pleasure (Phil. 2:13), which is always for our best, then change must also be good for God's people. Understanding this assures us that all things will work together for good for those who love God and are called according to his purpose (see Rom. 8:28), even the corrupt things that may have happened because of church conflict. Leaders therefore are urged to wake up to the fact that change is good because it serves the purposes of God.

A beloved pastor retired after many years in the church. Although this act would produce much change for the congregation, the elders saw it as good. They hired a transitional pastor to help them to discover their personality as a church, to revisit and recast their vision, and to rework their philosophy of ministry in order to carry out their vision. Once policies were reviewed and the philosophy established, a pastoral search committee was formed and charged with finding a pastor that fit their personality, vision, and philosophy. Change was not something they feared. They saw it as God's providentially working out his purposes to reorder and revitalize the church's ministry in order to find a pastor most suited to the congregation's reformulated values and vision.

God used the disruptions and changes in the apostle Paul's life over and over again for good. Even the conflict that he had with Barnabas over John Mark (Acts 15:36–41) turned out for the better for all parties involved, for God multiplied the missionary outreach to Gentiles two-fold. Paul sharply disagreed with Barnabas and, as a result, chose Silas to accompany him. Because of God's providence, both John Mark and Silas became mentored by seasoned missionaries, which gave them vision and turned their lives around. John Mark, for instance, needed a second chance and evidently proved worthy and a great help to Barnabas. In fact, he and Paul became reconciled, and Paul described him as "very useful to me for ministry" in his second letter to Timothy (2 Tim. 4:11).

TREATMENT FOR THE FEAR OF CHANGE

Leaders who allow fear to control their lives yield to anxiety and forget what Jesus said. Anxiety cannot "add a single hour to [one's] span of life" (Matt. 6:27). Various medications are used to treat anxiety disorders, including such drugs as benzodiazepines, antidepressants, and beta blockers. A beta blocker is used to control heart rhythm, causing the heart to beat more slowly, thereby reducing blood pressure, which rises with anxiety. God has allowed these discoveries to help those who are suffering mental and physical disorders.

A Christian's beta blocker is not a pill that lessens worry and apprehension caused by change. It is Jesus himself, for God gives us a new heart (Ezek. 36:26) that beats with security, courage, and perspective. Perfect love casts out fear (1 John 4:18), and the epitome of perfect love is Christ. Having Jesus as our beta blocker helps us to overcome whatever fears we have, especially the fear of change.

Security

The first component in the beta blocker of Christ is security. If we are Christ's sheep, then we are safe forever (John 10:27–28). Christ ransomed his life so that we may live (Matt. 20:28); our perpetual destiny is guaranteed because nothing can snatch us from his hands. To further assure us, Christ said, "My Father, who has given them [his sheep] to me, is greater than all, and no one is able to snatch them out of the Father's hand" (John 10:29). Why is this so? Because the Father and Christ are one in their ability to preserve the sheep (John 10:30)!

If our security is in Christ, then we have nothing to fear—for if Christ is for us, who can really be against us (Rom. 8:31)? Even when trials and conflicts come, we can persevere and weather the storms because Christ, who is for us, will direct the events for our good. Since nothing can separate us from the love of Christ (Rom. 8:35–39), all things will work together for the good of those who love God and are called according to his purposes (Rom. 8:28). Why do things work for our good? Because God has predestined us to conform to the image of his Son (Rom. 8:29)! Since we have the security of knowing that God is in charge of all things, including change, we have nothing to fear because even change ultimately works out for our best.

Courage

The second component in the beta blocker of Christ is courage. Once security is understood and accepted, a man after the heart of Christ is to exercise what is already his for the taking—boldness to do the right thing. Courage is the strength of purpose that enables us to overcome fear and difficulty because our purposes are aligned with Christ's. Physical bravery, therefore, is grounded in spiritual maturity, which is doing what is right and pleasing to God. The courage to change or to face change is a matter of discerning God's will and having confidence that he is the author of change. It is he who directs our steps even though we plan our ways (see Prov. 16:9). It is he who turns the king's heart in whatever way he wishes (Prov. 21:1), and it is he who declares the end from the beginning (Isa. 46:1). So, change is part of his declaration as he providentially governs his creation.

Perspective

The third component in the beta blocker of Christ is perspective. If God is the author of change, then our perspective must be the same as his. We are to view change from a heavenly point of view, as accomplishing God's eternal purposes—generally, for the enhancement of his kingdom on earth, and specifically, for the benefit of his sheep. Perspective comes only from a proper relationship with Jesus, who is perfect love. If we don't live to please him, then change will be seen from a standpoint of self-interest. Since God is behind the change, we should accept it and seek to please him by delighting in his ways (see, for example, Prov. 23:26), which means adapting to change for the right reasons. Conflict and transition in a church is, in a sense, change and is to be seen within the providence of God, and therefore must be purposeful. Our growth as Christians and as leaders depends on our choices in response to the changes in our lives and in our churches.

Mismanagement of Change

Although change is unavoidable and occurs within the sovereign purposes of God, leaders will still be held responsible for the way change is implemented. Here, the plurality of leadership acting with one mind (that is, the mind of Christ) will cause change to be more manageable. Conflict in churches easily happens when change is mismanaged or crammed down the throat of sheep. A pastor, for instance, may attend a church growth seminar or read a book on revitalizing his ministry and then attempt to implement his new discoveries without laying a proper biblical foundation for the change that he desires. He must involve his leadership in discussions as well as in the process for executing the change. Leaders are called to work together to determine the mind of Christ and then to perform and execute it for the betterment of the sheep. If consensus cannot be reached on the pastor's ideas, then any action should be postponed and more prayer about the project offered to God.

Conflict may also arise when a new pastor is called to a church and then tries to put into operation new ideas and ministries without first winning the confidence of leaders and staff. Pastors are wise to build trust by ministering to their flock and relating to their people for at least a year before any major paradigm shift is instituted. Proper management of future change follows a plan that should be implemented one step at a time. Steps for administrating paradigm shifts are known as the five *P*'s of managing change.

Preparation. The first *p* is *preparation.* Pastors and leaders are to prepare the sheep for any coming change by understanding possible reactions to the change and by spending time with people to lessen the shock of it. Jesus said that he knows his sheep and that, when they hear his voice, they follow him (John 10:27). Leaders are to know their sheep so that they will follow them throughout the process of change. This will not occur without proper involvement with the flock. Sheep do not particularly like change, for it upsets the status quo and brings uncertainty with it. Perceiving how people may react to the projected change helps in proper planning. Elders are to be as wise as serpents and as innocent as doves (Matt. 10:16); therefore, they must investigate the ramifications of change among church members. If a new pastor doesn't spend time getting acquainted with his sheep, he will not know what to expect when he tries to bring about a shift in the church's ministry. Spending time with people will give leaders insight on how to strategize and determine the best way to communicate the coming changes. The first tendency among sheep is to resist any major change, but when they are included in the process, sought out for their feedback, and asked for their participation, resistance is lessened and fears diminished.

A young and visionary pastor was called to serve a growing, trendy, Bible-centered church located in a city and near a prestigious university. When the pulpit committee called him and the elders affirmed his calling, the congregation experienced new excitement for the future of their church. The elders, however, gave this man carte blanche to institute whatever changes he felt necessary to move the church in the direction that he personally felt best. This man was not from the area, did not know his sheep, and had not developed the respect that he would need to present major changes to the congregation. He changed the persona of the church from a teaching and fellowship model to one that focused more on approaching faith in a cerebral and intellectual manner, so as to win academics from the local community. The results were devastating, for although the sheep were very knowledgeable in the Word and very accomplished in their secular pursuits, 70 percent of them were not urbanites who desired modern intellectual approaches to ministry in order to win a group of people that had nothing in common with their suburbanite lifestyle.

Change is to be introduced when the leadership believes it is the will of the Lord to do so. Moving a local flock to another pasture or having them accept a monumental change in the present pasture will take individual involvement by leaders, personal care of the anxious, and proper prodding of the stubborn. To uproot a flock of sheep without preparation and to drive them into an unknown pasture is foolishness.

Partnering. The second *p* in managing change is *partnering* with influential leaders and key stakeholders in the upcoming change. Scripture tells us that two are better than one because there is a greater return on their laboring together (see Eccl. 4:9). For a pastor, this means rallying others to participate in his plan. Nehemiah did this when he took a few men with him to investigate the condition of the walls of Jerusalem at night. Without knowing what was in Nehemiah's heart, these chosen men probably became part of his plan in convincing the officials and inhabitants of Jerusalem that the walls needed rebuilding. They could testify to the dilapidated condition and the lack of secure gates, making Nehemiah's appeal more urgent. (See Neh. 2:12–18.)

Reality forces pastors to partner with key church people so that others will feel more comfortable with the new change. Key people are not just those who are closest to the pastor, for they may be considered his "yes men." Partnering must be with key leaders outside the inner circle of the pastor. Once these key people are in place, it should be their voice that the sheep hear the most with regard to the proposed change. If they are truly shepherds and involved with their sheep, then the sheep will more likely follow them during the process of change. The people whom the pastor enlists as partners, therefore, must be natural leaders whose opinions are heard, appreciated, and accepted.

Publication. The third *p* in managing change is *publication* of the plan. Overcommunication is the key and is crucial in managing change successfully. Planning is vital, but publishing the plan is imperative. Sheep need to hear about the proper implementation of change over and over again and, in some cases, in different ways before the reality of newness sets in. Wisdom dictates the passage of time in order to give people opportunities to mentally process the change and thoroughly discuss it among themselves. In other words, psychological preparation is necessary. Leaders who allow time for proper communication are wise and will, in the long run, be honored for their decision (see Prov. 3:35). The time differential between the announcement of the coming change and the actual implementation of it will vary depending on the complexities of the change. In the meantime, leaders are to be prepared to answer questions such as "Why the need for change?" and "Why now?" and "Is there any other choice?" It is essential, when leaders are communicating the importance of change, to include the negative effects of not changing. Asking people what they may see as beneficial consequences of change incorporates them in the process and lessens the anxiety that change will bring. People want to be heard before they follow. Furthermore, elders are not to lord their authority over their sheep by instituting de facto change, for sheep need reassurance that their leaders have their best interests in mind. Change must therefore be beneficial to the sheep.

I have a friend who accepted a call to a church whose congregation fluctuates in attendance between summer and winter. He followed a beloved man who had retired from the ministry. Although his personality would be characterized as totally opposite to the former pastor's and his ministry style very dissimilar, he was wise in his plan for change. He assured the leaders of the church, as well as the congregation, that there were ten things that he would not change in instituting his plan for the church. When he listed the ten things, all of which were dear to the congregants, he not only alleviated their fears of drastic change but also endeared himself to them for considering their feelings and interests. In vision casting, leaders are wise to include those things that they would not change.

Plotting progress. The fourth *p* in managing change is *plotting progress*. Changes that are made must be monitored and analyzed. In one sense it is counting the cost of what we are doing, for Jesus exhorts us to assess the cost of being his disciples (Luke 14:28–33). If we are not willing to track the effectiveness of change for kingdom purposes, then the change should not be initiated in the first place. Everything that we do to bring about change must be done with the gospel in mind (see Col. 3:17). Part of the feedback process should include not only what leaders think but also what opponents to the change have observed, for their input may be valuable for future decisions.

After instituting two separate and distinct worship services, leaders of a church in the Midwest set times for congregational feedback six months later. Although the initial establishment had not been without controversy, the majority of the comments were actually favorable. The two services had not caused a major exodus; people had adapted and accepted the leadership's explanation and submitted to the vision. By having an opportunity to make comments, the congregation felt included in the process and realized that the leaders had the best interests of the people in mind.

Pliability. The fifth *p* in managing change is *pliability*. Leaders are to be flexible and willing to stop the changes from being made if they prove ineffective, caustic to the body, or schismatic. If the first four steps have been followed and instituting change at first seemed acceptable but has now become controversial for various reasons, then the leadership must reassess and be willing to stop what they're doing. Nothing should be considered permanent, because God's will is active, and he is continually working for the good of his people. What leaders thought was plan A might have been only a small step in God's plan B for the congregation. What was learned in the process, and how character was honed and perfected, may have been God's intent all along. We plan our own direction with perceived changes, but God directs our steps to include a new path, which allows us to participate in his kingdom's work (see Prov. 16:9).

Daniel is a good example of a person who accepted change as part of God's sovereign plan.[4] Surely he had not planned to be captured and sent in exile to the Babylonian kingdom. Because he served under a number of kings, he had to be flexible in various situations, for he understood that God was in control. He labored for the governmental authorities with diligence and forthrightness. Although in a foreign culture, he kept constant his relationship with the living Lord. If at any time the king's edicts conflicted with the dictates of God's Word, Daniel would obey God rather than men, with no hesitation. But if there was no conflict, he demonstrated his flexibility in managing adversity and adapting to the situations that God had providentially planned and engineered.

Daniel's friends, Shadrach, Meshach, and Abednego, also accepted their destiny as God's doing, and so they made the best of their captivity. They were appointed magistrates in Babylon to the dismay of the local satraps, who plotted their demise. When faced with the choice of worshiping the gods of Nebuchadnezzar or suffering the fiery furnace, they chose the furnace. The king offered them a second chance, but they still refused to bow before pagan gods. Entrusting their undesirable change in circumstances to God's providence, they told the king that their God was able to deliver them from the worst of fates. But even if

---

4. Daniel said, "He changes times and seasons; he removes kings and sets up kings; he gives wisdom to the wise and knowledge to those who have understanding" (Dan. 2:21).

God chose not to do so, they would trust him anyway (Dan. 3:16–18). They believed that God was the author of change, and therefore they acquiesced to his purposes in spite of the evil calculations of men. Church leaders, in like fashion, are to surrender their desire for control to God's sovereign hand, trusting that all change will work for good, whether they like it or not.

GOD'S CHURCH ALIVE

The Lord loves his church and will not desert it, regardless of its inner turmoil and unrest. Christ's church is never dead, for his Spirit resuscitates those who still have breath. And a church with Christ's Spirit is active and will rise from the ashes of division to spread the gospel within its local community. Pity the man who causes church dissensions, for he snubs the appeal of Paul, who entreats the people of God to set aside divisions (1 Cor. 1:10). Factions denigrate the name of Christ and bring condemnation on the church's witness. The next chapter will consider the matter of leaders who are unwilling to engage in reconciliation—and how it is a flaw in leadership.

8

Reconciling Differences

Therefore, since we have been justified by faith, we have peace
with God through our Lord Jesus Christ. (Rom. 5:1)

THE GLORY OF RECONCILIATION

Redemption is one of God's extraordinary themes woven throughout the Bible. From the Old Testament through the New Testament,
a gracious God demonstrates his love for wayward people by offering
appeasement, which is achieved in the death and resurrection of Christ.
Reconciliation of God to man and of man to God is described in Scripture and illustrates the glory of God. Peace with a holy God is a central
biblical theme. It brings armistice with God to those alienated from
him by their sin. God's offer of amnesty, however, came at the cost of
Christ.[1] And if Christ gave his life to reconcile us to God, then, as his
disciples, we are to promote reconciliation within his church.

When people resolve their differences, they bring glory to God.
A friend demonstrated this when he approached me to intercede on his
behalf with his ex-wife. He and his wife had been divorced and separated for a number of years, but he realized that the estrangement was
not God's will. This was reinforced in weekly meetings with an older

1. "For in him all the fullness of God was pleased to dwell, and through him to reconcile
to himself all things, whether on earth or in heaven, making peace by the blood of his cross"
(Col. 1:19–20).

Christian brother and mentor, who stressed accountability in living for Christ. What echoed in the mind of my friend was the question, "Whom do you live for—yourself or Christ?" His mentor stressed his responsibility before Christ to his ex-wife, stating that divorce was not an option in God's Word. His mentor advised him to get out of God's way and to live what was right by Scripture. Without biblical grounds for divorce, my friend reluctantly acceded to the will of Christ and sought mediators on his behalf.

Desiring to live for Christ, my friend understood that he had to submit to the Savior's will. He was therefore moved to attempt reconciliation with a wife for whom he had no feelings. He had been happier separated, but now he had to put his feelings aside, do what was right, and trust God for the results. He learned that submission was placing his will under Christ's, even when it was tough; otherwise, it was mere agreement.

When his wife agreed to be reconciled, my friend proposed that my wife and I should counsel him and his wife. Eventually, I performed the ceremony of remarriage, bringing glory to God. My friend and his wife are approaching fifty years of marriage. Both are active in their church, and he has been an elder for several years now. Forgiven sinners, my two friends were reconciled to God and then to each other; but Christ received the glory.

DRAGONS

In spite of Marshall Shelley's book titled *Well-Intentioned Dragons*, there appear to be very few such dragons, for dragons seldom intend to be sweet and gentle. They are totally unpleasant creatures that breathe fire, which destroys the very air around them. Shelley describes his dragons as "often sincere, well-meaning saints, but they leave ulcers, strained relationships, and hard feelings in their wake."[2] Typically pillars of the community with strong personalities, dragons bring continued strife, clouding the vision of the church. As dedicated church members, they

2. Marshall Shelley, *Well-Intentioned Dragons: Ministering to Problem People in the Church* (Minneapolis: Bethany House, 1994), 11.

are convinced that they are serving God and doing what's right, but the fire that they breathe causes nastiness and conflict.

Dragons often befriend the pastor initially, but later demonstrate unhappiness with him. Thinking that they know congregational concerns, they are sure to inform him of the "real situation in the church."[3] Dragons are self-serving and controlling, and they believe those with contrary opinions are wrong. After three decades of ministry, I have come to the conclusion that there really are no well-intentioned dragons, but only ill-intentioned intimidators who are destroying churches, disheartening pastors, and disillusioning the family of faith. It doesn't matter how pleasant or well-meaning they are in their own minds; their premeditated and harmful actions are normally motivated by pride and are, therefore, sinful.

One of my dragons assailed me in my sixth year of church planting. "You belong in a seminary, not in the church," was the accusation. "Go teach seminarians and leave running a church to us," the dragon directed. The "us" was a reference to him and another elder, who desired to change the focus and vision of the church.

For several months and without my knowledge, the dragon had maligned my character, given a twisted interpretation of my motives, and generally stirred up strife within the leadership and the congregation. After years of ministering to his family, involving him in the inner circle of leaders, and training him in biblical leadership, I thought there was a trusted bond between us. The last thing I expected was betrayal and deception.

Having persevered through the trauma of my daughter's broken back, my wife's cancer, and a small group that had turned grace into legalism—all within the preceding two years—I was exhausted and exasperated. After much prayer and counsel, I decided that it would be best for my family if I resigned from the church that I had planted and labored in for seven years. The fire breathing of the dragon had taken its toll. Though painful for my family, the struggle became especially agonizing for the church, which continued to struggle for many years.

Reconciliation is difficult with dragons that continue to believe that they are right. But the attempt to seek reconciliation is still the

3. Ibid, 43.

responsibility of both parties. Our duty before the Lord is to do what we can to repair relationships. Whether we succeed or not is up to the other party and to God's grace. I surely did not want to re-affiliate with my dragon. Feelings say, "Stay away from the dragon and avoid him at all costs." However, a relationship with our Savior speaks more directly: "Be reconciled if possible, and enlist others to assist if needed."

SYMPTOM #7 OF POOR LEADERSHIP: UNWILLINGNESS TO ENGAGE IN RECONCILIATION

Another symptom of failed leadership is the refusal to be reconciled with another. When leaders carry around an unforgiving spirit and entrench themselves in the hardness of their own hearts, they not only commit the sin of bitterness but also fail to model the character of Christ, which is a requisite of leadership in the church. Furthermore, such men actually demonstrate their disqualification for office by their pride and stubbornness. When elders fail to rebuke a brother among them or within the church fellowship for resentment toward others, they feed the disease of poor leadership. Simply turning a deaf ear and a blind eye to a problem that needs addressing will not make it disappear. Elders are truly God's instruments for applying wise discipline to those who veer from truth and act like unbelievers.

When I sought advice about disciplining the ill-intentioned dragon described above, I was asked to forgo filing charges on the premise that it would hurt the church even more. The congregation, it was argued, needed healing, not a trial. I complied with the request and thought that my love could cover his sins. I was wrong, and to this day I regret not seeking church discipline as an attempt to reclaim this man to ministry. Church discipline is not punitive, but is intended to retrieve the person; and I did not give this person an opportunity to repent and be reclaimed for kingdom purposes. Although others had told this dragon that he was wrong, church discipline would have formally given him the opportunity to defend himself and possibly to see the situation through more objective eyes.

As an interim pastor, I once combated a couple of ill-intentioned dragons who refused to adjust to the new direction of their church after the resignation of a beloved pastor. They believed that the pastor, a personal friend, had been compelled to leave the church because of the discontent of other elders and congregants, and their loyalty blinded them to the will of God for the church.

While investigating this charge, I asked the former pastor if he felt that he had been forced to leave the church. He informed me that he had left because he believed it was God's will for him to assume another ministry position. He in no way had felt constrained to leave the church. I then conveyed my findings to the discontented elders, who refused to accept them. They then accused me of siding with the dissidents. I tried to reason with these men, but they rebuffed all attempts. Such leaders' unwillingness to receive truth and to resolve issues calls into question their spiritual maturity as shepherds of God's sheep.

Dragon leaders are caught up in their own self-importance, connections, and agendas. They think they are in the right, and they manipulate others to agree with them. In one sense, they are bullies—spoiled children pushing people around in order to get their own way. But unlike children, they are actually wolves in sheep's clothing, destroying and fracturing the church of the living God.

Tim Witmer, professor of practical theology at Westminster Theological Seminary in Philadelphia, Pennsylvania, contrasts these rapacious bullies with faithful shepherds.

> Faithful shepherds protect their flocks not only from harmful outside influences but from the self-serving among the sheep. Many congregations have experienced the intimidation of bullies within their midst when leaders fail to take responsibility to shepherd the flock. It is often the strong-willed, outspoken, highly opinionated folk who fill the void. There will always be leaders—the issue is whether they are the leaders called and gifted by God to shepherd his flock or those who push themselves forward so that they can push others around.[4]

4. Timothy Z. Witmer, *The Shepherd Leader: Achieving Effective Shepherding in Your Church* (Phillipsburg, NJ: P&R Publishing, 2010), 23.

TREATMENT FOR THE UNWILLINGNESS TO BE RECONCILED

Hydrogen peroxide is a powerful oxidizer that kills bacteria, viruses, and fungi on surfaces. It may be used as a disinfectant in the kitchen and the bathroom and as an antiseptic on wounds. I read a study once that concluded that this versatile household product is extremely underutilized in the home and is often replaced with products that are higher priced, yet less effective. Apparently the reason for this is that the packaging is not as appealing as the more expensive items touted by advertisers.

The "hydrogen peroxide" that churches need, in order to overcome leaders' unwillingness to achieve reconciliation, is church discipline. The outside package seems unattractive to many churchgoers, and therefore it is underutilized—but it is a wonderful product that may be summarized in an adage based on God's Word: "Spare the rod; spoil the child." There are some spoiled brats in church leadership—leaders who think they are privileged and untouchable, but who need the firm hand of discipline.

I dealt with one such elder brat, who resigned from the session because he could not submit to a decision, after which he attempted to recant his resignation. In his recantation, he stated that he would take a leave of absence until the issue was no more. In its collective wisdom, the session explained that there was no provision in the church documents and bylaws for an elder to summarily and arbitrarily take a leave of absence because of a disagreement with policy. His resignation stood, and he was removed from the voting board.

A godly professor and fellow elder, commenting on the matter, said that the behavior of this elder was akin to a child in a sandbox who allowed only his favorite friends to enter and play with his toys. This spoiled brat defended his turf, hoarded the toys, and invited only children of his choosing to play with him. When another child forced entry into his box, he picked up his toys and departed. Dictating when, and under what conditions, this man would serve the church was the action of a spoiled brat who would play with others only upon his terms and conditions. Confronting childish behavior requires discipline, for "Whoever spares the rod hates his son, but he who loves him is diligent to discipline him" (Prov. 13:24). Loving this elder meant confronting him in his sin.

A leader who refuses to forgive and be reconciled with his brothers reveals that iniquity is bound up in his heart, and the only way to remove it is by biblical discipline (2 Sam. 7:14). As a loving father chastises his children, we must not hold back discipline on a brother in Christ. Even though it may seem harsh at first, it is for his benefit and the larger good of the congregation, in order for him to be restored to ministry if possible.

Formal discipline is an act of love, for as the Lord loves us and applies his scourge at times (see Heb. 12:6–7), we as the church, acting in the Lord's name, must apply correction to straying members of the flock—including leaders. Failure to apply discipline breeds illegitimate children (Heb. 12:8) and prevents the sinner from experiencing the goodness of the holiness (Heb. 12:10) to which we are called, as well as from enjoying the peaceful fruit of righteousness that it yields (Heb. 12:11).

Most importantly, church discipline is a means of holding members and leaders accountable to the vows they have taken, serving also as an exhortation to obey the Scriptures they have affirmed to uphold. Leaders seriously fail in their calling when they refuse to exercise biblical procedures in keeping their flock accountable to the teaching of the Word of God. If an elder is unable to manage and discipline his own family (1 Tim. 3:4), he will not manage the church well (1 Tim. 3:5). Good family men discipline their children; good church leaders discipline their members.

Harder still is the use of discipline on elders. Yet they are the ones who in all likelihood need it most. Abusive leaders are those who are dictatorial and demand obedience to them rather than to Scripture, who conspire with others in secret to assure success of their selfish plans, who refuse to be accountable to other leaders, and who make wild accusations against elders whom they consider to be in opposition. It is they who stir up strife among the brothers and who disturb the peace and unity of the church (see Prov. 6:16–19).

Another form of abuse is found in elders who cater to the whims of authoritarian dragons. Such men are the drovers who favor the cattlemen and who fear being seen as contrarians to those who are more influential. They allow another's will to dominate the church, without considering Christ's will in the matter. Elders who breach the peace of the body should be disciplined for breaking their vows of pursuing peace, purity, and unity within the church.

My Peacemaker friends tell me that they have numerous case studies in which some elders refuse to be reconciled with others. These leaders maintain their antagonistic spirits even when confronted with their ungodly attitude, and if charges are filed against them, the normal tendency is for them to quickly leave the church. Those who stay and fight their case, usually for the principle of the matter, cause further division in the church, making it nearly impossible for reconciliation to take place.

When elders are not confronted with their sinful behavior according to Scripture, conflict in the church is inevitable. Sin is compounded and spreads like wildfire, often causing irreversible suffering to the sheep and loss in membership. Adhering to scriptural principles is the farthest thing from the minds of dragons, and so antagonism multiplies, leading to further schism.

The Bible, however, is profitable for teaching, reproof, correction, and training in righteousness (2 Tim. 3:16). The process of discipline begins with an informed congregation. Congregants must be taught what church discipline is, told what Jesus said they should do if they discover a brother in sin, and encouraged to ask forgiveness for any bitterness they may have themselves toward others.

If we are adherents of God's Word, then we must understand that church battles are not against flesh and blood but against powers and principalities that have as their goal the destruction and impotency of the church. Our love for God and for each other ought to compel us to reprove those who we know are sinning and to repent from our own irreverence. We are not to turn a deaf ear to unrighteousness, for we are called to be emissaries of Christ, standing for righteousness and combating transgression.

Instruction, therefore, is the first step in the employment of church discipline. The second step is pursuing loving confrontation. If a brother sins, we are instructed to go and reprove him in private (Matt. 18:15). In doing so, we would be wise to use the four *G*'s in the "Peacemaker's

Pledge" by Ken Sande.[5] In approaching any sinner, we are to be committed to *glorify* God (the first *g*) (1 Cor. 10:31), to *get* the logs out of our own eyes (the second *g*) (Matt. 7:5), to *gently* restore if possible (the third *g*) (Gal. 6:1), and to *go* and be reconciled if we are involved (the fourth *g*) (Matt. 5:23–24).

I recall a situation in which two good friends took me to lunch and lovingly counseled me to approach a dragon and seek reconciliation. When I became defensive, they cautioned me about the logs in my own eyes. "What logs?" I demanded. "Bitterness, hurt, austerity, pride, and self-righteousness," was their response. I hadn't expected to hear this, for I was the embattled pastor, scarred and scorched by the dragon. I was the innocent party, and the dragon should be seeking my forgiveness. They agreed that the dragon was wrong but maintained that my response was just as sinful. My attitude was improper, and my own pain blinded me. Bitterness is like acid that eats the container from the inside out. The hurt that I felt was not bothering the dragon; it was only destroying me.

The advice of these friends struck as a wound (Prov. 27:6), but I could not forsake their entreaties, for "the sweetness of a friend comes from his earnest counsel" (Prov. 27:9). They had my best interests in mind and reminded me that, as the mirror reflects the face, the heart reflects the character within (see Prov. 27:19). I was encouraged to do what I could to mend fences, and so I did.

The third step in the employment of church discipline is third-party confirmation. If the person remains in an irresoluble mood after being confronted, then we must take another with us to witness the sinner's recalcitrance (Matt. 18:16). If the sinner repents, we have won the brother; but if he remains defiant and impenitent, we have secured a witness to his contumacy.

I was consulted in the case of a pastor who allegedly offended a number of his congregants with his authoritarian attitude. They approached him individually with his offense, according to the admonition of Jesus in Matthew 18:15. Never admitting wrong or apologizing for his lack of concern, the pastor continued his ways, driving a number of sheep

5. Ken Sande, *The Peacemaker: A Biblical Guide to Resolving Personal Conflict*, 3rd ed. (Grand Rapids: Baker Books, 2004), 259–60.

from the congregation. When a presbytery committee became involved and investigated the complaints, he told the inquisitors that no charges could be formally made against him because Scripture said that two or three witnesses had to be produced. Although more than five people were personally offended by the pastor, he claimed that there were no other witnesses to his alleged offense against each individual. Although five or six had come to him independently, he still maintained that there had to be witnesses to each individual occurrence; otherwise it was his word against his accusers'. Even though the allegations had come from separate incidents and may have been circumstantial, the number of complaints warranted investigation, especially as it related to his character. What the parishioners should have done was to bring a witness with them in a second confrontation, in order to have testimony against the pastor for his contumacy in refusing to change his behavior.

The fourth step in the employment of church discipline is a trial by peers. Jesus said that if the person refuses to listen to the allegations after two or three other people are brought for witness confirmation, then the church must be informed (Matt. 18:17). In Presbyterian churches, the elders represent the congregation, and therefore they are to receive the complaint against the sinner.[6] The elders then appoint a prosecutor and begin proceedings to bring the unrepentant sinner to trial. If, during trial, the accused fails to confess and repent and is found guilty, then his censure could be removal from office, exclusion from the Lord's Table, or expulsion from the church. Discipline is to be taken seriously, because Christ delineated its procedure to help cleanse his church from unrighteousness.

Paul instructed the Corinthians to remove an incestuous fornicator from their fellowship by expelling him from the church. This appears harsh, but the purpose of excommunication is not punishment, but spiritual reclamation—to redeem a fallen sinner and to save him in the day of the Lord (see 1 Cor. 5:1–5). If leaders are unwilling to exercise biblical discipline within the church, the result will be additional

6. "Taking it to the church" may be defined differently depending on the individual church or denomination. Appropriate church bylaws and denominational procedures should be followed in meting out church discipline.

conflict. Sides will be taken, the peace and unity of the church will be shaken, and the very witness of Christ will be eroded. Church conflicts, typically occurring every few years, are best resolved when people follow godly leaders who truly believe that Scripture is sufficient for life and godliness (see 2 Peter 1:3). Within the visible church, we may say there are dragons as well as sheep and wolves. The elders are the watchmen on the virtual wall of every church body, and therefore they must protect the sheep from the evil schemes of man and the Devil, which frequently come from within the local body.

Discipline is not just for sin within the church, but also to be applied for actions outside the church. Businessmen, professionals, and tradesmen cannot separate their church involvement from their professional lives. As members of a local church, they profess Christ and therefore should demonstrate Christian ethics in their business dealings. The church elders should confront those who cheat people and who demonstrate unprincipled practices. The reputation of Christ is at stake when Christians display behavior unbecoming of a follower of Christ.

My friend, who mediated many a church conflict in his days with Peacemaker Ministries, tells of a situation in which church leaders were disciplining a man for unethical business practices. Initially, the man was furious and saw the intervention as an invasion of privacy, for he was adamantly against discussing his financial and business dealings. When less formal attempts at altering the person's business practices failed, the elders filed charges and conducted a fair and open hearing. The Holy Spirit began changing the heart of the beguiler as details were revealed about his treatment of vendors and suppliers.

By the end of his formal trial, and after much teaching by concerned friends who spent time in showing him how to behave as a Christian businessman, the former recalcitrant openly repented. He responded by paying back with interest what he had wrongfully withheld.

Not only were the fruits of his repentance seen in his business and the protection of the reputation of Christ's church, but his marriage benefited as well! His wife told the leaders how much happier and less stressed he was at home, how he began to read the Bible more, and that he even had more patience with their children. God was at work! This man was rescued and renewed.[7]

Leaders must remember that redeeming church conflict is not just about resolving specific problems, but more about seeing struggles as a vehicle by which God matures his saints, causes them to grow in holiness, and continuously conforms them into the image of Christ. Leaders should therefore model God's truth and demonstrate the practicality and worthiness of Scripture to the flock, not just at church, but also in their public business.

ABUSE OF DISCIPLINE

Of course, discipline can be used improperly as a club to maintain strict compliance to the harsh rule of a few. Arbitrary treatment of antagonists by spiteful leaders is not uncommon. Conflicts necessarily arise from the abuse of authority by leaders who generate an air of secrecy in their manner and inspire fear through an attitude that says, "Submit to our rule—we are God's anointed."

Churches that have authoritarian rulers stifle Christian liberty, enact their personal preferences into law, and suppress joy within the community. When other leaders (drovers, in this instance) defer to the authoritarian ones (for example, the cattle barons), the local church becomes a corral, penning the sheep and causing discomfort and disarray. With the threat of destructive discipline hanging over their heads, sheep look to break out, eventually leaving the church.

Leaders who strive to have their way are the ones who need to be confronted with discipline, but there are few in cattle-baron churches who have the audacity and willingness to do so. It is easier to abandon the church and find more restful pastures than to fight those with power and influence.

A wonderful church once thrived in ministry. It had numerous elders who were involved with shepherding and with determining vision

---

7. Tara Klena Barthel and David V. Edling, *Redeeming Church Conflicts: Turning Crisis into Compassion and Care* (Grand Rapids: Baker Books), 161.

for the community of faith. A few cattlemen took control, grew in influence, and became the ruling elite. Leaders and congregants who did not like their decisions and vision for the church were systematically disenfranchised and told to leave if they couldn't submit to their decisions. Such authoritarian dictates are a form of abuse. Rather than cause greater conflict, a good number of elders chose to leave the church, followed by many sheep. The exodus of people was, in a sense, tacit church discipline, for it purged the congregation of those who were against the philosophy and policies of the elite few. The cattlemen won, the church suffered, and the glory of Christ was tarnished.

COMMUNICATION

A lack of communication with the sheep is a major complaint in the local church. Although oral and written communication from leadership is important, modeling truth is also a form of communication, for actions do speak louder than words. Poor modeling is poor communication. Leaders who joyfully shepherd will easily have good relationships with the congregation, which in turn facilitates communication and increases loyalty among their sheep. Disagreeable and uninformed elders typically have poor interaction with the sheep, thereby contributing to the overall disease in the church: poor leadership.

One of the more egregious forms of non-communication is the cloistered pastor. He exiles himself in his study and further distances himself from his sheep. The next chapter will deal with the eighth symptom of poor leadership: intellectual exile.

9

The Bookworm Pastor

Give your servant therefore an understanding mind to govern your people, that I may discern between good and evil, for who is able to govern this your great people? (1 Kings 3:9)

JESUS, THE GOOD SHEPHERD

When Jesus said that he is "the way, the truth, and the life" (John 14:6), he was directing his followers to the only path to the Father, which is through the Son. That path includes truth and life, indicating that a relationship with Jesus in earthly life is the only certainty for everlasting life. Jesus, as the leader of his disciples, taught truth and modeled relationship.

Jesus, therefore, is not only truth; he is relationship. Although he retreated at times to his quiet places, he soon engaged with people again, for it was through his relationships (both formal and informal) that he taught truth about God, the correct interpretation of Scripture, and how to live according to God's Word. He is the example for pastors to follow. They are to be versed in his truth but relationally involved with their flock. Involvement allows the sheep to hear the voice of their shepherd and respond to the truth that is fed to them.

PASTOR-SCHOLAR

John Calvin held a high view of the gospel ministry and believed that nothing was more urgent for the church than reforming pastoral ministry. He believed that most ministers in his day were blatantly ignorant of Scripture, making them ill-prepared to proclaim the gospel. He desired to be different and promoted the idea of the pastor-scholar, a minister who was both caring and informed. He believed that an educated minister had the duty to relate doctrine to the lives of the people. Ministers were "God's hands" in that they were instruments performing the saving and sanctifying work of God in the world. Philip Ryken, in an article for *Tabletalk* magazine, commented that Calvin was the model of a pastor-scholar by serving as God's agent in ministering to the people of Geneva.

> Based on his reading of Ephesians 4:11, Calvin made a clear distinction between "shepherds" (who served as shepherds of a local church) and "teachers" (who served the wider church by interpreting God's Word, defending true doctrine, and training other men for ministry, much like seminary professors today). But since Calvin held both of these offices, he set an example as a pastor-scholar that Reformation churches have followed ever since.[1]

Richard Baxter (1615–1691) respected Calvin's model of the pastor-scholar. Although he was a prolific writer and an eminent intellectual, he also held a pastoral role and acted as peacemaker to bring unity among Protestants during a time of English civil wars and religious nonconformity. He wrote more than two hundred discourses on doctrine; yet he believed that society was a large family to be cared for under the loving hand of the Father.

Because his parents did not think highly of learning, Baxter mainly educated himself, eventually attending a free school and then the royal court. His scholarship and pastoring skills were well known and were highlighted in his devotional classic, *The Saints' Everlasting Rest*, which is reputed to have been one of the most widely read books of his century. He believed in the practice of scholarship, which is seen in his

---

1. Philip Ryken, "The Pastor-Scholar," *Tabletalk*, July 1, 2009, http://www.ligonier.org/learn /articles/pastor-scholar/.

liturgical work, *Reformed Liturgy*, and culminated in his pastoral guide, *The Reformed Pastor*.

John Colquhoun (1748–1827) was another pastor-scholar. Shortly after his conversion, he felt constrained to walk fifty miles from Luss to Glasgow in order to purchase a copy of Thomas Boston's *Human Nature in Its Fourfold State*. This book, which greatly influenced Colquhoun's early Christian life, depicted four states of human nature: (a) Primitive Integrity; (b) Entire Depravity; (c) Begun Recovery; and (d) Consummate Happiness or Misery. Realizing that he was elevated from depravity into relationship with Christ by grace, Colquhoun dedicated his life to ministry, which included writing and pastoral calling. His books *The Uses of the Gospel and the Law* and *Treatise on Spiritual Comfort* demonstrate scholarship at a practical level.

Thomas Boston (1676–1732), whose book influenced Colquhoun, was a Scottish Puritan known for his pastoral scholarship. He represents the typical Puritan who merged scholarship with pastoral duty. Although we have had a resurgence of Puritan scholarship, we should not forget that our Puritan forefathers were actively engaged in ministering to their people. Scholarship was practical, not merely theoretical, for the sheep were to be fed food that they could swallow and digest.

John Piper is a modern-day Puritan, exemplifying the calling of the pastor-scholar. He served as pastor for preaching and vision at Bethlehem Baptist Church in Minneapolis, Minnesota, for over thirty years. He has written numerous books, including his bestsellers, *Don't Waste Your Life*, *The Passion of Jesus Christ*, and *Desiring God*. He undertook his doctoral work in New Testament studies at the University of Munich, writing his dissertation, *Love Your Enemies*. Writing theology as viewed through the lens of a practical and applied biblical response has always been his goal. Although a scholar, he is also a pastor who desires that his sheep learn truth and respond to the grace of God in their lives.

Piper is also an example of a shepherd who fed his sheep the richness of the gospel. Although he has written many books, he is known as having been a loving pastor of a large congregation. Pastors are to be scholars, especially of the Bible, but not to the detriment of relating to their sheep. If a pastor becomes a bookworm, he may have his nose in a theological treatise, sniffing out sermons and feeding sheep food that they may have a hard time digesting.

BOOKWORM

"Bookworm" is a popular designation for a person who loves reading, studying, and devouring books. The term is derived from the mistaken belief in an insect that bores through books. A number of insects do eat wood or paper, but actual book-boring insects are rare. The concept, however, of eating God's Word is biblical (for example, see Jer. 15:16), and we should bore through it to gain knowledge of God and his purposes. Pastors who concentrate on "knowing," however, may easily become reclusive intellectuals, desiring to teach to the exclusion of building relationships with people. The mere study of God's Word doesn't necessarily guarantee that a person will become a good teacher; and poor teachers should not be chief shepherds, for feeding the sheep is their primary responsibility. Preachers, though they are scholars, must relate the Bible to everyday living. If they do not make the application of God's truth relevant to the common person, then sheep will become emaciated and unable to cope with life's demands. Pastors with a cerebral approach may have difficulty relating truth to life's circumstances and may discount the fact that shepherding is a "no-nonsense," highly practical vocation.

There is an ongoing tension between being a shepherd and being a scholar. J. Gresham Machen, the founder of Westminster Seminary, believed that a pastor should be a scholar. In other words, the pastor-scholar was to be an expert in the Bible and the doctrines that are gleaned from its study. His emphasis, as was John Calvin's, was still on the pastoral side, which meant that the pastor was foremost a shepherd to the local flock. An ignorant pastor, however, would not be very helpful to his sheep, because he would be unable to feed them the truth of God's Word and to explain how doctrine helps them practically through the trials of life. Yet the emphasis was primarily on "pastor" and only secondarily on "scholar." The local shepherd was to be involved relationally with his sheep and, hopefully, with the people of the surrounding community. This is all because good relationships and proper interactions with people will foster opportunities to study doctrine as it relates to daily life and will answer questions of eternal significance.

Although Machen and others believed in the pastor-scholar model, statistics reveal that men of the cloth are often inadequately prepared for the shepherding ministry. Dr. Richard J. Krejcir, in a study performed for the Francis A. Schaeffer Institute of Church Leadership Development,[2] found that pastors are in the most dangerous occupation because of the high percentage of those who burn out, experience conflict, and are ill equipped. Some 89 percent of the pastors surveyed in Reformed and evangelical churches said they had considered leaving the ministry at one time or another, while 57 percent of that number would have forsaken the pastoral call if a better opportunity had presented itself.

In fact, 80 percent of seminary and Bible-college graduates who enter the ministry will leave the vocation within the first five years.[3] These shocking statistics lead to two possible conclusions: either these disaffected men are not truly called to the pastoral ministry, or they are poorly trained for the rigors of shepherding. Tending sheep is a tough and nasty job because sheep have minds of their own and tend, on occasion, to bite! An involved pastor has the wisdom and courage to lovingly confront the sinfulness of the sheep while protecting them from the wiles of the world and the schemes of the Devil.

Shepherding is a lonely job (70 percent of pastors allege that they have no close friends[4]) that involves interpersonal skills, which apparently are not the focus of seminaries. Though the local church and the denomination are ultimately responsible for ordaining people to the pastorate, the seminary is the boot camp for determining whether a person can endure shepherding. Theological institutions are the gate-keepers to the battlefield of shepherding. Scholarship is part of the preparation, but spiritual life, teaching skills, and shepherding abilities are integral in preparing a person for combat duty, where he will

---

2. Richard J. Krejcir, "Statistics on Pastors: What Is Going on with the Pastors in America?," Into Thy Word, last modified 2007, http://www.intothyword.org/apps/articles/?articleid=36562&columnid.

3. Ibid, quoting the research of Barna, Focus on the Family, and Fuller Seminary.

4. Ibid.

experience ill-intentioned dragons, church conflict, disgruntled sheep, and disenchanted leaders. The emphasis in seminary should therefore be on "pastor" first and "scholar" second, because the critical need in the church is to train leaders and shepherds.

Paul David Tripp, in *Dangerous Calling*, surmises that over the years theological education has morphed. A hundred years ago, seminary professors were also churchmen, coming to the lectern by way of the pastorate. They carried a love for the local church into the classroom and taught with the hearts and lives of people in view. They included within their scholarship the experiences of joy, pain, and sorrow in ministry, and they demonstrated the scars of doing battle in the trenches. Pastoring was not easy, but it was rewarding. Then, over time, theological training became more specialized and departmentalized.

> Over the years more and more professors came to the seminary classroom with little or no local church experience. They got to the classroom not because they were successful pastors and therefore equipped to train and disciple the next generation. No, they got to the seminary classroom because they were experts in their field. So the energy in the classroom was not cloning a new generation of pastors but cloning experts in apologetics, ethics, systematics, church history, and biblical languages.[5]

The danger, says Tripp, is an "academized Christianity," which puts hope in knowledge and skills while disconnecting the heart from ministry. Many churches in conflict have had pastors who, armed with knowledge, have shot truth at disturbed sheep rather than soothing them with the balm of Gilead. Being low in relational skills, these disaffected pastors have had difficulty handling disagreements, which has then caused more fissures in the church. Scholarship is wonderful, but unless it is tempered with a true love for people, it will become puffed-up knowledge that is devoid of human understanding and will lead to unrest in the flock.

---

5. Paul David Tripp, *Dangerous Calling: Confronting the Unique Challenges of Pastoral Ministry* (Wheaton, IL: Crossway Books, 2012), 53.

Most seminary websites specify that they form men for the gospel ministry but are unclear how that will impact tending the flock. The emphasis is undoubtedly on educating people for service, which in and of itself is good. Academics are important, but how do they translate to service as a shepherd? The pastor is to be a scholar, according to B. B. Warfield, who once said, "A minister must be learned, on pain of being utterly incompetent for his work."[6] Warfield meant that academics for the pastor should reveal themselves in practical application. The pastor as scholar is important, but an emphasis on pastoral work, not scholarly accomplishments, must be preeminent. The seminarian is purportedly trained for leading and tending a flock. He is no earthly good if he becomes an egghead who is unable to relate his learning to the struggles of a flock that may be under his future care. A pastor who is entirely intellectual, with few shepherding skills, contributes to the main disease in the modern church, which is poor leadership.

SYMPTOM #8 OF POOR LEADERSHIP: INTELLECTUAL EXILE

The US military, and specifically the Marine Corps, is committed to the principle that, in combat, a man cannot fight alone and survive long. Marines are famous for persevering in major battles when the odds are against them, because within each Marine is instilled "Esprit de Corps" (the Spirit of the Corps). This motto stresses the importance of the unit over individualism and the significance of each man within the unit. "All are for one" and "One is for all." There is no such thing as a "Lone Ranger Marine." Even snipers have spotters who crawl with them, suffer with them, and risk their lives for them. The term *isolation* is not in the vocabulary of a Marine, for battles are fought with brothers, which immensely increases the chance of victory.

Pastors who isolate themselves in their studies will eventually face church conflict alone. They will not have built the brotherhood, the "Esprit de Corps," needed to combat the issues that invariably face the church. Ministry is a battlefield, and pastors must realize that they war

---

6. Quoted in "What We Believe," Westminster Theological Seminary, accessed November 13, 2015, http://www.wts.edu/about/beliefs.html.

not with flesh and blood but with the spiritual forces of evil (Eph. 6:12). They therefore must build a combat force of brothers around them to fight the battles that will arise. Bookworm pastors who closet themselves in their libraries will find themselves isolated on the battlefield and unprepared for skirmishes that inevitably arise because the church is at war with the Devil.

Bookworm pastors are academicians, first and foremost, with little regard for interpersonal shepherding and boot-camp training of their sheep. Being theologically sound is a must, but theology that is not taught for life and godliness is intellectual drivel. The mission given by Christ is to make disciples—not intellectual outcasts—who will fight the forces of evil and persevere in the struggles of life.

Christianity has never won a culture through cerebral lectures and sermons. God empowers his people to model truth before they win the right to teach it as a daily lifestyle. Pastors who spend more time preparing sermons than being with their sheep are in danger of allowing their scholarship to become an obstruction to their shepherding. In a sense, they impose upon themselves an intellectual exile, which is a symptom of poor leadership.

Theology (the study of God) must be practical, for God is immanently and personally involved with his people. If statistics show that pastors are demoralized because seminaries are failing to train them adequately to manage, counsel, and shepherd the flock, then our schools are missing the mark. They may believe they are training pastors for the next generation, but a high number of their graduates think otherwise. Some feel that knowing doctrine and preaching the truths of Scripture are practical matters, and therefore pastors need only to sufficiently feed their sheep. This is like taking a raw recruit and showing him how to load his rifle, but never teaching him how to shoot it. There is so much more to shepherding than Sunday preaching, and much of it involves the application of interpersonal skills.

To have a shepherd's heart is to love people. If pastors are distancing themselves from people because of excess study, criticism by sheep, and conflict in the church, then they are not long-suffering in the call given to them by Christ. If they avoid ministering to sheep, especially to the unpleasant ones, then the question arises whether they are truly called to pastoring, which is a people business.

Preaching is essential and is the primary method of feeding sheep, but if sermons are merely academic studies in doctrine that bore people, then the shepherd is not feeding his flock tasty meals but rather is spoon-feeding them the ugly-tasting cod liver oil that many of us as children hated. To bore sheep with foul-tasting suppers is a sin. Ministers are to present God's Word in such a way that it is relevant, interesting, and alive. Relevancy will occur only by living with the sheep and interacting with them during fun times, hard times, and disastrous times.

Elders have the responsibility of ministering to their pastor and helping him to become a better preacher and shepherd. If elders are spending time with the sheep, they will know how effective the lead shepherd is. They are not to entertain gossip about their pastor, but they will get a sense whether they need to approach him about preaching more practically or shepherding more tenderly. Some pastors are insecure and do not take criticism well. But that is the problem of pride and of not trusting God, who puts people in our lives to help mold us into better preachers, pastors, and Christians.

Controversy in some churches that are marked by conflict arises because of the pastor's style of leadership. As an intellectual, he may like to spend more time in the study than in the field where his sheep are. Time spent in sermon preparation for these pastors may average between eighteen and twenty hours per week. (This amounts to approximately two days of seclusion out of a five- to six-day workweek.) If the pastor is also preparing another sermon or a Sunday school lesson, then at least another half or full day can be added to his isolation. The average pastor works fifty to sixty hours per week, which means that close to half his time is spent preparing sermons and lessons. Preparation is important, but it must be balanced with all the other duties of a shepherd—managing staff, directing committee meetings, visiting at hospitals and in the home, counseling the struggling, comforting the grieving, and attending various functions where the sheep will be found.

Tim Keller, of Redeemer Presbyterian Church in Manhattan, New York, has amazing insight as well as good advice for the pastor of a smaller church. He comments that, as a pastor of a large church, he spends fifteen or more hours a week in sermon preparation. When he had no staff, he spent only six to eight hours on a sermon. He believed that more time in his study translated to less time with people, which actually made for a poorer preacher.[7]

> It is only through doing people-work that you become the preacher you need to be—someone who knows sin, how the heart works, what people's struggles are, and so on. Pastoral care and leadership (along with private prayer) are to a great degree sermon preparation. More accurately, it is preparing the preacher, not just the sermon. Through pastoral care and leadership you grow from being a Bible commentator into a flesh and blood preacher.[8]

Elevating the "scholar" part of the pastor-scholar model to the neglect of the "pastor" portion of the minister's job description often results in his intellectual exile and his becoming distant from the sheep and other leaders. Churches often choose intellectual pastors, thinking that they are doctrinally knowledgeable and will preach theologically correct sermons. In reality, many of these men have theoretical knowledge but lack the "field sense" that a shepherd needs. A frequent consequence of intellectual exile is future conflict that challenges the pastor's ability and authority as a shepherd leader.

TREATMENT FOR INTELLECTUAL EXILE

The "academic" pastor is challenged to make a personal and heart-felt examination concerning his calling. Does he truly want to be the shepherd of the flock? Or does he mainly want to study and be a pulpiteer? If he really wants to be a shepherd, then the treatment for intellectual exile is "forced discomfort." Physical therapy is like that—it is compulsory distress for the purpose of bringing an injured part of one's body back

---

7. Tim Keller, "Preacher-Onlys Aren't Good Preachers," *The Gospel Coalition Blog*, October 19, 2009, http://blogs.thegospelcoalition.org/blogs/tgc/2009/10/19/preacher-onlys-arent-good-preachers/.

8. Ibid.

to normal operation. Part of the restorative process for a broken bone or torn ligaments is physical therapy, which is unpleasant and hurtful, but is necessary for complete healing.

Physical therapy in the treatment of intellectual exile is the forced discomfort of relating to others. If pastors find more comfort in their studies perusing theological books, then in all likelihood they are introverts. Since introverts have a harder time relating to people, the forced discomfort of properly interacting with others will seem harder and more intense. But it must be done in order to bring oneself back from intellectual exile. Although introverts will never become extroverts, they can learn extroversion through compelled relationships.

The congregation may see pastors who pride themselves on their intellect as being out of touch with their needs. Such men will be accused of being aloof and having an uncaring attitude, when this is probably not the case. A pastor should be known as a shepherd, not a bookworm, and therefore must get out of the office and into the field in order to know his staff and his sheep and to properly care for them both. One of the major complaints from people who leave the church is the feeling of not being cared for. What makes them feel this way? Probably a lack of involvement from their pastor and other leaders in their lives!

Bookworm pastors find it more difficult to train elders as shepherds, because they have difficulty being shepherds themselves. The result is foreseeable—a confused, restless, and unappreciative flock. The pastoral ministry is a people ministry. If pastors or elders have a hard time relating to people, then they should question whether they belong in the shepherding profession. But if they truly believe that they are called to ministry, then the following suggestions may help them relate better.

- *Consider how best to focus sermon preparation.* To do this, pastors may have to learn to look at a passage of Scripture differently and to preach sermons by firing a high-powered rifle, not a scattergun. Sermons should have a purpose and an objective statement, with points that clarify or explain the purpose. Most sheep are not looking for lectures that provide doctrinal information, contribute to boredom in the pew, and have no relevancy to the struggles and burdens of their lives. They want truth, but in the context of relationship, which actually is the model that Christ provided. With shorter sermon preparation, the pastor will have to rely more on the Holy Spirit's leading than on his own intellectual prowess.

- *Ask close friends to invite you and others to dinner.* Some churches have "Dinner 8" ministries through which, once per month, four couples meet at a host's home to enjoy dinner and conversation. I was with a church that assigned different couples each month to various homes. The host family prepared the main course, and others contributed with salads, vegetables, and dessert. If our schedule fit the dinner night, my wife and I had an open invitation to attend. Sometimes we would have to choose between two different groups. By attending these informal dinner parties, I not only enjoyed the fellowship but also learned more about the sheep I was called to tend.

- *Schedule visits to the elderly at home, and spend at least an hour with them if appropriate.* The older we get, the more we need contact with people. Shut-ins are isolated from their church and from most of their friends, and they feel like their purpose in life is shattered. The elderly like visits from their pastor, but they want their pastor to stay for at least an hour and to give them the latest news on other families and happenings in the church. The shepherd must show authentic concern and can do so by asking questions about the person's spouse, what attracted them to each other, what they liked to do when they first started dating, what favorite restaurants they liked to frequent, what vacation spots they preferred, and what amusing family moments they remember.

- *Visit people in the hospital and talk to them about pain, prognosis, family, and matters of scriptural interest.* Ask for their favorite Scriptures to read, and then pray accordingly. A pastor once asked family members if he could visit their hospitalized mother, who had been attending another church for some time. She had been a founding member of the church that he was pastoring on an interim basis, but for convenience's sake she had started attending a fellowship nearer to her home. The answer that the pastor received from the mother was amusing and a bit disconcerting, "Of course, please have Pastor Interim visit, but don't send Pastor So-and-So!" Upon further exploration the Interim discovered that Pastor So-and-So was not very personable and did not seem to enjoy the visits. He would hurry through his visits by asking how she was and what he could pray for. He would then pray and leave. He would never converse, and he hardly seemed concerned for his parishioner. Of course, discernment is important while visiting someone at home or, especially, in the hospital. Some people are hurting or are tired, and want only a quick visit. Yet most people want to be loved and to feel that the pastor is genuinely interested in them.

- *Learn some icebreaker questions to ask when you meet new people.* This will help to ease conversation. I love to ask couples how they met and what attracted them to each other. I'm interested in their upbringing—what they cherished and what they disliked about it. I also want to know what attracted them to the church as well as what led them into the field in which they are working. Let others talk, and listen carefully for clues that will help you to keep the conversation going. If a person likes sports, talk about sports. If the person likes cooking, ask questions about cooking.

- *Manage your staff by being involved with them.* Show genuine interest in the staff and in their families. Leave your office, on occasion, and pop into theirs. Ask if they have a moment to talk; and, if they do, ask them about their job, their families, and their frustrations with the church. Ask how you can better serve them. Have staff luncheons once a month, either at the church or at a local restaurant. Ask a fun or witty icebreaker-type question to which staff members are to reply. A person's answer gives a glimpse into his life and promotes conversation among staff. It helps in the process of team building as well as fostering camaraderie. Some sample questions are listed below:

- What is your favorite movie, and why?
- What is the last book you completed reading, and why did you read it?
- Describe an embarrassing moment and how you responded.
- Tell us about a trip that went bad.
- Who is your favorite superhero (besides Jesus), and why?
- What Bible character (besides Jesus) impresses you the most, and why?
- What Bible character do you relate to the most?
- Name a villain or sad character in Scripture, and tell us what strikes you most about the person.
- What is your favorite cartoon character, and why?
- Describe your favorite room in a house you have lived in.
- Describe the type of person who you dislike and why.
- Who is or was the most influential relative in your life, and why?
- What is your favorite saying?
- What is your favorite meal, and what makes it your favorite?
- What is the most important advice you have ever received?
- What type of automobile really appeals to you, and why?
- What is your favorite zoo animal, and why?
- Describe yourself using just one word, and explain why you chose it.
- Describe the person to your right (or left) using just one word, and explain the reason you chose it.
- Imagine that you are at a Chinese restaurant and you crack open a fortune cookie. What does it say?

- *Make disciples by meeting weekly with a potential leader.* Each of us should have a mentor whom we may call with questions at any time. We should also have those whom we are discipling. Although general discipleship may occur from the pulpit, personal discipleship is more effective in changing lives for Christ. Pick one or two men (preferably younger ones) to encourage to grow in Christ. Spend time each week with the person or persons, teaching them from Scripture about being a good husband, the best of fathers, a wonderful boss or employee, and a potential leader in the church. Talk about their struggles and how to overcome them.

- *Become a member of an accountability group.* Join with trusted friends who will not cater to your wishes but will love you enough to point out your idiosyncrasies, your faults, and your sin. Meet frequently to talk about Christ and about your growth or lack of growth as a pastor, Christian, husband, and father. Remember, it is an accountability group you need—not a discussion group on sports, church activities, or favorite books.

- *Join the Chamber of Commerce or a local club.* I'm amazed that most churches are not members of local chambers of commerce. We say that we want to reach the local community for Christ, yet many of us are uninvolved in the same community. We avoid non-Christians, but it is they who need the gospel most. A church pastor or staff member participating in the activities of a local chamber or familiar club will demonstrate concern for the community. I realize that it may be uncomfortable for some, but involvement with unbelievers is necessary to understand the culture of those who desperately need the gospel. I remember, as a chamber member, participating in the local rodeo by manning a booth and selling tickets. By being involved with a community project, I met many people, participated in interesting conversations, and had opportunities to pass out literature on the church. Some in the chamber started attending my local congregation, and one in particular became a good friend and eventually an elder in the church.

RELATIONSHIPS MEAN INVOLVEMENT

Relationships are important and must be modeled by pastors. Paul exhorted his disciple Titus to pick leaders who were above reproach and were not quick-tempered, but were hospitable to others (see Titus 1:6–8). In other words, elders and pastors must be involved with the community in order to have a reputation that is above criticism. It is involvement that demonstrates a warm and welcoming personality and presents a Christlike model for proper relationships. This is done not in the pastor's study but out in the community where the sheep live and struggle.

A great example of a modern shepherd pastor is Frank Barker, retired minister of Briarwood Presbyterian Church in Birmingham, Alabama. Dr. Barker is highly educated, and he authored *A Living Hope* (a study guide on 1 Peter); *The Gospel of John for Group Study*; *First Timothy: Pure Heart, Good Conscience, Sincere Faith*; and *Encounters with Jesus*. He remains active in retirement by teaching Old Testament at Birmingham Theological Seminary. Although a scholar, he is appreciated for his pastor's heart. Humble and unassuming, he is known as a prayer warrior with a passion to share the gospel with the lost.

Barker was not always modest and self-effacing. Although he grew up in the church, he abandoned the principles taught to him as a child and became a rebellious teenager, a college profligate, and a hardened pilot in the Naval Air Corps. He did not grasp the freedom presented in the gospel in his early years, and he lived irresponsibly until the Lord radically saved him. Barker had never doubted the truth about God or the Bible; it had just never had a great effect on his lifestyle. It wasn't until the Lord jerked him into reality through the untimely and reckless deaths of two air force pilots that he saw the necessity of living the truth. After his conversion, he eventually went to seminary, received two masters' degrees, and founded Briarwood Church. This hard-nosed fighter pilot became a gentle, loving, and devoted pastor. His story is chronicled in *Flight Path: A Biography of Frank Barker Jr.*[9]

Frank Barker has always been a pastor first and a scholar second. He is beloved of his people because he spent time with them. Although he preached thousands of sermons and loved the pulpit ministry, he expended most of his energy in meekly serving his flock. The result was a ministry blessed of God in one church for forty years. He loved people and tried not to cloister himself in a study to the detriment of ministering to hurting sheep.

---

9. Janie Buck and Mary Lou Davis, *Flight Path: A Biography of Frank Barker Jr.* (Fearn, Ross-shire, UK: Christian Focus, 2004).

John Calvin, mentioned at the opening of this chapter, was a Protestant Reformer of the same theological persuasion as Frank Barker. He, like Barker, exhausted himself in preaching the gospel and pastoring his sheep. Most people have an impression that Calvin was a reclusive egghead. Yet he is a wonderful example of a preacher who balanced his study time with practically applying his theology to the problems and conflicts of Geneva's society.

Many people today don't think of him as a forceful leader who participated in the life of his people. Although he placed much emphasis on expository preaching as central to his ministry, he also spent much time sitting as a member of the community governance council and hearing hundreds of cases brought by the city elders. He listened with his fellow pastors to various disputes, family quarrels, and accusations of sinful behavior. He made judicial decisions about the lack of church attendance, mistreatment of widows, child abuse, and inheritance issues.[10] He applied his theology in resolving the cases before him. Calvin was not only an intellectual; he was a wise leader, a church statesman, and an involved shepherd. His life, though not perfect, should be a great encouragement and stimulus to bookworm pastors in overcoming their tendencies to remain insulated in their studies, which contributes only to poor leadership in the church.

LEADERSHIP FOR MEN

Pastors are disciplers of men, who follow their lead. Being cloistered in an office will not produce godly leaders. Rather, the pastor is charged with identifying and training leaders in the church. The next chapter will review the current situation in the church—the lack of male involvement—and will propose a prescription for actively involving men in the leadership positions that the Lord has reserved for them.

10. Williston Walker, *John Calvin: The Organiser of Reformed Protestantism; 1509–1564* (New York: The Knickerbocker Press, 1906), 281–82.

10

"Man Up"

Be watchful, stand firm in the faith, act like men, be strong.
Let all that you do be done in love. (1 Cor. 16:13–14)

THE "STUFF OF LEADERSHIP"

The "stuff of leadership" is authority—how it is acquired, employed, and transferred to others. The authority of Jesus came from the Father. "For I have not spoken on my own authority, but the Father who sent me has himself given me a commandment—what to say and what to speak" (John 12:49). Jesus, however, used his authority to confront evil and to invest further authority in his followers, teaching and motivating them to act in his name and for his sake. His empowering leadership is validated every day as millions around the world continue to serve him faithfully. Bob Briner and Ray Pritchard, in their book *The Leadership Lessons of Jesus*, call the empowerment of Jesus "brilliant leadership," for leadership that is not invested in followers is failed leadership.[1]

The authority of Jesus was given to his followers to "make disciples of all nations, baptizing them in the name of the Father and of the Son and of the Holy Spirit" (Matt. 28:18–19). Teaching others what Christ had commanded them to observe would not be an easy task. They would

---

1. Bob Briner and Ray Pritchard, *The Leadership Lessons of Jesus: A Timeless Model for Today's Leaders* (Nashville: Broadman & Holman, 2008), 41–42.

have to summon for themselves the "stuff of leadership" to weather the storms of adversity that would assail their ministry. Today is no different. Leaders will have to summon the courage and persistence to teach the gospel and to transfer their authority to the next generation.

THE GIDEON FACTOR

There are many men in the Bible who had "the stuff of leadership" and who, in the face of adversity, stood tall, relied on God, and persevered despite their circumstances. Gideon was such a man. He answered the call of God to raise an army to deliver Israel from the harassment of Midian. While he was encamped by the spring of Harod, the Lord spoke to Gideon, saying, in effect, "You have too many men for me to deliver Midian into your hands. In order for Israel not to boast of a victory in her own power, I want you to shrink your force and keep only the number I tell you to retain." After twenty-two thousand men were told to go home, the Lord informed Gideon that there were still too many men in his army. He then instructed Gideon to take only those who lapped from the water like a dog. In other words, Gideon was to go to battle with three hundred questionable simpletons—not the smartest and not the best, but still the choice of the Lord (Judg. 7:1–25).

Imagine the expression on Gideon's face and what he must have thought! "I went to a lot of trouble to raise thirty-two thousand troops; and now I'm down to three hundred hayseeds!" What Gideon did not do was to question the judgment of the Lord. He manned up, did what he was told, and secured a victory that sent a superior force away in defeat.

Men in the church need to remember the Gideon Factor—that one person with God on his side makes a majority that can conquer any foe. We need men like Gideon in the church—men who will become involved in the expansion of God's kingdom on earth—men who will lead the church and take responsibility for pushing forward against the gates of hell. Yet many Christian men have succumbed to pursuing personal happiness, wealth, and worldly prestige. Men are being lured with false illusions of satisfaction that keep them from church or keep them inactive in church. According to David Murrow, who founded the website ChurchforMen.com, the typical congregation in the United States draws an adult crowd comprised of 61 percent women and 39 percent men.[2] Sadly, on any given Sunday, 25 percent of married women will visit church without their husbands.[3]

Furthermore, 70 percent of the male children of church-going families will cease to attend during their late teens and twenties.[4] These same boys grow into men who might profess belief in God but who see no need for Sunday worship. Without enough men, there will be a paucity of male leadership and few Gideons who have the verve and the love for Christ to lead others in the battles of life. Many pundits have attributed the lack of male involvement in the church to the feminization of the church. The cause of feminization is debatable, but one thing is sure: many men have relinquished responsibility in the family, which does have a carryover effect in the church. Women fill the gaps left by males, and these gaps include leadership in the church.

Hanna Rosin agrees that women have ascended to leadership in all facets of life, including the church. In an article she wrote in *The Atlantic Monthly* titled "The End of Men,"[5] Rosen quotes statistics that show that women hold the majority of positions in the US workforce for the first time in history. For every two male college graduates, there are three women with degrees. She claims that the modern, postindustrial society is better suited to women than to men. Women exceed men as managers, and in the largest cities, young, single, childless women actually earn 8 percent more than their male peers.[6] The increase of women leaders in the marketplace has flowed over into the church.

2. David Murrow, "Quick Facts on the Gender Gap," Church for Men, accessed December 13, 2015, http://churchformen.com/men-and-church/where-are-the-men/; quoting "Key Findings: Who Worships in the U.S.?," U.S. Congregational Life Survey, October 29, 2003, http://www.uscongregations.org/blog/2014/02/17/key-findings-who-worships-in-the-u-s/.

3. Murrow, "Quick Facts on the Gender Gap."

4. Ibid., quoting Scott McConnell, "LifeWay Research Finds Reasons 18- to 22-Year-Olds Drop Out of Church," LifeWay, August 7, 2007, http://www.lifeway.com/Article/LifeWay-Research-finds-reasons-18-to-22-year-olds-drop-out-of-church.

5. Hanna Rosin, "The End of Men," *The Atlantic Monthly*, July/August 2010, http://www.theatlantic.com/magazine/archive/2010/07/the-end-of-men/308135/.

6. Andrew Romano, "Why We Need to Reimagine Masculinity," *Newsweek*, September 20, 2010, http://www.newsweek.com/why-we-need-reimagine-masculinity-71993.

The need for male participation in church may not be a concern for local congregations, but it might be a sign of church deterioration. According to Jeff Iorg, who promotes the Antioch model of church leadership, strong and transformational churches have men in obvious leadership roles. He doesn't discount the contribution of women in the ministry of Jesus, but he underscores the pattern of strong churches having men in leadership roles. "The more significant problem in most churches today," he says, "isn't the absence of women in leadership; it's the declining number of men who will lead."[7] Coincidentally, denominations with the smallest number of men, which equates to fewer men in leadership, have been losing the most members. In contrast, churches that have healthy male involvement are generally growing and more vibrant.

Some may find this surprising, for women are the backbone of congregations. They keep the ministry going and the church operating smoothly, for they sing in the choir, care for the children, teach Sunday school, organize potluck suppers, collate the bulletins, and serve on various committees. On any given Sunday, 13 million more adult women than men attend church services in the United States.[8] Although we thank God that women are a vital and needed force in the congregation, God has nevertheless appointed men to lead his church. When men fail to accept their calling and to lead according to God's directions, a price is paid—and that price has become the ineffectiveness of the church as a force to transform culture.

SYMPTOM #9 OF POOR LEADERSHIP: ABDICATION OF AUTHORITY

Men who lack the "stuff of leadership" will abdicate their headship and responsibility. This will affect the church, making her more effeminate and weaker in the battle against society and the Evil One. Wayne Grudem, cofounder of the Council on Biblical Manhood and Womanhood, sees "evangelical feminism" as a new path to liberalism.

7. Jeff Iorg, *The Case for Antioch: A Biblical Model for a Transformational Church* (Nashville: B&H Publishing Group, 2011), 152.
8. Murrow, "Quick Facts on the Gender Gap."

As a movement, feminism claims "no unique leadership roles for men in marriage or in the church."[9] Blurring these roles leads to egalitarianism, which undermines the authority of Scripture. Accepting women in male roles, especially in positions of headship in the family and in the church, necessarily leads to reinterpretation of Holy Scripture. Redefining gender roles in this way is in accord with J. Gresham Machen's definition of "applied Christianity." Machen used this term to describe how Christianity was being morphed into pragmatism to reflect societal mores that have evolved from the initial creative act of God.[10] As a way of life, Christianity had become centered in social justice by promoting the concept that everyone, no matter his or her religious persuasion, is a brother or a sister. Machen thought that this broad-minded thinking was the greatest menace to the Christian church, for liberalism, he said, was not Christianity but a new religion.[11]

John Calvin, in his commentary on 1 Timothy 2:12, clearly taught that a woman was excluded from the office of teaching, which was reserved for men only. This did not prevent women from instructing their families, but when it came to holding church office, they were not permitted to do so. In answer to critics who refer to Deborah (Judg. 4:4) as an example of a woman in leadership, Calvin stressed that unusual acts performed by God do not set aside the general rule that men are granted the office of rule and teaching in the church. God, however, is above all law and may, at his discretion, appoint women to accomplish his purposes in particular cases for peculiar times.[12]

Teaching, Calvin said, implied the rank of power or the position of authority, which according to 1 Timothy 2:13 women were not given, because Adam was first created. The creation decree that Paul referred to placed men over women. Calvin said that women were therefore formed

---

9. Wayne Grudem, *Evangelical Feminism: A New Path to Liberalism?* (Wheaton, IL: Crossway, 2006), 15.

10. J. Gresham Machen, *Christianity and Liberalism* (Grand Rapids: Eerdmans, 1923; repr. 2001), 155.

11. Ibid, 160.

12. "1 Timothy 2:11–15," in John Calvin, *Commentary on Timothy, Titus, Philemon*, available online at Christian Classics Ethereal Library, last modified June 1, 2005, http://www.ccel.org/ccel/calvin/calcom43.iii.iv.iv.html (see v. 12).

to obey (that is, to be in subjection to men) by the ordinary ordinance of God. The instruction by Paul for them to learn in quietness (1 Tim. 2:11) meant that women were to keep within their own rank and not usurp the authority of men.

The mainline Protestant churches have a plethora of women in positions of authority, both at the local level and at denominational headquarters. Paul's instruction about women and teaching, according to mainline churches, was a cultural issue, which does not apply to modern society. Tom Ascol, in an article for Ligionier Ministries, counters this argument by saying,

> While Paul's restrictions on women's roles are out of step with the egalitarian spirit of our age, the foundation of his argument makes it clear that his instruction is not culturally conditioned. "For Adam was formed first, then Eve; and Adam was not deceived, but the woman was deceived and became a transgressor" (1 Tim. 2:13–14).[13]

The order of creation and the motives for the fall specify the reason that women are not to exercise authority over men, either at home or in the church. This does not mean that women are inferior, but it does mean that God's wisdom dictates certain roles to be performed by the sexes, with headship belonging to the man.

It so happens that denominations with women in leadership roles are consistently losing members, which confirms the Hartford Seminary study that found that a lack of involved men in the congregation correlated with church decline.[14] The shortage of male participation in church is a symptom of the greater disease—poor leadership. Men, for the most part, have abdicated their responsibility to lead, which has obligated women to fill the vacuum. Without greater male involvement, local congregations will decline into irrelevance and leadership will be

---

13. Tom Ascol, "The High Calling of Women," *Tabletalk*, June 1, 2009, http://www.ligonier.org/learn/articles/high-calling-women/.

14. C. Kirk Hadaway, *FACTs on Growth* (Hartford: Hartford Institute for Religion Research, 2006), 4, available online at https://faithcommunitiestoday.org/sites/all/themes/factzen4/files/CongGrowth.pdf.

relegated to women. Biblically functioning males will continue to fade from view and therefore from influence on church and family.

How has male abdication been manifested in the church? Men are quite comfortable to allow women to lead, which has caused the church to become more docile. Passivity and gentleness are encouraged, to the detriment of boldness and assertiveness—two normal and important male characteristics. The focus on sensitivity and nurture has led to a family focus, which is praiseworthy, but which has retarded the development of self-assured and purposeful churchmen. Although Scripture has much to say about loving one's wife and caring for one's family, it also portrays men as pursuing adventure, fighting battles, and accomplishing objectives. It describes men as leaders in the church, in the community, and in the nation.

BS

Generally speaking, men yearn for significance and pursue risk, while women desire security and understanding. The modern church, however, promotes calmness, relationships, and sociability, which are honorable traits, but ones that appeal more to a woman's psyche than to a man's need for meaning. Generally, women are not driven to establish their own importance; rather, they socialize and seek peace and harmony. Yet the church is at war and needs male leadership to lead congregants against the attacks of the enemy: "For we do not wrestle against flesh and blood, but against the rulers, against the authorities, against the cosmic powers over this present darkness, against the spiritual forces of evil in the heavenly places" (Eph. 6:12). It wasn't Deborah who picked up the sword against Sisera and the Canaanites, but Barak. Although she spoke for the Lord, God gave instructions to Barak to enlist Israelites for battle against the army of Jabin (see Judg. 4:4–10). Barak manned up and led the Israelites to victory, defeating Sisera, Jabin's general, and forcing him to flee into the hands of Jael, who assassinated him.

Men who have grown up in church hardly notice its feminization, but male visitors are quick to detect womanly touches. They observe the flowers, the scents, the decorations, and the people who greet them. They read in the bulletin about activities that revolve around children and women, and they notice the lack of involvement by men. Most of all, they sit in what they may perceive as a dull worship service amid strange people who sing ancient hymns and hear sermons that have no relevance to their lives. Most men desire excitement in worship, more originality in liturgy, and meaningful sermons. Their exploratory natures crave programs that appeal to their manliness. Many are unsettled when asked to hold hands in a circle, to pray aloud in public, and to share their innermost turmoil, but that is what some churches promote.

Men who are involved in church may find it difficult to stand up and be men—to make judgments that are out of favor with female influencers. They may lean toward compromise and accede to the status quo rather than make decisions that are unpopular but biblically correct and best for the congregation. A church run by women is a symptom of men abdicating their call to leadership.

TREATMENT FOR ABDICATION

Jesus did not abdicate his authority. He made it known that he and the Father are one, and then he took the ridicule and the ostracizing from the Jewish leadership to the point of death. He stood firm, completed his mission, and passed his authority to those who followed. People in church leadership today are reluctant to admit that they lack fortitude and the manliness to remain steadfast. Yet the signs of abdication are present, for many men in the church display a decreased mental and physical energy to lead. They defer to the whims of others by refusing to make strong and, at times, unpopular decisions. They default to the status quo in fear of upsetting a few people, thereby distancing themselves from discontented and obstreperous sheep.

Jesus did not avoid his opposition. He confronted when the time was right and spoke with the tone appropriate for the occasion. Elders are to "man up" for the purpose of combating the evils of society and the intrusion of irrelevancy into Christianity. Early Christian thought divided the church universal into the church militant and the church triumphant. The church militant comprised those living Christians who struggled against the world, the flesh, and the Devil. These believers saw themselves at war, for their battles were against the wicked forces of darkness in the spiritual realm. They were not passive men but aggressive warriors in pushing back the gates of hell. Many elders today don't even think in terms of war. They are more concerned with pleasing people, maintaining a false peace, and making decisions that do not offend.

The church triumphant is the invisible church, which is composed of all believers, but especially of those who have died and are now in heaven—the reward for fighting earthly battles. Triumph, however, does not occur without engagement in the fight; and who better to wage war than men? Most men are naturally strong and protective, and, given the chance, they will fight to defend truth, preserve freedom, and protect family and church.

God called men to war—to wield the sword against societal evil! To Joshua, the Lord said,

> Moses my servant is dead. Now therefore arise, go over this Jordan, you and all this people, into the land that I am giving to them, to the people of Israel. . . . No man shall be able to stand before you all the days of your life. Just as I was with Moses, so I will be with you. I will not leave you or forsake you. Be strong and courageous, for you shall cause this people to inherit the land that I swore to their fathers to give them. (Josh. 1:2, 5–6)

God commanded Gideon, whom he addressed as a mighty man of valor (although he was hiding in a wine press), "Go in this might of yours and save Israel from the hand of Midian; do not I send you?" (Judg. 6:14). God also encouraged Jehoshaphat, through the prophet Jahaziel, to go to battle against the Ammonites and Moabites by saying, "Do not be afraid and do not be dismayed at this great horde, for the battle is not yours but God's" (2 Chron. 20:15). The church will be in constant battle with the forces of wickedness, but Jesus himself said that the gates of hell would not prevail against it (see Matt. 16:18). Christ has already secured the victory, but there will be constant skirmishes until the Commander-in-Chief returns to lead his final mop-up campaign and bring judgment against those who rebelled against his rule.

An imperative, therefore, for the local church is to harness the energy of men and to enlist them to fight the spiritual battles that continually confront the church. Leaders who take their calling seriously are to recruit men. This involves raising strong male leadership from men who are already in the church as well as the enlistment of more males from the community to join their ranks. Men need the church, but more importantly, the church needs men. The involvement of passionate men promotes church health, vibrancy, giving, and growth. How do we get men involved without abdicating responsibility? And, more poignantly, how do we attract more men to church?

First, Teach Men Biblically to Man Up

Scripture teaches that men have the power of family authority.[15] Abdication (renouncing one's authority) from being head of one's family will in turn affect leadership in the church. God in his wisdom created males and females equal in worth but different in roles. Adam was placed in the garden of Eden to cultivate it and preserve it (see Gen. 2:15). The responsibility of producing fruit from the garden was his. This would take initiation and ingenuity. Right from the beginning, man was to be the initiator, for that is a prerequisite of leadership. When God initiated redemption, he demonstrated executive ability in bringing people to salvation. In like manner, a husband is to provide initiation in his family management, for as Christ is his Head, he is the head of his wife (see 1 Cor. 11:3).

Man's role as a leader in the family also involves providing direction. He is the one charged with cleaving to his wife (see Gen. 2:24 KJV). It is his responsibility to hold the family together. Therefore he is the director of the family unit. His wife was created as his helper (Gen. 2:18, 20). She is the adjunct, the lieutenant, and the *aide-de-camp* to her husband. She influences him and gives advice, which a good leader listens to and acts upon when fitting.

The word *husband* is derived from words meaning "householder," and as such the man has the responsibility of protecting and providing for his family. He is to stand up for his wife and to take much of the world's pressure from her. When she needs him to intervene on her behalf, he

---

15. "For the husband is the head of the wife even as Christ is the head of the church, his body, and is himself its Savior" (Eph. 5:23). Elders are to be the husband of one wife (1 Tim. 3:2; Titus 1:6).

is to step in and do so. I remember a time when I received a phone call from my distressed and weary spouse. She asked if I could meet with the children's teachers at their school—a task that she normally did and took pleasure in doing. She had had an abnormally frustrating day and was exhausted. The last thing she wanted to do was to meet with teachers who would point out the needs of our children. My day was busy, but I could sense a great need in my wife. I told her not to worry about the parent/teacher meetings, that I would handle them, and that it was not a problem for me to rearrange my schedule. That little task helped to relieve the stress on my wife. With a little rest, she was raring to go the next day.

A husband also builds up his wife's self-worth and personal security by providing the love, care, and togetherness that she longs for. He accepts her unconditionally and communicates at deep levels to prevent loneliness and feelings of abandonment. Men are to be loving husbands, involved in family affairs and taking reign over issues that may detrimentally affect family stability.

Dr. Gary Yagel has taken the call of "men being men" seriously and believes in igniting men to action, both in the family and in the church. In 2002, after reading Bob Buford's book *Halftime*, he realized that God desired him to focus his energy on helping the church to disciple men. He is the executive director of Forging Bonds of Brotherhood, a ministry that helps men to become true brothers in Christ. He keeps busy speaking at men's retreats or leading men's seminars, such as "Rediscovering Biblical Manhood," "Winning at Home," and "Grace Transformed Sexuality."[16] He helps men to understand their biblical mandate, spiritual headship, and sexual wholesomeness. He is a man's man who teaches Christian husbands how to meet their wife's need for emotional intimacy.

Men who are good leaders in their families will make effective leaders in the church. Men who are terrible husbands and poor providers will make horrible elders and deacons. They will be more concerned for their own well-being and significance than with the care of the sheep

16. Gary Yagel also serves as the Men's Ministry Consultant for the Presbyterian Church in America. For many years he was a Field Network Trainer and a speaking faculty member for Man in the Mirror ministries. See "About," The Ministry of Gary Yagel, accessed November 15, 2015, http://www.forgingbonds.org/about.

entrusted to them. When men take responsibility at home, they in all likelihood will not abdicate their responsibilities at church.

Second, Exhort Elders to Mentor Younger Men

When men become elders, they are to shepherd the people whom God has placed under their supervision. Part of shepherding is finding younger men who exhibit traits of leadership and then mentoring them so that they become future leaders. Hearing that Timothy was well spoken of by the brothers at Lystra and Iconium, Paul decided to have Timothy accompany him on his ministry trips (Acts 16:2–3). This was the beginning of Paul's mentoring of the young believer. Church leaders should do the same, because inherent in leadership is the necessity of enlisting others to carry on the battles of faith and to protect the sheep.

Despite all that Paul was facing—abandonment by many of his friends for fear of oppression, the end of his ministry, and even death—he faithfully encouraged his spiritual son, Timothy, to be strong in the grace of Jesus and to pass the baton of truth to others (see 2 Tim. 2:1–2). To the end of his life, he mentored his disciple, assuring Timothy that in Christ he had the strength to do all that God called him to do. For the sake of propagating the gospel, modern churchmen are urged to mentor others to continue the battles that will rage until the return of Christ.

Mentoring men is no small task, for energy is required and encouragement is a necessity. Men often start strong but later fizzle out in their commitments. Finding men who desire to be mentored by an older Christian is not always easy, but those who do come forward with the desire to be discipled by another must ask themselves a number of questions, such as:

- Am I willing to meet regularly (preferably each week) for the next six months with my mentor?
- Am I willing to read and discuss what is proposed to me?
- Am I willing to submit to the leadership of another and to do what he asks me to do?
- Am I prepared to be vulnerable and to reveal my personal struggles, repent of sin, and repair broken relationships?

- Will I be brutally honest with my mentor by showing no guile but demonstrating the utmost integrity?
- Am I willing, within six months of my own mentoring, to mentor another man in order to share what I have learned?

Two of my most rewarding instances of mentoring involved two divorced men who eventually became reconciled with their former spouses. One man had been excommunicated from his church, became homeless, and lived under a bridge. By grace he was convicted of his folly, started attending church, and asked to be mentored. His goal was restoration with God and reconciliation with his wife and family. I told him that I would not approach his ex-wife about becoming reconciled with him until he had held a job for a year. He did everything I asked, confessed his most secret sins, repented, and became actively involved in the church. With encouragement, he met with his former church, of which his ex-wife was still a member, confessed his sins before the members, and asked that the censure of excommunication be lifted. The church acceded to his request and placed him under the care of my church and its session.

After a year or so, this man was reclaimed, and a ceremony of thanksgiving marked the occasion. I then approached his wife, who at first wanted nothing to do with him, for the hurt that he had caused her and their children was still ongoing. He openly admitted his sin and his failures to her. God started softening her heart, and, after another year, she agreed to be remarried to a husband who had been disciplined by the Lord and had recovered for the sake of his glory. The wife, against counsel from relatives, became reunited with her ex-husband, believing that marital reconciliation honored God.

This reclaimed, once homeless man is an active churchman today. A former abdicator of responsibility, he is enthusiastic for the Lord and desires to see other men live for Christ and return to church. Grace made a difference in his life, but that grace was shown through concerned and compassionate leaders. Churches that attract broken men have involved leaders who are not afraid to become trailblazers for Christ. They are unified in the mission of making disciples and are clear in their vision of becoming what Jesus would have them to be. Men are sheep and will follow a strong shepherd, and shepherds lead by example without abdicating their responsibility to care for their lambs at home and in the church.

Third, Reach Men for Christ and Involve Them in Ministries

Leaders are to consider worship styles, church activities, ministries, and vocabularies that appeal to the male psyche. This doesn't mean that it is necessary to make wholesale changes, but it does mean that it is advisable to think outside the traditional box without violating scriptural principles.

Men normally find significance in what they do. Therefore, they enjoy their work, hobbies, and recreation. Jesus ministered to men by going to their places of business and activities. He called some from the fishing industry, others from their accounting offices, and some, like Paul, from their "manhunts." He met them where they were and expressed interest in them. The church would do well to follow the example of Jesus and to meet men in their own environments.

Leaders must become proactive in reaching men in their workplace. To do so, the church needs to think in missional terms (to adopt the attitude, thinking, and behavior of a missionary in order to engage others with the gospel) and exhort men to reach companions at work by focusing more on interpersonal relationships. Josh Reeves, in an article offering thirty ways to bless the workplace, suggests some creative ways to become more involved with people at work. Some are simple and easy to institute, such as:

- Intentionally eat lunch with others and listen to their story.
- Encourage others when they do a good job.
- Bring snacks to give away.
- Bring donuts or a fast-food breakfast once a month to be shared by the office.
- Create a time to invite coworkers to meet after work for drinks and conversation.
- Start a regular monthly lunch-out program and rotate who chooses the restaurant.
- Reach out to the person who is regularly ignored.

- Visit coworkers when they are in the hospital.
- Lead the charge to help others in need.[17]

Furthermore, men will most likely talk about life and spiritual matters not in churches or in their homes, but in pubs and coffee houses, on golf courses, or at ballgames—places that are familiar and unobtrusive to them. Some Christians frown at the thought of going to places where alcohol is served; but isn't this what Jesus did? He supped and drank with sinners, causing consternation to Jews and Pharisees. At the beginning of the Reformation in 1520, a small band of English scholars began meeting at the Whitehorse Inn in Cambridge, England, to discuss Martin Luther's writings and Erasmus' recently completed Greek New Testament. Over a cup of ale, people like Robert Barnes, William Tyndale, Miles Coverdale, Nicholas Ridley, Hugh Latimer, Thomas Cranmer, and Thomas Bilney discussed the ideas and thoughts of Protestant theology. Here, the fire of the English Reformation was kindled. Because the works of Luther were the main topics of discussion, many referred to the meeting house and drinking establishment as "Little Germany."[18]

Understanding the draw of beer and fellowship, an elder in a Presbyterian Church sponsored a monthly meeting at his home where men gathered for Bible, banter, and beer. Food was served, and fellowship time was carved into the first half hour. Following the fellowship, the group discussed relevant cultural issues and how the Bible addressed them. Participants were encouraged to bring along a friend or neighbor to join in the following month's conversation.

In following the principles of discussing theology over liquid refreshment, Christ the King Presbyterian Church of Houston, Texas,[19] and Christ the King Presbyterian Church in Roanoke, Virginia,[20] have ministries called

17. Josh Reeves, "30 Simple Ways to Be Missional in Your Workplace," *Verge*, accessed May 19, 2013, http://www.vergenetwork.org/2011/08/16/30-simple-ways-to-be-missional-in-your-workplace/.

18. Shane Rosenthal, "The History of the White Horse Inn," White Horse Inn, accessed November 12, 2014, http://www.whitehorseinn.org/resources/free-articles/253-the-history-of-the-white-horse-inn.

19. Visit their website at http://www.christtheking.com.

20. Visit their website at http://www.ctkroanoke.org.

"Theology on Tap," in which men meet at a local pub to discuss theological issues while sipping a beer. Redeemer Presbyterian Church in Manhattan, New York,[21] schedules events at local pubs and invites those who are wrestling with questions about God or the claims of Christianity. Skeptics are welcomed at their "Theology on Tap," at which participants hang out over beer and hear a short talk on subjects such as "Isn't the resurrection just a myth?" or "Why would a loving God send people to hell?" or "Why is there suffering in the world?" A discussion follows with a question and answer time.

Not all churches can do this effectively, and some may not even agree with the strategy, but they can concur with the principle of going where men are to be found and thinking like men think in order to reach them for Christ. In sponsoring outreach activities for men, churches should first survey men in their congregation to determine their interests and what they like to do in their spare time. Retreats or events should include time to do what men often do—such as playing physical games, building things, watching sports, going cycling, playing cards, hunting, fishing, hiking, rock climbing, and sitting around a fire for conversation and refreshment.

Though he has been accused of being an open theist, John Eldredge, author of *Wild at Heart*,[22] understands the core longings of men, which include having a battle to fight, an adventure to live, and a beauty to rescue. Founder of Ransomed Heart Ministry,[23] Eldredge has designed his "Wild at Heart Boot Camp for Men" around these pursuits. He desires men to discover the heart of God, to recover their own hearts based in the love of Christ, and to learn to live and function as real men in God's kingdom. Churches need men to be men; the result is a church on fire for Christ, attacking the gates of hell, and developing the next generation of men to continue the fight for the gospel.[24]

---

21. Visit their website at http://www.redeemer.com.

22. John Eldredge, *Wild at Heart: Discovering the Secret of a Man's Soul* (Nashville: Thomas Nelson, 2001). Eldredge invites men to recover their masculine heart, which is defined in the image of a passionate God. And he invites women to discover the secret of a man's soul and to delight in the strength and wildness that men were created to offer.

23. Visit their website at http://www.ransomedheart.com.

24. Other ministries that have helpful insights for men are The Familyman (http://family manweb.com), Every Man Ministry (http://www.everymanministries.com), and Man in the Mirror (http://www.maninthemirror.org).

Local churches are encouraged to design activities for men that focus on how Scripture answers questions that are relevant to men. Men like camaraderie, challenges, and competition. Retreats built around popular male activities (both indoor and outdoor) will make it easier for church-going men to invite their non-church-going friends to attend.

A number of churches sponsor or participate in athletic leagues—softball, soccer, basketball, golf, or Ultimate Frisbee. This gives great opportunity for believers to invite their friends to join them in an activity that will not be too religiously overbearing. Rivalry and contest are built into a man's psyche, so friendly games and competition energize men and provide opportunities for building camaraderie, which is a primary step on the road to sharing the gospel.

Fourth, Deal with Reasons Why Men Don't Attend Church

I was amused with a cartoon that depicted a young lad standing in front of his friends, who were sitting under a large oak tree. He said, "Let's play church. I'll be the preacher; and you be the hypocrites." We may chuckle, but there is much truth in that cartoon, for many young men have the impression that the modern church is filled with hypocrites and wimps—people with whom they would rather not associate. Church-going men must realize that they are being watched and that their example of manliness and godliness will not go unnoticed.

Male visitors also frequently complain that worship services are too long and too boring. Leaders must understand that worshipping God should never be tedious, and therefore they should structure their services to be uplifting and joyous. Men have a hard time listening to a preacher who presents the Word in a dull manner with content that is irrelevant to their personal lives. Ministers of God's Word have the duty to prepare sermons that are true to Scripture, true to life, and relevant to both sexes, and also to take into consideration the various ways in which people in congregations learn: audio, visual, kinesthetic, and other such learning dimensions.

Another reason that men leave churches or refuse to attend them is the constant solicitation of funds. I once served a church whose fiscal year ended June 30. I was asked to write an article on stewardship each week for four weeks prior to the end of the fiscal year. This article appeared on the front page of the bulletin. Inside the bulletin was another highlighted box stressing the need to give! Then, during the worship service, a member of the Stewardship Committee spoke for five minutes on the value of giving. Although I protested the overkill about giving and informed the committee and the elders that men leave churches over the emphasis on money, I was overruled. This church did not understand that money follows ministry and that soliciting funds during summer months, when many people relocate and search for new churches, can quickly turn off visitors—especially men.

Fifth, Encourage Women to Be Women of the Word

Women are to submit to appropriate male authority and to receive instruction quietly.[25] As wives, they are to humbly place their wills under their husbands' as is fitting under the Lord.[26] Such behavior is a witness to men,[27] for guys don't want competitors but do desire encouragers. Women, according to Thom S. Rainer, do play a key and instrumental part in leading men to Christ.[28] The reason for this is the power of influence given to them by God. Such power of persuasion can be used negatively, as seen in Eve's inducement of Adam to eat the forbidden fruit,[29] or positively, as seen when Sarah influenced Abram (with the Lord's commendation) to send Hagar away to preserve family harmony.[30] Abigail was very much

25. "Let a woman learn quietly with all submissiveness. I do not permit a woman to teach or to exercise authority over a man; rather, she is to remain quiet. For Adam was formed first, then Eve; and Adam was not deceived, but the woman was deceived and became a transgressor" (1 Tim. 2:11–14).

26. "Wives, submit to your husbands, as is fitting in the Lord" (Col. 3:18).

27. "Likewise, wives, be subject to your own husbands, so that even if some do not obey the word, they may be won without a word by the conduct of their wives, when they see your respectful and pure conduct" (1 Peter 3:1–2).

28. Thom S. Rainer, *Surprising Insights from the Unchurched and Proven Ways to Reach Them* (Grand Rapids: Zondervan, 2001), 83.

29. "So when the woman saw that the tree was good for food, and that it was a delight to the eyes, and that the tree was to be desired to make one wise, she took of its fruit and ate, and she also gave some to her husband who was with her, and he ate" (Gen. 3:6).

30. "But God said to Abraham, 'Be not displeased because of the boy and because of your slave woman. Whatever Sarah says to you, do as she tells you, for through Isaac shall your offspring be named'" (Gen. 21:12).

the influencer in Nabal's household, and she preserved her husband's life by convincing David to refrain from killing a fool (1 Sam. 25:25–34). The misuse of the power of influence, however, is manipulation, which many men accuse women of engaging in. But when women fulfill their role as women, they win men to Christ, and the local church is the beneficiary.

Women, however, are not to usurp the authority of men. They are equal in worth, but they have different job descriptions. They may be better than men at many things, but in the economy of God they have been given certain posts to occupy. One such post or position is that of responder to appropriate male leadership. God said in Genesis 2:18, "It is not good that the man should be alone; I will make him a helper fit for him." The word for "fit" or "suitable" is *neged*, which literally means "before" or "in front of." The idea is an "opposite" or a "counterpart." Placed alongside the word *helper* or *helpmate*, it indicates that the wife is not a mere servant, but "one who corresponds" to the husband. Women are therefore created as the necessary and favorable responder to the headship of men. When husbands lead lovingly and correctly, women find it easier to support male leadership at home and in the church.

Behind great church leaders are remarkable women who properly influence and aid in the accomplishment of church vision, growth, and vibrancy. Women who are devoted servants of Christ may teach children, other women, and, on occasion, men as it concerns the principles of understanding the opposite sex. Furthermore, some individuals may expound on subjects specific to their skills and training, which will encourage male leaders to lead, love, and appreciate the female perspective. Because women may trust instinctively without first verifying the reasons for that trust, they are more likely to be deceived and hurt. Such a tendency may be the reason that Paul admonished Timothy not to allow a woman to teach men. "I do not permit a woman to teach or to exercise authority over a man. . . . For Adam was formed first, then Eve; and Adam was not deceived, but the woman was deceived" (1 Tim. 2:12–14). The tasks of teaching and exercising authority seem to point to the handling and explaining of Scripture. As man was appointed the head of the woman, he has the responsibility of spiritual oversight, which includes the explanation and elucidation of God's Word.

Women are not called to shepherd the people of God; men are. Women are, however, to help men in the care of the sheep. They are talented and gifted in many respects, but God in his providence chose men (as quirky as it may seem) to be leaders of the home and shepherds of the church. When women rebel against God's role for them, and when men abdicate their position of authority, the church suffers and the gospel is smothered by cultural expediency and political priorities.[31]

"SHEPHERD MY SHEEP"

Jesus chose men to lead his fledgling church. Although women were an important part of his ministry, the Lord appointed men to govern his church and to feed his sheep. Jesus exhorted Peter to feed, tend, and shepherd his sheep (see John 21:15–17). Peter remembered the Lord's admonition and encouraged his fellow elders to care diligently for the sheep entrusted to them (1 Peter 5:1–4). Church leaders, therefore, are to be actively involved with their sheep.

The Lord will judge churches with weak male leadership; and that judgment starts with the elders (Ezek. 9:6). Leaders who abdicate their shepherding duties may contribute to turmoil, disruption, and irrelevancy within the church. Woe to those leaders who do not feed their sheep with the truth of God, who do not care for the sick among them, and who scatter the flock because of self-interest (Ezek. 34:2–5)! God is opposed to such shepherds and will hold them accountable (Ezek. 34:10).

A vibrant church has manly leadership, male disciples, and active women involved in ministry and service. Leaders must "man up" with the courage to make decisions that not only will benefit the congregation, but will also attract faithful and steadfast men to become involved in the work of the church. This entails leaving the status quo and becoming what Christ wants his leaders to be. Men in leadership must remember that they are called to their positions by Christ to shepherd his flock.

31. The Presbyterian Church in America, through its Church Discipleship Ministry, has a vibrant women's ministry with helpful resources. See "Women's Ministry," CDM Discipleship Ministries, http://www.pcacdm.org/women/, for more information. Revive Our Hearts ministry is another resource for women's ministry; visit their website at http://www.reviveourhearts.com.

The church, therefore, does not belong to any human being in particular, but to Christ himself. Leaders have the responsibility to find the will of Christ for the local church, which invariably includes sharing the gospel with men in the local community.

PRESCRIPTION FOR LEADERSHIP

Elders need an involved pastor to demonstrate what shepherds do. They need a minister who is not only versed in Scripture but also involved in their lives—a brother who will help them to become better leaders in the church. A young pastor whose father was a great evangelist and pulpiteer in the church confessed that, if he were to pastor the church all over again, he would spend more time building relationships with his elders. The next few chapters will explain how leaders can be proactive in maintaining spiritual health while maturing as shepherds of their sheep. Spiritual vitamins will be suggested, the taking of which should help prevent poor leadership.

11

Faithful Leaders

Your throne is established from of old; you are from everlasting. (Ps. 93:2)

FIDELITY OF CHRIST

The Lord will not forsake his people, and he will not abandon his heritage (see Ps. 94:14). Isaiah described the righteousness of the Messiah as the belt around his waist, and faithfulness as the belt about his loins (Isa. 11:5). The total dependability and steadfastness of Jesus is shown in his personal character and demeanor and is made known by his words and actions. He is the same yesterday, today, and forever (Heb. 13:8); and, because he never changes, he is forever faithful. Therefore, we can rely on his Word, which helps us to persevere in our difficulties and gives us new perspective on our situations.

WATCH THE SHEEP

Every leader who is devoted to Christ is called to faithfully watch over and shepherd the sheep (see Acts 20:28). God, who is incomparably great and regards nations as less than nothing and emptiness (Isa. 40:17–18), nevertheless supports those whose hearts are blameless toward him (2 Chron.16:9). A leader's heart, therefore, should endear itself to his Maker, for the Lord expects shepherds to represent him faithfully in caring for his sheep.

Leadership involves moral integrity and doing what is right. Leaders are not to avoid the sharp edges of ministry, for those sensitive moments make the man and hone his skill as a leader. When conflict surfaces—and it will—elders intervene, listen to and counsel both sides, and then execute justice and righteousness. They act as peacemakers to redeem conflict and bring unity to the congregation. Following God's will takes courage, truthfulness, perseverance, and long-suffering, for verbal abuse often follows intervention. In other words, godly leadership trusts God and believes that he is sanctifying his people in the midst of congregational hurt, disappointment, and disagreements.

Conflict in a church occurs because people are sinners, and the enemy of Christ lurks in the background, trying to destroy unity among Christians. Building an immune system to prevent conflict will never be 100 percent effective. There are, however, daily preventatives that help leaders to maintain God's perspective.

DAILY VITAMIN F1: FAITHFULNESS

To be physically healthy, we eat right, exercise properly, and take daily vitamins to help build our immune system. To be spiritually healthy, we are to be proactive and strengthen our spiritual resistance to withstand the disease of poor leadership. Therefore, the first of three daily vitamins that leaders need is Vitamin "F1," which stands for *faithfulness*.

Faithfulness is adhering to the teaching of Scripture, performing the duty of a leader well, and demonstrating dependability as a true shepherd of God's sheep. Preventing poor leadership begins with the election of leaders who labor faithfully, who influence their sheep to do the right thing, and who trust God for results. President Dwight D. Eisenhower once commented that leadership was "the art of getting someone else to do something you want done because he wants to do it."[1] Shepherds should adopt a similar motto, for their calling is to lead sheep to green pastures, even though individual rams and ewes may want to veer toward rocky crags. Sheep are happy to be relatively inactive but will eventually

---

1. *Public Papers of the Presidents of the United States: Dwight D. Eisenhower; 1954* (Washington, DC: Office of the Federal Register), 477.

wander where new attractions lure them. They won't follow a shepherd whom they don't know and will certainly not do what he says if they are not familiar with his voice. Shepherds therefore must earn the right to be heard by faithfully tending their flock.

Faithfulness includes the adoption of God's perspective, for what happens (whether good or bad) is within his sovereign control. He is always at work accomplishing his good pleasure (Phil. 2:13), which will always turn out for good for those who love him and are called according to his purpose (Rom. 8:28). Thinking God's thoughts is to know Scripture and act accordingly! For instance, God desires peace and unity among his people; so leaders are, first, to be at peace with all men if it is within their power (Rom. 12:18) and, second, to stem conflict within the church by pursuing unity among the congregation.

Job tells us that people are born for trouble as surely as sparks fly upward (Job 5:7). In other words, there is no avoiding the adversities of life, which include church conflict and difficulties. We are therefore expected to weather storms for the sake and glory of our Lord. The question that confronts faith is this: does God actually control the events and circumstances of life? At times, it certainly does not look like it, for we often wonder whether a loving God would actually allow his people to experience distressing ordeals and schism in churches. Faithfulness therefore includes trusting God.

Trusting God through the heartaches of life becomes a challenge in our pilgrimage on earth. In order to trust him, we must love him, and loving him corresponds to our growth in knowledge of him and of his character. Only then will we come to view the circumstances of life through the eyes of faith rather than through the emotion of pain. In his book *Trusting God*, Jerry Bridges comments that faith to trust God during hardship and misfortune comes through the Word of God alone.[2]

It is from Scripture that we find an adequate view of God's involvement in our painful circumstances. It is from Scripture, applied to our hearts by the Holy Spirit, that we receive the grace to trust God in adversity. Truths that we learn from Scripture include: (1) God is completely

---

2. Jerry Bridges, *Trusting God: Even When Life Hurts* (Colorado Springs: NavPress, 1988), 18.

sovereign, even when bad things happen; (2) God works his perfect wisdom to accomplish his plans and purposes; and (3) God is good and perfect in his love for us.[3] Understanding and believing these three biblical principles is essential to trusting God during our struggles in life. Trusting God, as Jerry Bridges adeptly stated, can be pictured as a three-legged milking stool. Each leg represents one of the above truths, and the loss of any one truth will collapse our trust and will bring us into a crisis of faith.

Masking our real relationship with the Lord occurs when we pretend that our faith is alive and well, but for all intents and purposes it is wavering and causing us to doubt God's love and wisdom. We will not know the strength of our stool of faith, however, until a severe hurricane strikes the coastal areas of our lives. Needing all three legs to trust God in our storms, we have the tendency to shift our weight toward a missing or fractured leg. For instance, if we do not believe that God is sovereign and that he wills what is best for us in order to conform us to the image of Christ, then we will doubt his love and will not trust his wisdom. The stool of "trusting God" then collapses, and we find ourselves in disbelief, reaching for anyone and anything to help, and questioning God's providence and goodness. We may then turn toward the world for counsel and look for the easiest and swiftest way out of the pain. In other words, we seek immediate relief while avoiding the real cure, which is found in Christ and in his Word. It is only during times of struggle, turmoil, and affliction that the stool (that is, our trust in the Lord) is tried and tested.

Trusting God is looking at the issues and problems in our church as part of the Lord's sanctification process to make us better leaders and our sheep better followers of Christ. We are not to run from conflict but should attempt to see it from God's perspective of perfecting his people. What happened occurred! Whether the issues and conflict resulted from bad leadership and disastrous decisions, the events and consequences did not emerge outside of God's auspices. We must realize that God is still in charge and wants unity among his people. Leaders are therefore

3. Ibid.

charged with confessing their own faults, working with mediators if necessary, and confronting sheep with their own complicity in order for forgiveness to be sought and repentance to occur.

Church conflict may look unmanageable, but from God's perspective he is sanctifying his people to cause them to be conformed to the image of Christ (Rom. 8:29). People embroiled in church difficulties may feel helpless and uncomfortable, but God will work his way to accomplish his purposes for the church. Sheep are ultimately safe and secure because Jesus has conquered the world (John 16:33) and deprived it of any power to eternally hurt his flock.[4] Leaders who realize this have a big God and will submit to his direction. And who better to be in control of an evil situation than the God who overcomes evil (see 1 John 3:8)?

When conflict comes, leaders set the example by turning away from evil themselves, acting appropriately by seeking peace with others (Ps. 34:14), and trusting God for the best results. Peter concurs with this admonition and adds that the face of the Lord is against those who do evil (1 Peter 3:12). So church conflict may be the mechanism that the Lord uses to weed from the sheepfold those who are unruly and divisive and whose influence may be inflammatory.[5] If leaders are not peacemakers but instead incite further schism, then they may be the ones whom the Lord opposes. If, however, they are secure in their relationship with the Lord and trust in his sovereignty, then they need not fear the face of man, for such dread brings a snare (see Prov. 29:25).

Jeremiah 1:8 reads, "Be not afraid of their faces: for I am with thee to deliver thee, saith the LORD" (KJV). Elders need not fear man, especially when confrontation is needed. This Scripture encourages leaders to do what is right to pursue harmony in the church. Most people dislike conflict, but challenging someone who breaches the peace of the church is the right thing to do.

---

4. "I give them eternal life, and they will never perish, and no one will snatch them out of my hand. My Father, who has given them to me, is greater than all, and no one is able to snatch them out of the Father's hand" (John 10:28–29).

5. A friend of mine said that losing malcontents from the church should be looked at as "blessed subtractions."

THE PRODUCT OF FAITHFULNESS

Faithfulness is steadfastly adhering to the will of God, even when it seems fruitless. Great encouragement is found in Scriptures that tell of the lives of people who remained faithful to God in spite of their circumstances. Against all odds they trusted God and praised him for results, whether good or bad.

David's walk with the Lord brought him face to face with Goliath. He couldn't understand why the Israelite army was terrified of an uncircumcised Philistine who defied the armies of the living God. Faith says, "God will triumph; so why fear the likes of an enemy?" The years of protecting his father's sheep had prepared David for this moment of confrontation. When King Saul met the young David, he couldn't see how a youth of slight stature could fight a giant of a man. David's answer was, "The LORD who delivered me from the paw of the lion and from the paw of the bear will deliver me from the hand of this Philistine" (1 Sam. 17:37).

Goliath had no chance of victory over a man of faith, for God's favor of his own will bring about the result that he wants, which will be to his glory. The odds were against David, but the Lord was not. Goliath came after David with sword and spear; David came in the name of the Lord, believing that deliverance was from God (1 Sam. 17:45–46). When leaders confront adversity, believing that the results of their efforts are in God's hands, they cannot lose, for God honors faith.

Shadrach, Meshach, and Abednego faced insurmountable odds when cast into the fiery furnace. They had served King Nebuchadnezzar well, but because of the sin of others they faced the greatest challenge of their lives. Refusing to worship a golden image, they were given a chance to recant by the king himself. "Is it true," queried the king, "that you do not serve my gods or worship the golden image that I have set up?" (Dan. 3:14). The three servants needed no additional time to think about a retraction. They immediately replied,

> O Nebuchadnezzar, we have no need to answer you in this matter. If this be so, our God whom we serve is able to deliver us from the burning fiery furnace. . . . But if not, be it known to you, O king,

that we will not serve your gods or worship the golden image that
you have set up. (Dan. 3:16–18)

Faith trusts God for the results. Shadrach, Meshach, and Abednego
relied on God's sovereignty for their security—whether it was life on
earth or life after death. Knowing that God was with them eased the
pain of their decision, even if it meant their demise. Their deliverance
and testimony moved Nebuchadnezzar to bless God and to issue a decree
that anyone speaking ill against "the God of Shadrach, Meshach, and
Abednego shall be torn limb from limb, and their houses laid in ruins,
for there is no other god who is able to rescue in this way" (Dan. 3:29).
When leaders do what is right and trust God with the outcome, they
give testimony to the hand of God in the affairs of men.

Adversity in a fallen world cannot be avoided. Leaders are expected
to represent righteousness in any situation. Faithfulness demands it. Peter
and John, after Christ's resurrection and ascension, faced community
leaders who "charged them not to speak or teach at all in the name
of Jesus" (Acts 4:18). As faithful followers of Christ, they responded,
"Whether it is right in the sight of God to listen to you rather than to
God, you must judge, for we cannot but speak of what we have seen and
heard" (Acts 4:19–20). They were loyal to their calling and preached
the risen Christ when those around them forbade it. Faithful leaders
perform the will of Christ and risk ridicule for doing it.

THE SIMPLICITY OF FAITHFULNESS

Godly leaders exercise faith by doing what is right. This pleases
God (Heb. 11:6) and brings healing to situations of conflict. Elders
need not fear people in the exercise of their rule of the church or in their
shepherding of them. Loving righteousness and hating wickedness will
bring the anointing of God's joy upon leaders (Ps. 45:7).

Pastors should encourage leaders to step out in faith by doing
what the Lord wants and not what people desire. A faithless leader will
lack courage and decisiveness, contributing to the ineffectiveness of the
church. "I will show you my faith by my works," said James (James
2:18). The same goes for elders. Their faith is demonstrated by their

shepherding abilities and by their willingness to make godly, though at times unpopular, decisions.

Faithfulness is taking one's calling seriously and being steadfast in performing the duties of an elder or church member. I once met a Presbyterian elder from New England who told me how he remembered his vow of membership at the baptism of an infant. When the pastor asked the members to raise their hands in promising the young couple to help raise their child in the nurture and admonition of the Lord, this elder (like most members) raised his hand without thinking about the implications. Some seventeen years later, when this infant, now a rebellious teen, was arrested by the police for theft and vandalism, he suddenly remembered his vow and felt the pains of guilt for not coming to the aid of this family earlier when he had first seen signs of unruliness in the son.

With the parents' permission, he visited the teen in jail, not once, but a number of times. God rewarded his faithfulness by softening the teen's heart and allowing the words of the gospel to take root. By God's grace, the elder was enabled to lead the young man from apparent reprobation to redemption.

Faithfulness is giving comfort to a dying sheep. An associate pastor was instrumental in ministering to a dying Jewish man who had become a believer in Christ by reading Isaiah 53. Knowing that his life was coming to an end, the new Messianic believer wished to join a church and be baptized, much like the Ethiopian eunuch in Acts 8.[6] The pastor baptized him after he joined the church, and an elder was moved to include him in his fold—the families that he shepherded. This elder visited him once or twice a week, giving him comfort, helping him with the assurance of his salvation, and nurturing his faith in the face of death.

Faithfulness is having quarterly fold lunches after church. An elder friend sponsored periodic lunches after Sunday services for the families in his fold or flock. He and his wife provided the meat, and those who were attending provided the side dishes. The invitation was extended to all visitors or newcomers to the church. This elder took hospitality

---

6. "And as they were going along the road they came to some water, and the eunuch said, 'See, here is water! What prevents me from being baptized?'" (Acts 8:36).

seriously,[7] and the time spent in eating a meal together helped him to maintain contact with people and helped the people to grow in relationship with each other.

Faithfulness is mediating in family squabbles. An associate pastor at a large Presbyterian church was charged with discipling the people and helping them to mature in Christ. One of his duties was to intervene in family disputes and to help resolve issues. He partnered with an older elder who was gifted in peacemaking. This elder had a way of cutting to the chase without offending the parties. He was firm yet understanding. His bearing and demeanor commanded greater respect and authority. And the parties responded! Where the associate pastor may have butted in and quoted Scripture, the elder listened, clarified the issue, presented a plan of reparation or reconciliation, and encouraged following Jesus' example. He was a faithful elder who was instrumental in healing family disagreements.

Faithfulness is a leader meeting with family members at a hospital to console them after the loss of a son due to an automobile accident. Faithfulness is exercising one's giftedness to lead worship, volunteer in youth ministry, teach Bible studies, and organize work parties to aid widows. Faithfulness is the grace of God to persevere in ministering to people when people seem to care little for an elder's involvement in their lives.

PERSPECTIVE

When my eldest son, Joshua, was nine years old, we travelled to Williamsburg, Virginia, to visit the Olde Country, Busch Gardens. Like many Christian families, we prayed at the entrance to the amusement park. Part of our prayer was for God to watch over us and protect us from injury. We hadn't been in the park for one hour before Joshua was injured. He slipped while getting off a merry-go-round horse, and the iron step-stirrup gouged his thigh near his groin. The wound, which was so extreme that it looked as if it had been caused by shrapnel, took more than seventy-two stitches to close.

---

7. "Contribute to the needs of the saints and seek to show hospitality" (Rom. 12:13).

Josh whispered to me while waiting for the ambulance, "But Dad, we prayed!" He was questioning God and the power of our prayer. He didn't quite understand why he had to suffer such a gaping wound on a family outing. But the Lord knew what lay ahead and what he was protecting Josh from.

Unable to compete on the local swim team for four weeks, Josh was not particularly happy. A week after the incident, however, he complained about an earache. Knowing that he had a high threshold of pain, we rushed him to the doctor, who confirmed our suspicions of a serious ear infection. The doctor was amazed that Josh wasn't writhing in pain. In fact, he added that, if Josh had been swimming, he probably would have burst an eardrum, causing deafness. Josh quickly learned that God had protected him from a more serious injury by allowing his leg to be wounded. God did answer our prayer about protection, but not in the way we had first expected.

God, who controls all things, not only saw in his providence what was to happen to my son but also ordained the outcome by answering our prayer in a manner of unanticipated beneficence. He was always in control of the situation, although we were somewhat panicky. God is sovereign and has the power and right of dominion to rule over his creatures and to do what is good for them. His perspective is always right and best for his chosen people. His rule over the church, however, is delegated to those whom he calls as elders. Leaders therefore are to understand the God perspective, which states that, though events and circumstances may look bad at the moment, the eventual outcome will be good for those who submit to the governance of God.

Being ordained to serve the interests of God in building up the flock of Christ (Eph. 4:11–12) is an awesome task and is not to be taken lightly. As pastors will be held accountable for what they teach (James 3:1), elders will be answerable for their faithfulness in ruling the flock (see Heb. 13:7). And, if they are sincerely shepherding for the sake of the Lord, they will have an eternal perspective in all that happens within the church. So, even if bad things occur within the congregation, having God's perspective is realizing that he is in control and will work the issues for good.

Faithfulness in leaders is a preventative from getting the disease of poor leadership. But faithfulness must be shown in the godly decisions and tireless work of shepherds. Faithfulness, then, is leaders exercising faith by doing what they are called to do: to rule the church well (1 Tim. 5:17) and to shepherd the people sincerely, tenderly, and lovingly (John 21:15–17).

The next chapter will explore the benefit of Vitamin "F2," which is forgiveness—not mere lip service, but a true act of the heart. A forgiving heart is testimony to the love of Christ.

12

"Seventy Times Seven"

But you are a God ready to forgive, gracious and merciful, slow to anger, and abounding in steadfast love, and did not forsake them. (Neh. 9:17)

LOVE THE ONE YOU HATE

"Forgive and forget; that's the Christian way!" Don't you hate this reminder? Forgive and forget? No way! Revenge is sweeter. "Don't get mad; get even!" That sounds better to sinners' ears. Harboring hatred appeases us for the moment, for our minds act out our vengeance. We imaginatively slay the person, think ill of him, and wish bad to befall him. Yet we are Christians, and a mark of Jesus' disciples is forgiveness, for the Savior did say, "Love your enemies and pray for those who persecute you" (Matt. 5:44). Forgiving the dastardly is proof that we are sons of God, for only true believers can really love the one they hate (Matt. 5:45–46). Furthermore, Jesus said that if we harbor anger in our hearts toward our brother, we have basically murdered him and are guilty before the court (see Matt. 5:21–22).

When conflict arises in churches, sin increases and leaders either add to the problem or become soothing balm to heal the hurt. Hatred of the ill-intentioned dragons that cause the conflict will only stir up more strife, but loving them will cover their sins and ease the controversy (Prov. 10:12). In these situations, leaders must be strong yet humble, steadfast yet understanding, and decisive yet loving. If they have sinned, then they must model what confession and forgiveness look like, for the sheep (that is, true believers) will follow their lead and seek reconciliation with others. Those who fail to admit their sin and who harbor an unforgiving attitude will, in all likelihood, leave the church and retain their bitterness.

I once served a church that underwent a major split over worship styles and the direction of the church. The senior pastor resigned, but many of his supporters remained in the church, causing disquiet among the elders. After preaching a number of sermons on forgiveness and leaving the past behind, I asked the congregation during the confession time of the service to bow their heads, close their eyes, and raise their hands if they had transgressed God's law by sinning in the way I had described. I mentioned a litany of sins that broke fellowship and strained relationships with one another. Just about every hand went up. I then asked them to lower their hands, keep their eyes closed, and confess their sins silently before the Lord, asking for his forgiveness and for the power to forgive others who had hurt them. I had them open their eyes and look around the sanctuary. If they saw anyone in the congregation with whom they were experiencing strained relationships, and if they had just prayed to forgive that person, then they were to leave their seats and approach him or her to ask forgiveness.

The Lord's Spirit was moving in that church, and people stood up and approached those they had harbored bitterness toward. I heard the buzz of confession and the sobbing of joy as the Lord brought peace and unity to a torn congregation. I kept an eye, however, on two key families who were centrally embroiled in the conflict. They remained in their seats and were shocked when a number of people approached them, asking forgiveness for the bitterness they had carried. The hearts of the sitters had remained hardened, and they maintained their self-righteous attitude, which lodged them in the darkness of unforgiveness. The two recalcitrant families eventually removed their membership from the church. How sad for former leaders to harden their hearts and remain stubbornly unrepentant!

Lewis Smedes (1921–2002), a former professor of theology and ethics at Fuller Theological Seminary, once said, "When you forgive a

person who wronged you, you set a prisoner free, and then you discover
that the prisoner you set free is you."[1] How right he is! By not forgiving
the person who has seriously offended us or harmed our family, we
allow the bile of bitterness to eat us up. And when we are bitter, that
acid is not hurting the one we are angry at; it is hurting us. Freedom is
in forgiving; bondage remains for the impenitent.

DAILY VITAMIN F2: FORGIVENESS

The second daily "F" vitamin that leaders need to ingest in order
to build the immune system against the disease of poor leadership is
forgiveness. Forgiveness (let's call it Vitamin F2) is a character trait of
Christians and is to be exhibited by all church leaders. Those who have
trouble forgiving must look closely into a mirror and ask whether they
serve Christ or self. An unforgiving leader is a poor example for his
sheep, who need to see Jesus in their shepherd.

When leaders sin and foster schism in the church, they demonstrate
poor leadership. Once they recognize their sin, they should openly confess it at a congregational meeting or during a Sunday worship service.
Public confession is difficult, for we all fear humiliation, but elders
who humble themselves before the sheep will be forgiven and willingly
followed. Perfection is unattainable, but forgiveness is not. Leaders will
frequently sin and make foolish decisions. A good leader eventually
recognizes his foolishness and confesses his sin. Once it is confessed,
repentance is in order, which means to abruptly turn and go the opposite
way from which one was heading. And that opposite way is the way of
God's truth and righteousness.

I met an elder who had contributed to a horrendous church split.
I had heard many rumors about how intolerant he was and how unfair
he had been to the pastor. He had lost credibility when he vocalized his
opinion that the pastor had to go. The session then took sides, eventually
causing approximately two hundred people to leave the church, including this elder. Enjoying my conversation with him, I found it hard to

1. Lewis Smedes, "Five Things Everyone Should Know about Forgiving," *30 Good Minutes*, Chicago Sunday Evening Club, October 5, 1997, available online at http://www.csec.org
/csec/sermon/smedes_4101.

believe that he was the major cause of people leaving a beloved church. He then admitted to me that he had been wrong in what he had done, had apologized to the pastor, and had met with the session of the church and asked forgiveness from the elders.

I asked whether he had apologized publicly to the congregation, since it was a public sin he had committed. He told me he had offered to do so, but the elders had said it wasn't necessary. The elders may have thought that a public appearance could do more to harm the already fragile congregants. This elder was sincere, and he submitted to his brothers on the session. If the elders had decided that an appearance before the congregation was appropriate, then they would have had the opportunity to show solidarity among themselves while embracing the estranged elder with forgiveness for all to observe.

Sheep are followers and will follow their leaders in confession, thereby easing tensions and bringing peace to the congregation. Leaders who take a good dose of Vitamin F2 will model forgiveness and will foster peace and unity in a schismatic situation. If one or two leaders are moved by the Spirit to confess sin or admit bad decisions, but other elders adamantly refuse to do likewise, then further friction occurs and the church suffers. Fellow elders must confront each other in love for healing and reconciliation to occur. If elders refuse to resolve their disputes, then a peacemaker—an objective third party—should be invited to broker peace. An outsider is unbiased, has no proverbial "dog in the fight," and will more easily admonish according to God's Word.

ANGER AS AN OBSTACLE TO FORGIVENESS

Many pastors resign their positions rather than facing or causing further conflict in the church. They think this the better course of action, but in reality the split will occur anyway. Eighty-five percent of pastors in a study by Maranatha Life Ministries said that they were "tired of dealing with problem people."[2] Such difficulty in dealing with uncooperative people was confirmed by John La Rue, who asserted that

2. "Don't Become a Statistic," *Life-Line for Pastors* 1, no. 2 (April 2003): http://www .maranathalife.com/lifeline/03-04-p.htm.

the seven main reasons for a pastor's forced exit involved some form of conflict.[3] When it comes to dealing with problem people, pastors often do not find it worth persevering, and so the result of a pastor's departure is a victory celebration for ill-intentioned dragons.

I once confided in a pastor friend about some problematic people and leaders in my congregation. My friend's advice was to weather the controversy and stand firm. He related his own experience of confronting an influential but ill-intentioned dragon, whom he told, "One of us is leaving the church, and I am going nowhere." My friend reminded me that I was called to shepherd the people in good times and in troublesome times. He further commented that, when he had left his prior church to take a new call, he had frankly been happy to leave some of the difficult people behind. He continued, "Yet I wasn't in my new church six months before I saw the same people in the congregation. There they were—sitting out there—staring back at me. Different faces, different names, but the same cantankerous attitudes!"

The point is that there will always be people who will try our patience and will dislike our preaching, our vision, or our shepherding. As leaders, we will have to deal with the complaining spirits, confront their unhealthy attitudes, and fight our own unforgiving hearts. Bitterness, not the irritable malcontents, will become our enemy; and so we will be constantly battling our own unforgiving hearts.

Since the fall of Adam and Eve, it has not been the nature of man to forgive easily. Part of the reason is the anger we carry against the offender. As long as we remain full of ire, we will find it difficult to forgive. Pride gets in the way and influences our behavior by convincing us that we have a right to be angry. To forgive an evil person is an act of humility, for it requires us to deal with our anger, bury our pride, and reach out with the love of Christ. Even though vindictive people malign us, we are to forgive them, for Christ has forgiven us (Luke 24:46–47; Col. 2:13; see also Matt. 6:14–15).

3. John C. LaRue, "Forced Exits: A Too-Common Ministry Hazard," *Your Church*, March/April 1996, 72, http://www.christianitytoday.com/cbg/features/report/6y2072.html, cited in Ken Sande, "The High Cost of Conflict Among Christians," Peacemaker Ministries, last modified February 18, 2015, http://peacemaker.net/project/the-high-cost-of-conflict-among-christians/.

WHAT FORGIVENESS IS NOT!

Forgiveness is not an option. We do not have the luxury of deciding whether we will forgive or not. A Christian forgives, because forgiveness is a mark of a disciple of Christ. When Peter asked how many times we are to forgive, Jesus said seventy times seven (Matt. 18:22), effectively making the point that we are not to keep a count. Jesus went on to say that the kingdom of heaven is like a king forgiving a servant a debt of some 10,000 talents (Matt. 18:23–35). We dare not refuse to forgive others when the Lord has forgiven us an immeasurable number of sins.

Forgiveness is not a feeling. We don't wait until we feel like forgiving, because love dictates that we forgive regardless of how we feel. Love doesn't keep a record of the wrongs suffered at the hands of others (see 1 Cor. 13:5). We are to have a short memory and to offer forgiveness even though the culprit doesn't deserve it. Giving forgiveness, therefore, means going against our ill feeling and potential bitterness in order to extend grace to the one who has sinned against us (Heb. 12:15).

Forgiveness is not long-suffering. It is not patiently waiting for the other to ask forgiveness, nor is it patiently waiting for the right opportunity to extend forgiveness. We do not wait for the victimizer to come to us. Rather, we go to him, express our hurt, and attempt reconciliation (Matt. 18:15–17). If he doesn't give it to us, it becomes his problem, for it is as if we have just heaped coals upon his head (Rom. 12:20).

Lack of forgiveness will become internalized anger—an acid that eats the container (us) from the inside out. Bitterness, therefore, is the poison that we eat while preparing it for others.[4] It is rebellion against God and is therefore equated with the sin of witchcraft (see 1 Sam. 15:23). Our resentment will lead to broken relationships, not just with the offending party but also with others associated with him or her. The greatest fracture, however, is with God, because he commands us to forgive, and refusal to do so means that we are not forgiven by him (Matt. 6:15). Leaders must therefore model the grace of God by extending forgiveness to those who have slandered their name and challenged their authority.

---

4. Thomas Chalmers once said, "Unforgiveness is the poison we drink hoping another will die" (quoted in Gregory Scott, "The Poison We Drink," *Gregory Scott Blog*, October 1, 2010, http://gregoryscottblog.com/miscellany/the-poison-we-drink/).

THE ATTITUDE OF FORGIVENESS

Forgiveness is the medicine that softens hearts, which then creates opportunities to restore broken relationships (see 2 Cor. 2:5–10). Temperate hearts lead to changed attitudes, which are the ingredients necessary in extending forgiveness to others. With the right attitude, leaders portray their calling and are seen by others as God's shepherds to the flock. Wrong attitudes will have the sheep questioning an elder's call as an officer of Christ's church. Chuck Swindoll once said of attitude,

> The longer I live, the more I realize the impact of attitude on life. . . . Attitude, to me, is more important than facts. It is more important than past, than education, than money, than circumstances, than failures, than successes, than what other people think or say or do. It is more important than appearance, giftedness, or skill. It will make or break a company . . . a church . . . a home. . . . The remarkable thing is you have a choice everyday regarding the attitude you will embrace for that day. . . . We cannot change our past . . . we cannot change the fact that people will act a certain way. We cannot change the inevitable. . . . The only thing we can do is play on the one string we have, and that is our attitude. . . . I am convinced now that life is 10% what happens to me and 90% how I react to it.[5]

When we reach out to forgive our victimizer, our action should be accompanied with a proper attitude. The first attitude that attends our forgiveness is forbearance (see Col. 3:13), for we are to put on the heart of compassion in order to bear the hurt of another. So, just as the Lord has forgiven us, we must forgive others and continue to bear the hurt if necessary. If someone asks for our forgiveness, we must commit to forgive immediately (Luke 17:3–4). We do this by not dwelling on the offense, but rather dwelling on the promise of God to free us from any resentment because we obey his Word (John 8:31–32).

5. This popular quotation can be heard in context in Charles R. Swindoll, "Strengthening Your Grip on Attitudes, Part 1" (sermon, May 30, 2014), available online at http://www.insight.org/broadcasts/player/?bid=1970.

A second attitude to accompany forgiveness is kindness, which is a fruit of the Spirit (Gal. 5:22). This is demonstrated by the conduct of Joseph when he told his brothers not to worry that they had sold him into slavery, for God had arranged the incident in order to provide for them during the famine (Gen. 45:5). Although he had been treated badly by his brothers, he provided for their families. This was an act of kindness that accompanied his forgiveness.

A third attitude is forgetfulness. Once forgiveness is given, we are to forget the incident as best we can. God not only forgives, he also forgets, which means that he chooses not to hold our sins against us. He not only wipes out our transgressions, but he also says he will remember them no more (Isa. 43:25; Jer. 31:34). In our situation, we have a hard time forgetting. Not remembering means not to use the sin against the victimizer in the future, even though it may come to mind. How can we do this?

We learn to forget what others have done to us by actively loving them. We accomplish this by overlooking the act (Prov. 19:11) and by allowing love to cover the sin (1 Peter 4:8). We also refrain from rejoicing when calamity befalls our adversary (Prov. 24:17). Rather, we are to reach out in love to be of help in his or her taxing situation (see Matt. 5:44). Furthermore, we do not to seek revenge (Prov. 24:29), but we allow the Lord to be our vindicator. In this way, we love our enemies by doing the unexpected—feeding them (Prov. 25:21), blessing them (see Matt. 5:43–44), and doing good to them (Luke 6:27). To love the unlovable, we must put aside malevolent feelings about them by thinking positive thoughts and by praying for the dragon we have forgiven.

WHEN FORGIVENESS HAS OCCURRED

Although we may not feel like forgiving another, we understand that we have done so when we no longer experience anger or resentment upon thinking about our victimizer. Our thoughts are not bombarded with the abhorrence of this person, for we have actually turned him or her over to the Lord and wish no evil in return.

Second, forgiveness has occurred when we no longer have sinful feelings toward our adversary when we are in that person's presence. I recall a former elder in my church who intentionally caused dissension.

My hurt carried on for a while until I accepted the situation as having occurred within the providence of God. I had something to learn from this incident, and, until I realized that God was in control of the situation and was preparing me for future ministry, I still carried antipathy. I knew that the resentment was gone when I met this person in another church, said hello, and asked how he was. His facial expression conveyed surprise, confusion, and guilt. He didn't know what to say, and he actually said nothing. He acknowledged me by the shake of his head and the pain in his eyes, and then he moved on.

Third, forgiveness has occurred when the past hurt no longer controls our present thoughts and actions. I did not think unkindly of this elder whom I providentially met. I did feel sorry for him, for he had never dealt with the pain or the sin of the situation.

Fourth, forgiveness has occurred when we start loving the offender. For most people, to love an adversary is to pray for him and to ask the Lord for an opportunity to be reconciled. I recall praying for an elder who had left the church under disagreeable circumstances and had moved to another state. Then, amazingly, the Lord arranged a "chance" meeting in a hotel in a city far away from home. We had booked reservations at the same hotel for different occasions—he was there for a music festival, and I to perform a wedding ceremony. Now, who is in charge of our lives? The Lord arranged the opportunity, and we were able to take advantage of it. The former elder and I arranged breakfast together, had a pleasant time reminiscing, and repaired our relationship. Nothing happens by accident! If opportunities arise to reconcile a relationship, then by all means we are to do so, for we are called to be at peace with all men if possible (Rom. 12:18).

FORGIVENESS FRUSTRATES THE ADVERSARY

Although many of our adversaries may still carry resentment toward us, we are helpless to change their thoughts and attitudes. If we know that there is something between us, our duty is to attempt reconciliation (Matt. 5:23–24). If they refuse, then our love for Christ is to cover the depth of their sin.[6] Otherwise, retained bitterness will stir up strife

6. "Above all, keep loving one another earnestly, since love covers a multitude of sins" (1 Peter 4:8).

within us, denigrating our other relationships. Love, however, covers all offenses (Prov. 10:12). Loving our enemies is unexpected, but when we do so, we disarm them from further complaining against us.

Forgiveness is sweet and is the hallmark of a Christian who has been forgiven by God through Christ. It is a daily vitamin, because it builds a mindset of compassion, tolerance, and pardon toward others. Forgiveness frees leaders to focus their attention on the mission of the church, which is to make disciples. The third daily F vitamin is *focus*, which means being single-minded in accomplishing the mission and is the subject of the next chapter.

13

Focused on Making Disciples

And Barnabas and Saul returned from Jerusalem when they had completed their service, bringing with them John, whose other name was Mark. (Acts 12:25)

THE CHARGE OF CHRIST

To the church at Sardis, Jesus said,

> I know your works. You have the reputation of being alive, but you are dead. Wake up, and strengthen what remains and is about to die, for I have not found your works complete in the sight of my God. Remember, then, what you received and heard. Keep it, and repent. (Rev. 3:1–3)

Sardis had lost its vision of being what Christ desired it to be. Its prosperity in the manufacture and dyeing of wool and carpets had led to self-satisfaction and apathy. The church was not under persecution and, from all appearances, was religiously active. The problem was its nominal and inoffensive Christianity, which may have been compromised with the culture.

A calm and sedated church loses the vision of reaching society with the gospel of Christ. Paul warned Timothy of people who seemed religious enough but who denied God's power (2 Tim. 3:5). A congregation that merely plays church—that is, one that engages in religious activities while lacking vision—has no future, for disciples are not being made. The charge of Jesus to his disciples was to make and equip other supporters for expanding the kingdom of God. In his High Priestly Prayer to the Father, Jesus prayed for the setting apart of his followers.

> As you sent me into the world, so I have sent them into the world. And for their sake I consecrate myself, that they also may be sanctified in truth. (John 17:18–19)

Those who are in Christ are sent into their own communities to declare the good news of salvation. The focus, therefore, is the gospel of Christ; and focus becomes the bridge to the future in bringing others into the brotherhood of faith.

ONE MISSION

Lynn Anderson, founder of Hope Network Ministries,[1] tells a story about a shipload of travelers who sailed across the ocean sometime in the seventeenth century and landed on the northeast coast of North America. For the first year the people worked hard at establishing a town site. The following year they elected a town government to manage the new community. The third year the elected officials decided to build a road five miles westward into the wilderness. Well, this seemed strange to the townspeople, who in the fourth year of their existence organized to impeach their town officials. They thought that a road to nowhere was a waste of public funds. Who needed to go five miles into the wilderness anyway?

What happened to these people, who had once been visionaries— who had ventured into a wilderness, crossing unfriendly waters and settling a place that had never been inhabited by Europeans? They had the focus to see three thousand miles across a wide expanse of sea and the fortitude to overcome great hardships in order to maintain that vision. But, after just a few years of sedentary living, they lost their pioneering

---

1. Visit their website at http://www.hopenetworkministries.org.

spirit and could not see a mere five miles out of town.[2] Without a clear vision of what Christ would have us to be in our community, we as a church will remain riveted to our status quo, hardly venturing forth with the gospel of Christ.

When we lose the focus of making disciples in the location where God has placed us, a listless torpor sets in that frustrates the congregation.[3] Stagnant or declining congregations have, for the most part, forgotten their mission, which according to Christ is to "Go therefore and make disciples of all nations, baptizing them in the name of the Father and of the Son and of the Holy Spirit, teaching them to observe all that I have commanded you" (Matt. 28:19–20).

When problems arise in a church, leaders tend to lose focus on their mission. Like the apostles before us, we have but one mission, and that is to make disciples. Each church may go about the task differently, for each community is diverse and unique. A church's vision, therefore, is to be what Christ desires it to be in the community where the church is located: to make disciples.

PINELANDS

As mentioned earlier in this book, when Harry Reeder went to Pinelands Presbyterian Church in Cutler Bay, Florida, he inherited a dying church that had lost focus on the mission of making disciples. In fact, he relates that some of his key people were not even disciples themselves. Although some led worship and some were officers in the church, they were not true believers. They may have thought that they belonged to Christ, but in reality they belonged to the world.

Suspecting that some of his parishioners were unconverted, Reeder focused his first sermon on the necessity and nature of having personal faith in Christ Jesus. Taking his text from 2 Timothy 1:12,[4] he stressed that saving faith consists of knowledge, conviction, and trust.

2. "Sermon Illustrations: Vision," Higher Praise, accessed February 4, 2011, http://www.higherpraise.com/illustrations/vision.htm.

3. "Where there is no prophetic vision the people cast off restraint" (Prov. 29:18).

4. ". . . which is why I suffer as I do. But I am not ashamed, for I know whom I have believed, and I am convinced that he is able to guard until that Day what has been entrusted to me" (2 Tim. 1:12).

Finally, I shared that our faith has only one proper object, which is Jesus Christ. "I know whom I have believed." Not what, when, or that I have believed. Paul did not put his confidence in his approbation of facts (*what*). He did not put his confidence in a conversion experience (*when*). He did not put his confidence in this faith (*that*). His confidence was rooted in the only proper object (*whom*), Jesus Christ—who He is and what He has done to save us from our sins.[5]

That day, both the church organist and the chairman of the deacons came to faith. The following Sunday, a deacon came forward and gave his testimony. Then the deacon's wife came forward, and twenty-eight of the fifty-five people in church proceeded to the front. Reeder was focused on God's grace converting sinners. God was focused on revitalizing the Pinelands Church.[6]

When leaders lose the focus of disciple-making, the church withers, becoming ineffective in promoting the gospel to its community. Loving people is not some platitude to be preached but not lived. Loving people means loving the city, the town, and the area in which God has placed the church. It means involvement beyond one's comfort zone—engaging the surrounding culture and influencing it for Christ.

DAILY VITAMIN F3: FOCUS

The third daily "F" vitamin that leaders need in order to bolster their immune system against the disease of poor leadership is *focus* (Vitamin F3). Leaders have the tasks of maintaining focus, of promoting the mission of the church, and of establishing vision for the local congregation. When the church becomes inert and moribund, the focus has definitely been misplaced, and leadership is at fault. Too many times a church gets overly involved in programs that have no connection to making disciples. Energy is consumed and activity becomes the enemy of mission. The programs may be wonderful, but if they fail to accomplish

---

5. Harry L. Reeder III, *From Embers to a Flame: How God Can Revitalize Your Church* (Phillipsburg, NJ: P&R Publishing, 2008), 60.

6. Ibid., 61–63.

the objective, then they become a subtle tactic of Satan to make the church an ineffective factory for crafting disciples.

Leaders must therefore be frank and honest and must have the fortitude to remain dedicated with single-mindedness to the mission of making disciples. If the church has drifted from this all-important objective, then leaders are to take steps to revitalize their churches in order to recapture the fervor of disciple-making. Focus, according to Thom Rainer and Eric Geiger, is "the commitment to abandon everything that falls outside of the simple ministry process."[7] The ministry process is to make disciples, and anything that obstructs this mission is to be discarded. Leaders therefore must be willing to pare down church programs to keep their mission for Christ simple.

To keep the church focused, leaders must be personally focused on maintaining a passionate and intimate relationship with Christ. The apostle Paul was cognizant of this fact and refused to be gripped by his checkered past, choosing rather to press on to attain the upward call of Christ (Phil. 3:13–14). His focus was on Christ and on what Christ desired. Leaders who are focused on Jesus can't help but catch the fervor of disciple-making. If programs are contributing to the decline of raising followers of Christ, then leaders must say no to them and prune them from the ministry of the church.

One church had a wonderful reputation in its denomination. It had multiple ministries in place—to the inner city (although the congregation lived miles away), to the culture with a Christian heritage renewal theme, and to the public at large with a movement to salvage the Bible for daily life. All were wonderful programs, but the leaders, in enacting and supporting them, had lost their true mission—making disciples in the local community. The church had no protracted and pointed outreach agenda that would catch the attention of the surrounding community and demonstrate that the church had a genuine interest in the people's temporal and eternal welfare.

There were no ministries for young mothers, for premarital couples, for seekers, for new believers, for divorce care, for grief recovery, for

---

7. Thom S. Rainer and Eric Geiger, *Simple Church: Returning to God's Process for Making Disciples* (Nashville: Broadman & Holman, 2006), 203.

improving marriages, or for overcoming the trials of life. Leaders were not involved in community programs or agencies such as the Chamber of Commerce, Rotary Club, or Lion's Club. At one time the church had been instrumental in reaching professionals and business leaders for Christ, but it no longer supported or involved the people in this form of outreach. What had happened? The leadership had lost focus. The immediacy of preaching and living the gospel locally took a back seat to dreams of expansion and countrywide agendas that promoted the church's prominence within its denomination while losing its effectiveness in reaching the local community.

Like the first-century church in Ephesus, this local congregation needed revitalization—but when a consultant mentioned this, some leaders rebelled, claiming that it was a great church and needed no changes. Such an attitude was fraught with guile and delusion. The elders were not focused on making disciples and were certainly not frank with themselves or with the congregation in seeing their need for rejuvenation. There is nothing wrong with admitting the need for renewal. If the Ephesus church needed it, and if she was the best of the New Testament churches, then in all likelihood the local church in the United States needs it as well.

Jesus requires us to take a good, hard look at ourselves. Just because our church has been vibrant in the past doesn't mean that it still is. Christ spoke frankly about the church at Ephesus in Revelation 2. After commending the believers for their perseverance and for not putting up with evil men, Jesus admonished them for leaving their first love (Rev. 2:2–4). He then exhorted them to remember from where they had fallen and to repent from their backslidden state to recommit to what they had done at first (Rev. 2:5). What was that? They had loved Christ so much that they wanted others to know about him. But they had lost their vision for accomplishing the mission of making disciples. In order to reclaim that mission, they had to be revitalized and to reestablish their vision.[8]

8. Dr. Harry Reeder's ministry, From Embers to a Flame (http://www. emberstoaflame .org), is designed to help revitalize the local church.

THE NEED FOR VISION

Although every church has the same mission to make disciples, local congregations will vary in how they go about doing so. Since churches are located in diverse communities, the vision of making disciples will differ. Having vision, therefore, is defined as being the local church that Christ desires for making disciples. George Barna concurs that "vision is a result of having spent much time absorbing the facts about the community, knowing the resources upon which the church can call (people, funding, facilities, equipment, etc.), and devising sound but creative strategies for moving forward."[9] A purposeful church, therefore, is a congregation designed around a clear-cut and planned process that moves people in the community to a knowledge of Christ, then to spiritual maturation, and finally to equipping them to reach out to their neighbors, friends, and family.

When a church lacks vision, the people will be rudderless and will do what pleases them most. Leaders must direct the vision and discern the will of Christ for their local congregation. They must be flexible by frequently reviewing their strategy for making disciples, because culture and communities are constantly changing, and change creates more opportunities to present the gospel to a dying and desperate world. Without assessing vision, leaders will, without much thought, approve programs, ministries, and activities that, although good, divert the church from the purpose of making disciples.

One church's "Vision and Mission" brochure had, for its motto, "Proclaiming the Word and Reclaiming the World." The motto suggests making an impact on the world, but it does raise the question of the local surrounding community. What vision did this church have for making disciples of the people nearby? Although the brochure attempted to describe the purpose of the church, it failed to tell how disciples would be made. It proposed that the congregation could reach the world through teaching every member to obey Scripture. Though obeying Christ is a character trait of a disciple, there must be a vision

9. George Barna, *How to Find Your Church* (Charlotte, NC: World Wide Publications, 1989), 104.

for making potential attendees of the church into disciples. Otherwise teaching becomes moralistic and enigmatic for those seeking answers in life.

In discovering what Christ would have a church to be in a local community, leaders must discern the Lord's will, and they can do so by applying the following recommendations:

- Look at the giftedness of the pastor and determine how this could be used to reach those living in the surrounding community.
- Determine the spiritual gifts and talents of the congregation, and then plug the people into church and local ministries that best serve their giftedness. Encourage congregants to become involved in their town, in their arts, and in their neighborhood in a warm and friendly way.
- Study the demographics of the local area to determine the type of people residing nearby. Have the pastor incorporate in his preaching the biblical and practical answers to the typical issues that confront these people!
- Institute outreach programs, such as divorce care, premarital instruction, marriage counseling, grief workshops, senior services, English as a second language, job training, or soup kitchens, that would attract those who fit the local demographics.
- Structure a worship service that will be pleasing to God while also having some appeal to those who may visit the church because of your outreach programs. Too many ancient hymns that are hard to sing will make it difficult to worship (and will therefore be unappealing) to seekers or new believers.
- Encourage authentic worship and expository preaching, for God uses both to draw people to himself. Preach to answer the questions of the local culture, and demonstrate why the Bible is relevant to those who sit under its teaching.
- Establish small groups that have the purpose of reaching their neighbors. Encourage these groups to have block parties and neighborhood get-togethers that attract others who might not otherwise attend a church-sponsored function.

- Develop an attractive website with pictures of singles, families, seniors, and the community in which the church is located. Eye-catching and dynamic websites are indicative of outward-looking congregations who are not afraid to modify their approach to reach the community for Christ.

REDEEMER CHURCH

Maintaining focus is what Tim Keller has done at Redeemer Presbyterian Church in New York City. The church began with a Bible study on the upper east side of the city in 1989. The founders believed that people need "meaning in life"—something bigger than themselves. Significance is fostered in three ways—spiritually, socially, and culturally. Since the least reached people group is the young urban single professional, Redeemer was fashioned to bring the gospel to these urbanites, thereby helping them to grow in significance, which in turn would have an effect on the culture of New York.

In 2001, Keller reiterated three goals for the church. First, they were to be a church not just for themselves, but also a place where their friends who did not yet believe in Christ would be made to feel welcome. Second, they were to be a church for the entire city. Their goal was to build not just a great church, but rather a great church for a great city. Having a love for the people in the locale where God had placed them was a necessity in order to reach people with the gospel of Christ. Third, they were not to be just a single church, but a movement of the gospel that planted and helped other churches. They believed that the church is inclusive of all ethnic groups, and Redeemer would reflect this—if not at the main campus, then through satellite churches that connected with and promoted the philosophy of reaching all people groups.[10]

Over the years, Keller would reiterate the vision through a series of sermons. He did not want his parishioners to forget why Redeemer exists. In 2005 he preached a sermon from Jeremiah 29, reminding the people that they were part of Redeemer not for themselves but for the people of

10. Tim Keller, "2002 Redeemer Vision" video, Redeemer Presbyterian Church, accessed July 11, 2013, available online at http://www.redeemer.com/learn/about_us/redeemer_history/past_vision_updates/.

New York City. Jeremiah's letter to the exiles in Babylon emphasized that the Lord himself had sent the Israelites to the foreign city.

> Thus says the LORD of hosts, the God of Israel, to all the exiles whom I have sent into exile from Jerusalem to Babylon: Build houses and live in them; plant gardens and eat their produce. Take wives and have sons and daughters; . . . multiply there, and do not decrease. But seek the welfare of the city where I have sent you into exile, and pray to the LORD on its behalf, for in its welfare you will find your welfare. (Jer. 29:4–7)

Keller's application was that the members of Redeemer had not materialized in the city of New York by chance. They may have come with their own individual reasons, future hopes, and ideals; but they hadn't come by accident. They had been sent on a mission for the glory of God, not for the grandeur of self. His parishioners, if united with Christ, were to be missional. They were sent by God and were to seek the welfare of the city by becoming involved with helping people and sharing the gospel. This sermon brought the people back into the original focus and vision of the church—to love the city of New York and to bring the gospel to all ethnic groups.[11]

In September 2009, Redeemer launched its RENEW Campaign in order to fund the first phase of a ten-year plan. Although Redeemer will remain one church, it will have three locations known as "generative" congregations on the East Side, West Side, and downtown. The purpose of having three campuses is to employ and cultivate more leaders in order to reach more friends and serve more neighborhoods. In a video promoting RENEW, Dr. Keller restated the focus to love the city. Since cities have great diversity, the church must be open to reach the diverse aspects of the city. Leaders and people should be energized by the city in order to influence people with the gospel of Christ. The good news is to be presented in an intelligent but also sincere and warmhearted way in order to address the concerns of both Christians and non-Christians.

---

11. Tim Keller, "2005 State of the Vision and Vision Campaign," Redeemer Presbyterian Church, accessed July 12, 2013, http://download.redeemer.com/audio/Redeemer_State_of _the_Vision_2005.mp3.

Leaders and congregants are to remember that they are a church for friends and associates who don't believe. They are to have a strong social concern for the city and to express it through their deeds and words. They will therefore deal with the physical and spiritual needs of the lost, the poor, and the broken. The church will remain culture-friendly by encouraging Christians to pursue excellence in their jobs, their vocations, their arts, and their involvements in order to influence the culture for Christ.[12]

Tim Keller has never lost sight of the "why" of Redeemer Presbyterian Church. Focus is important, and as long as leaders keep their eyes on Jesus and discern his will for New York City, then the movement of the gospel will continue and will not return void. Other churches are not Redeemer and are not given the same vision. Yet church leaders are to have focus and to concentrate on the vision that Christ has given them in the locale where he has placed them.

OUTWARD LOOKING

Leaders who are inward looking rather than outward focused are not concerned with the community around them. Not all churches are to be facsimiles of Redeemer in New York, for every church is called to its own unique location. Vision therefore varies, but focus does not. Maintaining the focus of bringing the gospel to the local community and making disciples for Christ will keep the church and her people excited for the gospel and concerned for local unbelievers. When a church becomes comfortable in her present ministries and programs that serve only congregants, decline is forthcoming.

Since culture is constantly morphing, the church must frequently adapt in order to influence the people around it for Christ. In order to be focused, leaders must be frank with themselves and be flexible to meet the changing times without compromising the gospel or diminishing truth. The secret of church growth is not to spotlight the fruit (namely, the target group of people), but rather to focus on the environment that

12. Tim Keller, "2009 Redeemer Vision Talk and RENEW Campaign," Redeemer Presbyterian Church, accessed July 12, 2013, http://download.redeemer.com/audio/Redeemer _Vision.mp3.

produces the fruit. This requires the involvement of leaders and sheep in the local community, for if we care little about outsiders we will in all likelihood become an ingrown church. Although only God can build his church, we—his people—must be willing to lay bricks according to the blueprints provided by Christ.

The next chapter will concentrate on the shepherd and his duties. As a leader of leaders, the senior pastor has many functions to perform in helping to build and equip the local church.

14

The Shepherd's Duties

And he gave the apostles, the prophets, the evangelists, the shepherds and teachers, to equip the saints for the work of ministry, for building up the body of Christ, until we all attain to the unity of the faith and of the knowledge of the Son of God, to mature manhood, to the measure of the stature of the fullness of Christ. (Eph. 4:11–13)

THE MODEL OF THE SHEPHERD

Christ is the Good Shepherd who knows his sheep, and his sheep know him (John 10:14). Pastors and elders are to model the shepherding of Jesus, which places a high priority on knowing the sheep. The more they know their sheep, the more the sheep know them. Likewise, elders are to be involved with their sheep, spending more time developing relationships than making business decisions for the church.

A church consultant once asked me this question: "What do you think is the percentage of time that an elder in the local church spends doing the work of governing [that is, ruling] compared to doing the work of a shepherd?" He had recently spoken at a church leadership conference and had surveyed the participants by asking them the same question. My answer was the typical 80/20 percentage ratio, thinking that leaders would probably say that they spent 80 percent of their time doing the business of the church and the remaining 20 percent shepherding the flock. He chuckled and said that the figure was 90/10.

The consultant wasn't surprised with the results, but he was concerned with the lack of time that elders spent being shepherds. Scripture is explicit that elders are primarily appointed to shepherd God's people, which means caring for their temporal and spiritual needs. Often they spend too much time in meetings and not enough time with people. Pastoral ministry is first and foremost a relational ministry. The emphasis therefore is on people, not on business, even though business must be conducted. If leaders have difficulty relating to people, they should reexamine their call, for the work of an elder is primarily interacting with and caring for people. The pastor, if necessary, must help to reorient his leaders to pastoral ministry, while at the same time shepherding his elders, managing his staff, and being a peacemaker to those who need reconciliation.

THE SHEPHERD/LEADER

In one sense, the church is a hospital, for within its walls are ailing members and sick leaders. The pastor assumes the role of hospital administrator in supervising the staff, helping to set policies with the trustees (the church leaders), and strategizing how to reconcile conflict. As a hospital manager, he serves as liaison between board members and the medical staff (the church employees) and maintains contact with key donors (the congregation).

As an administrator, the pastor reviews policies, reads minutes, and coordinates the agenda for board meetings. All in all, he has the best interests of the hospital/church in mind. A very important job for the administrator is to train personnel in human resource particulars and to participate in the hiring of department heads at the hospital. In similar fashion, the pastor has the responsibility of training leaders for the work of ministry in the church and of helping to hire assistants to implement the policies set by the governing board.

A new pastor is encouraged to read the minutes of the elder meetings from the past four or five years in order to grasp what has transpired within the church, to identify parties involved in any conflict, and to define issues that need addressing. He should review the church bylaws and policies that have already been established. Doing so is part of the administration process of familiarizing oneself with the operation of the church. Not to do so is to be naïve, for much information can be gleaned from the corporate minutes and bylaws of a church. Reading minutes may be laborious, but it is doing due diligence in learning more about one's new assignment.

Although the business side of church is a necessity, an elder, truly called of God, is to shepherd first and govern second. Shepherding, however, begins at home, for an elder is to lead his own family if he expects to lead a number of families in the church. The pastor has the responsibility of encouraging and training his elders to become better husbands and spiritual leaders in the family, which will have the residual effect of making them better leaders in the church. He is to encourage them to love their wives as Christ loved the church. An elder who loves his wife selflessly will, in all likelihood, diligently care for his sheep as well.

On the one hand, many pastors have the tendency to relate to their elders only on a superficial level. They socialize with some, spend little time with others, and assume that all is well with their families. Even if pastors have suspicions that things are not very healthy in an elder's home, they may turn a blind eye to this, for it is more appealing to have a friend and voting partner than to have to expose cracks in a marriage. Being liked and appreciated is a stronger human yearning than confronting unrighteousness. Elders, on the other hand, may turn a deaf ear to a pastor friend who may need confrontation over sinful or foolish behavior. A senior pastor in a small rural church, when confronted by an assistant and an elder, refused to acknowledge the lack of discipline in his own children, which was evident in a disruptive daughter and a philandering son. He rationalized that his parenting style was not wrong, but was only different from those who were more rigid in rearing their children. His other elder friends accepted his explanation, fired the assistant, and neutralized the accusing elder. The church eventually split, and the pastor started another church.

A pastor in another church was blinded to the fact that one of his elders had a bad reputation in town. He was accused by others, including members of the church, of behavior that was unbecoming an elder. The pastor was a close friend, and he believed the elder when he denied these accusations against him. Rather than forming a committee to investigate the charges, he convinced the elder board that such allegations were frivolous and not worth pursuing. An investigation might have cleared the elder of false accusations, but because no investigation was made, a cloud remained over the reputation of this elder.

Elders who are "yes men" for the pastor become antagonists to leaders who question the pastor's decisions. When an elder was confronted by a brother elder concerning inappropriate behavior, he snapped at his adversary, became quite incensed, accused him of fabricating the charges, and caused a split in the leadership. Rather than admitting sin, or at least the possibility that his behavior was unbecoming, this elder went on the offensive, defended himself, and refused to be reconciled. Scripture explicitly states that elders are to be above reproach, self-controlled, and not quarrelsome (see 1 Tim. 3:1–3). Not only did this elder violate his ordination vows about maintaining the peace and unity of the church, but his incivility also put in question his qualifications for office.

Elders, truly called of God, are charged with shepherding the people of God, not with being the business partner of the pastor. Pastor Tim Witmer, in his book *The Shepherd Leader*, distinguishes between "macro-shepherding," which he says is the oversight of the flock as a whole to include the corporate and organizational concerns of the congregation, and "micro-shepherding," which is the personal ministry of the elders among their sheep.[1] He goes on to say, "Unfortunately, many agree to serve as elders with the misconception that they are only being asked to serve in macro, corporate functions."[2] Although these business and ruling functions are necessary, they are not as important as involvement with the sheep.

Leadership training must therefore concentrate on making shepherds, which surprisingly leads to better church statesmen. When the sheep know their shepherd, they will respond to his voice and will follow

1. Timothy Z. Witmer, *The Shepherd Leader: Achieving Effective Shepherding in Your Church* (Phillipsburg, NJ: P&R Publishing, 2010), 103–4.
2. Ibid., 104.

him, even during difficult times. Sheep who have not seen their shepherd will not recognize his voice and, consequently, will not follow him. The uninvolved shepherd contributes, unknowingly, to the discontent of the sheep, which in turn can lead to conflicts in the church.

Witmer identifies four areas of an elder's responsibility: knowing, feeding, leading, and protecting the sheep.[3] Each area functions in relation to the macro and micro activities of shepherding. For instance, knowing the sheep from a macro perspective means maintaining accurate membership rolls and understanding the flock's corporate strengths and weaknesses. Knowing the sheep from the micro perspective means being personally involved with them by having a strategy of regular contact and care. Feeding the sheep from a macro viewpoint includes the pulpit ministry of the church as well as having a Christian Education program. In a micro sense, feeding occurs through individual discipleship, mentoring, and participation in small groups.

Leading the sheep occurs at the macro level through vision casting, maintaining the mission, making ministry decisions, and chairing church committees. On the micro level, leading is modeling righteous behavior and counseling hurting sheep. Protecting the flock at the macro level takes place through public instruction and warning by scriptural admonition, by exposing and providing protection from wolves masquerading as sheep, and by performing church discipline. On the micro level, protecting transpires by private ministry to individuals displaying unrighteous behavior and then by gently restoring wandering sheep, if possible, by the application of Matthew 18:15–16.[4]

Those who feel that personal shepherding is too tiring and cumbersome should not aspire to the office of elder. It is a work of ministry that will be judged by the Lord (Heb. 13:17), and he takes no pleasure in watchmen of the flock who shirk their responsibilities.[5] If a man desires

3. Ibid., 189.

4. "If your brother sins against you, go and tell him his fault, between you and him alone. If he listens to you, you have gained your brother. But if he does not listen, take one or two others along with you, that every charge may be established by the evidence of two or three witnesses."

5. "But if the watchman sees the sword coming and does not blow the trumpet, so that the people are not warned, and the sword comes and takes any one of them, that person is taken away in his iniquity, but his blood I will require at the watchman's hand" (Ezek. 33:6).

most to do the business of the corporate church, he would best serve as a corporate trustee or be appointed to serve on a policy governance committee. Such work is important, but it is not the main function of a shepherd. To be a true shepherd, a man must have the heart of a shepherd, which impels him to be personally involved with his flock, tending to their spiritual health and helping them to grow in Christ.

CHURCH MANAGER

The pastor also serves as supervisor to his staff and director to his elders. In this sense he is a manager with various responsibilities, including (but not limited to) leading elders, overseeing staff, setting policies with church leaders, and strategizing how to reconcile conflict. Providing leadership to the elder board is a major task of the pastor, but in doing so he is not to usurp the authority of the elder board. God calls pastors and elders to sit together in session for the purpose of finding his will, not to automatically approve the requests or ideas of a pastor.

Pastors manage sheep, not cattle. They are shepherds, not cattlemen. They do not herd parishioners; they lead them by loving them and being involved with the flock. Although pastors are highly educated people and usually score high in intelligence, it is not their intelligence quotient that will make them successful shepherds, but their emotional intelligence, which is the ability to identify, assess, and control one's emotions while personally relating to others. Pastors with high emotional intelligence are more effective in ministry because they are adept at social skills and at interaction with people.

Daniel Goleman, in his article "What Makes a Leader," which appeared in the *Harvard Business Review*, stated that "emotional intelligence is the indispensable condition of leadership."[6] He claims that it is not the most highly intellectual managers or executives who are the most successful, but those with the best relational skills. A pastor, for instance, can have the best education, a superb systematic and incisive

---

6. Daniel Goleman, "What Makes a Leader," *Harvard Business Review*, January 2004, http://hbr.org/2004/01/what-makes-a-leader/ar/1.

mind, and an infinite stream of creative ideas, but he will not excel as much as the person with exceptional relational skills. The pastor who is an involved shepherd flourishes with a longer ministry in the local church.

Ken Sande has redefined "emotional intelligence" as "relational wisdom," which he says is the "ability to discern emotions, interests and abilities in yourself and others, to interpret them in the light of God's Word, and to use this insight to manage your responses and relationships successfully."[7] He believes that possessing relational wisdom is what allows some people to have closer and more enduring friendships and marriages. It is what successful business people have, which quickly advances their careers.

Pastors, to be good managers, must have relational wisdom. Blessed is he who has this wisdom and gains understanding of those around him. Such wisdom is more precious than jewels, will lead to riches and honor, and will make the ways of its possessor pleasant and peaceful.[8] If a pastor is able to relate well to his staff and elders, this will reap dividends for him. A relaxed and amiable work environment leads to a devoted and appreciative staff. An uninvolved and nonrelational minister who is confined to his office or retreats to his home could generate a tense and unpleasant office, eventually contributing to disgruntlement in staff and conflict in the church.

Relational wisdom could be called the "street smarts" of the shepherd. He knows himself, understands his sheep, is interested in his charges, and involves himself with the interests of the flock. Jesus is the epitome of relational wisdom, for he is truth in the context of relationship. As his disciples, pastors are to emulate Jesus, who involved himself with the people, teaching them truth while caring for their hurts.

Although most pastors are not trained in management, they are expected to be proficient when it comes to managing people and situations. Effective leaders understand that various situations and diversity among elders require different approaches to management. Good leaders

7. Ken Sande, "Discover Relational Wisdom," Relational Wisdom 360, accessed November 16, 2015, http://www.rw360.org/discover-rw.
8. See Prov. 3:13–17.

are able to adapt and minister according to the circumstances. In doing so, they are proactive—not reactive, which makes handling situations all the more difficult.

A pastor cannot be an autocrat, for he doesn't have absolute authority or unlimited power. To the contrary, he must demonstrate a participatory style of leadership as he interacts and works with church leaders. As he builds relationships and grows in influence, he becomes more assertive and directive. Participation, however, doesn't mean that the pastor capitulates to the more dominant elders on the church's board. He must remember that he is God's emissary, called to serve in a particular place and to lead men in shepherding sheep who long for the greener pastures.

MEN AT WAR

The pastor is a leader among leaders, and he realizes that he must prepare his elders for warfare. The church is constantly in battle with spiritual forces (Eph. 6:12) that seek to disable the army of God and to render the church helpless and ineffective. As David drove off lions and bears that sought to destroy his sheep (1 Sam. 17:36), pastors are to be vigilant and to train their leaders to recognize possible intrusions into the sheepfold. Leaders are to deploy for guerrilla warfare, for the enemy is alive and well, and he prowls around seeking to devour the unsuspecting (1 Peter 5:8).

In his book *The Leadership Dynamic*, Harry Reeder describes three types of combat leaders required for military victory. The visionary leader gives direction, the strategic leader develops a plan, and the tactical leader implements the plan.[9] Pastors, whether they anticipate it or not, will find themselves in spiritual combat. It therefore behooves them to understand the principles of leadership that they need when they face church conflict.

As a visionary leader, the pastor is to identify his objective in preparing the church for spiritual warfare. He will have to organize

---

9. Harry Reeder III, *The Leadership Dynamic: A Biblical Model for Raising Effective Leaders* (Wheaton, IL: Crossway, 2008), 130.

and manage a staff, help leadership to formulate a vision, and exhort the men to lead their sheep in being what Christ would have them to be in the local community. In order to see where he needs to take the leadership, a new pastor must understand where the church has been. To this end, he is to familiarize himself with the church's past—the good, the bad, and the ugly. He discerns what issues have surfaced in the past and how they were handled, and he identifies people who may have been offended in the process or who caused conflict. He will then have to formulate a course of action to seek healing, reconciliation, and peace between conflicting parties if necessary.

As a strategic leader, the pastor develops a plan to aid in revitalizing the church, which includes helping the congregation to reconnect to its past in a good way, showing where repentance is needed, and encouraging leaders to recover their first love, Jesus, by getting back to the basics of gospel preaching and outreach. I once took a number of elders to a "From Embers to a Flame" conference in order for them to see what revitalization looks like and to encourage them to follow the principles discussed. Although most did not think that their church needed revitalizing, their eyes were opened and they finally admitted that the church was stagnant and needed stimulation. All churches need constant renewal, for warfare never ceases, and the church militant is assigned the task of assailing the gates of hell, which is tiring, painful, and uncomfortable work.

Revitalization cannot begin until leaders admit that they need it. Leadership must regroup and determine what Christ desires for the local church. This is what vision planning is all about—discerning what God wants his people to be in the local community. Church elders, because they know their sheep, their giftedness, and their strengths and weaknesses, are in a better position to cast a general vision than a new pastor is. Furthermore, any pastor looking at the possibility of coming to the church has already reviewed the church's website, read printed versions of any vision and purpose statements, and decided that he fits the character of the church. A new pastor, therefore, should basically agree with the general vision of the church and truly believe that he can put flesh to it and lead others in pursuing it.

As a tactical leader, the pastor implements his plan for training elders, caring for the sheep, and managing staff. He works with the elders in establishing the curriculum and schedule for teaching men how to be shepherds of Christ's church. He maintains office hours and an open-door policy so that congregants may come for counsel and advice. He visits the sick and shut-ins, and he arranges for the sheep to be visited by elders. He proactively encourages the staff and helps them to become the best at what they do.

A pastor's open-door policy is an invitation to interrupt what he is doing. Although most people will make appointments, leaders and staff are frequently in and out of the church office. A pastor is to be approachable and should give people the freedom to speak to him at a moment's notice on any issue. People are too important to keep at a distance. An open door says, "You are important to me, and I want to hear what you have to say."

"But won't the pastor get stressed if his sermon preparation is interrupted, forcing him to cram or hurry completion?" is a typical question. Sermons are words woven around the gospel to be delivered to people who are to be encouraged through grace. When people want a pastor's attention and opinion concerning matters and issues dear to them, he hopefully responds by living the gospel that he preaches. Sermons are not only for Sundays but are dispensed during the week to people who seek godly advice and need encouraging words to persevere in the spiritual battles that they constantly wage. Disruptions do bother some pastors, but having an open door doesn't mean that quiet and study intervals are not built into a schedule. Shut doors are needed at times, especially when a pastor is preparing for a sermon. The idea behind open doors is about approachability and availability.

An accessible pastor demonstrates biblical leadership by loving and tending his sheep. In discipling his officers to be shepherds, he is also training them to be soldiers of the cross. The pastor's leadership may be likened to that of a military officer who influences others to accomplish the mission by establishing an objective, providing direction, and supplying motivation. He supports the overall task by demonstrating his confidence in those who serve under him and by looking out for the welfare of those fighting alongside him. Tom Landry, the legendary coach of the Dallas Cowboys, once said, "Leadership is a matter of having people look at you and gain confidence, seeing how you react. If you're in control, they're in control."[10] Pastors must exude confidence in performing a most difficult job to which they have been called by God. The measurement of success in any particular church is not how big the numbers are, but how faithful leaders are in living out their call.

BLESSED ARE THE PEACEMAKERS

Although pastors are encouraged to have a military mindset in fighting spiritual battles, they are, foremost, servants of the living God and as such must also do the work of peacemakers. Spiritual warfare produces causalities among the sheep. Pastors, therefore, must diligently seek to reconcile estranged people. According to Life-Line for Pastors, 1,500 pastors per month leave their pulpits. Another 50 percent of pastors said that they would leave the ministry if they had viable alternatives. The main reason cited by departing and frustrated pastors was the difficulty in dealing with problem people and dissatisfied leaders.[11] Yet a pastor is not to run from difficult relationships. He is to confront them as a peacemaker and to apply the balm of Gilead to hurting congregants. He is to encourage the estranged to become reconciled in their relationships, which may include his own alienation from ill-intentioned dragons.

Many pastors flee conflict because it is unpleasant. They act as peacekeepers, maintaining the status quo and containing fires of conflict rather than putting out the flames. They hope that problems will fade away, not realizing that the embers of discontent are smoldering and will, in all likelihood, flare up. Sheep can be unpleasant creatures, biting one another. They are to be shepherded, disciplined, and reconciled in order for the flock as a whole to thrive.

10. Quoted in "Sports of the Times: Landry Was in Control as Cowboys' Coach," *The New York Times*, February 13, 2000, http://www.nytimes.com/2000/02/13/sports/sports-of -the-times-landry-was-in-control-as-cowboys-coach.html.
11. "Don't Become a Statistic," *Life-Line for Pastors* 1, no. 2 (April 2003): http://www .maranathalife.com/lifeline/03-04-p.htm.

I've known unpleasant sheep, both on my grandfather's farm and in the church. As a young lad, I loved visiting my grandfather's homestead, playing in the haystacks, catching flies off the backs of cows, playing baseball in the hollow, and chasing sheep. There was one unpleasant ewe that didn't take kindly to my being around. In fact, every time I climbed in the sheep pen, she would come after me, butting with her head and nipping with her teeth. It was a hilarious scene to my siblings and cousins, for this ewe didn't bother them, only me. They further heckled me by naming her Bob, after me.

Knowing more about sheep now than I did then, I know that I could have easily frightened that ewe by hiding around the corner of the cote and jumping out to scare her when she appeared. But the ewe probably would have dropped dead of fright, and I would have had to answer to my grandfather's strap.

Practically every pastor has known a few biting ewes and butting rams in their church. They are contentious sheep, backbiting, gossiping, and causing distress among the flock. These sheep must be lovingly but firmly confronted, called to account, and encouraged to reconcile with those they have offended. Conflict cannot be avoided; it must be faced. Pastors are to promote reconciliation in order for the church to prosper and for Christ to be honored.

The Peacemaker Ministries' approach to conciliation is a helpful and very valuable thing for pastors and leaders to know. Teaching the four *G*'s mentioned in chapter 8 and having leaders apply them in reconciling conflict is critically important.[12] Ken Sande's acronym PAUSE[13] is a beneficial tool for carrying out cooperative conciliation between disputing parties in the church. Alfred Poirier, author of *The Peacemaking Pastor*, believes that PAUSE is the simplest way to negotiate peace between parties in conflict.[14]

12. The four *G*'s are: (1) *glorify* God; (2) *get* the log out of your eye; (3) *gently* restore; and (4) *go* and be reconciled. Ken Sande has provided a checklist for summarizing and applying the principles behind the four *G*'s of peacemaking in his book *The Peacemaker: A Biblical Guide to Resolving Personal Conflict*, 3rd ed. (Grand Rapids: Baker, 2004), 263–69.

13. Ken Sande, *The Peacemaker Church Implementation Manual* (Billings, MT: Peacemaker Ministries, 2005), 101.

14. Alfred Poirier, The Peacemaking Pastor: A Biblical Guide to Resolving Church Conflict (Grand Rapids: Baker, 2006), 165.

The *P* in PAUSE is for *Prepare*. Preparation begins with prayer, after which an investigation of the facts must be made that includes hearing both sides of the controversy.

As simple as the matter of prayer may seem, many pastors neglect this weapon of warfare. They are so busy counseling others, attending committee meetings, and preparing sermons for Sundays, devotionals for women's ministries, and Bible studies for men's groups that they neglect to carve out time for their own self care—including prayer and private devotional time. Pastors must pray not only for their flocks, but also for their own souls and their family situations. A relatively small prayer life may well produce a correspondingly large and overly busy church life that is full of conflicts.

Bob Burns, Tasha Chapman, and Donald Guthrie, in their book *Resilient Ministry*, point out that many pastors feel like failures and imposters when it comes to their prayer life.[15] Pursuing spiritual formation for themselves is not a high priority for pastors, because the pressures of work and the corresponding responsibilities of ministry prevent it. Yet, if our preparation for anything that we do is not bathed in prayer, we have basically decided that we can do what we do without the help of God, the very one who called us to ministry in the first place. Leaving God out of our preparation is either the height of arrogance or the epitome of stupidity.

Preparation also includes seeking godly counsel from those who are wise, objective, and not embroiled in the issue or conflict at hand. There will always be nemeses in ministry, for spiritual warfare assures it. Wherever people gather in a church, there will be problems and discontent. Pastors are not to avoid conflict or sweep it under the rug as undesirable dirt, but are to face it with the strength of Christ. One aspect of facing the issues is to seek counsel from those with greater experience, who have the scars of fighting similar battles in their past.

Options and strategies are to be developed and a plan of action adopted when handling conflict and facing malcontents. Know what

---

15. Bob Burns, Tasha Chapman, and Donald C. Guthrie, *Resilient Ministry: What Pastors Told Us about Surviving and Thriving* (Downers Grove, IL: Intervarsity Press, 2013), 52.

you will say beforehand, and have the Scriptures to back your position. Preparation in any mediation is a must and the first step to successful reconciliation.

The *A* in PAUSE is for *Affirm Relationships*. When parties agree to meet to discuss differences, the mediator is to remind participants that the first relationship to honor is the one that they have with Christ. It is Christ who is to be glorified in the process. Secondly, the relationship that people have with Christ must filter down to their relationships with other brothers and sisters in the faith. The parties are to respect each other, not to gossip, not to interrupt when the other is telling his or her story, and not to denigrate the character of the other.

The *U* in PAUSE is for *Understand Interests*. When varying narratives are told, the mediator is to identify the concerns, desires, needs, fears, or interests of each party. He then attempts to have each side acknowledge the concerns of the other. Once each story is told, the focus should be on clarifying the issues so that each party understands the critical concerns of the other. If a party confesses sins or faults during the process, the mediator is to mention how thankful he is for the person's humility and willingness to admit his or her sin in the situation.

Stubbornness, born of pride, is a major block toward understanding another's position. We love to be right, and we blind ourselves to the views of others. A number of times, when counseling couples about marital difficulties, I have had to stop a spouse from looking at me while directing his comments at his wife. "Hold it!" I would say. "Turn and face your wife, and tell her what is on your heart." It is amazing how many times I have heard a spouse say to the other, "Honey, I never knew that you felt that way." Listening is the partner to understanding; without truly hearing the other's viewpoint, understanding will never occur.

I have used a tennis ball to facilitate understanding by placing it in the hand of the person who is first to speak. When done, the speaker tosses the ball to the other, indicating that he has completed his discourse. The one catching the ball (the listener) must repeat what he thinks the speaker has said. Once he has done this, he tosses the ball back to the first speaker, who then says, "Yes, that is what I meant," "No, I didn't say that," or, "Let me clarify for you." When done, he throws the ball back to the listener, who may then ask questions, say that he understands, or respond with his interpretation of the facts. The ball will be tossed back and forth until each party acknowledges and comprehends the other's position and viewpoint.

The *S* in PAUSE is for *Search for Creative Solutions.* If each party understands the position of the other, then a cooperative solution should be explored that will help each. If sin is involved, then it must be confronted gently but firmly. If misunderstanding was the genesis of the problem, then workable solutions can be brainstormed and implemented. The mediator is to point out complicity and responsibility for the consequences of each party's actions. He then states a reasonable and biblical solution that is godly and fair and exhorts the parties to accept it and to glorify God in living up to it. Invariably bitterness is an issue, but bitterness is the sin of the person carrying it, even if it has been caused by the other party. Forgiveness for this internalized anger must be encouraged in order for relationships to be healed.

Creative solutions are win-win situations in which both parties feel that they have pleased the Lord and received acceptance and understanding from their adversary. "How can you love me after what I have done?" asked a repenting husband. "It won't be easy," replied the wife. "I feel betrayed, soiled, and used. But when I said, 'I do,' it was forever. I have forgiven, but trust is another issue. As we build back our lives together as one, I am trusting that the Lord will give me a new and deeper love for you, knowing that the more I love you, the more I will trust you."

"I understand," he said, "and that is fair. I don't even deserve that. I am thankful that the Lord has forgiven me, and, in time, your forgiveness will be manifested in a closer relationship with me." Being received back into the family was a win situation for the husband, and having a repentant husband who was willing to humble himself was a win situation for the wife.

The *E* in PAUSE is for *Evaluate Options Objectively and Reasonably.* After discussing several options and possible solutions to the issues at hand, the mediator asks if the parties are ready to move toward a final agreement. A written settlement is recommended (but not necessary), which delineates the issues that were resolved, the biblical principles that were followed, the actions that both parties commit to, and the time frame for completing the action. A future appointment between the parties should be scheduled in order to discuss the results and evaluate the reconciliation that was accomplished. Follow-up is so important, for even though the parties have come to a resolution, Satan is lurking to devour whatever good has been accomplished.[16]

I once mediated between two elders of the same church. One elder had spoken up in a meeting that challenged the pastor in his priorities. The other took offense and called him out at a session meeting. The first elder asked other elders if they all felt the way that the challenging elder did. All remained silent. The elder, thinking that he was alone in criticizing the pastor, left the meeting and never returned to the church, causing a major rift. Some elders were shocked; others were relieved. Schism among leaders leads to cracks in the foundation of the church. A number of sheep followed the disenchanted elder, leaving the communion of the church and the committees on which they served. When I learned about this breach in the brotherhood, I began a process of reconciliation.

I used the principles of PAUSE to resolve the split between these two popular leaders. My preparation, after much prayer, was to hear both sides of the story and to interview other elders in order to garner their perspectives. I affirmed both elders separately and encouraged them to do what was right according to God's Word. Both these men were principled and wanted to please Christ. Yet both were also stubborn and, at first, would not be mollified. After meeting with each individually, I arranged for a meeting together, in which each was allowed to tell his view of things without interruption from the other. I clarified the issues, pointed out sin on each part, and brought both parties to an understanding of the other's position. When they recognized their sin, they confessed and asked forgiveness of the other. I thanked them for their humility and submissive spirits.

16. "Be sober-minded; be watchful. Your adversary the devil prowls around like a roaring lion, seeking someone to devour" (1 Peter 5:8).

The solution was not only to reconcile two brothers, but also to reintroduce to the congregation the one who had left the church. When the sheep saw leaders and families fellowshipping again, they stopped their own gossip and became more actively involved in the life of the church. In evaluating the options, I did not think that a written agreement was needed, but I did encourage the elders to meet on occasion for lunch and to speak highly of the other in mixed company. I followed up with both elders by meeting them for lunch and dinner on numerous occasions to ensure that their relationship was healed.

A PASTOR'S PASSION

Pastors are to be passionate about leading sheep and doctoring them when needed. Loving people is one thing, but dealing with them is another. Leaders and sheep can be inconsiderate, insensitive, and exasperating. A pastor, therefore, must develop a persevering mind-set in order to weather the storms that will confront him and to minister to the sheep that God has brought to the pasture known as the local church.

Pastors, as leaders, are to be enthusiastic about their calling, collegial in their work with elders, and caring in their oversight of sheep. To help their elders and congregation to face critical issues and resolve conflict takes courage, fervor, and wisdom. A pastor who is lackadaisical in his attitude, uninterested in his task, and indifferent toward people will not withstand the onslaught of criticism or the guile of conspirators. A pastor is to love and fight for his people, who at times will be frustrating, unlovable, and irksome. In doing so, however, he will reap the fruit of trust, respect, and unity. C. H. Spurgeon sums it up:

> If the service of God is worth anything, it is worth everything. We shall find our best reward in the Lord's work if we do it with determined diligence. Our labour is not in vain in the Lord, and we know it. Half-hearted work will bring no reward; but, when we throw our whole soul into the cause, we shall see prosperity.[17]

17. C. H. Spurgeon, *Cheque Book of the Bank of Faith: Daily Readings* (Fearn, Ross-shire, UK: Christian Focus, 1996), 48.

Jesus is our model for leading and loving others. He epitomizes the character traits of a pastor and leader. Next, in the conclusion, we will see how modeling Christ is the perfect antidote for all the symptoms of poor leadership.

CONCLUSION

The Leadership of Jesus

For by the grace given to me I say to everyone among you not to think of himself more highly than he ought to think, but to think with sober judgment, each according to the measure of faith that God has assigned. (Rom. 12:3)

JESUS AS LEADERSHIP MODEL

"We love because he first loved us" (1 John 4:19). Jesus loved his church so much that he "gave himself up for her" (Eph. 5:25). But occasionally Christ's church appears stagnant and not to be fulfilling his lofty expectations. Could it be that, at these times, the leaders of his church have lost their first love—that is, Jesus—and have ceased being all that their Lord would have them to be as shepherds of his people?

There is but one perfect leader—Jesus. Elders and pastors must accept the fact that they are fallen creatures and, therefore, imperfect leaders. Understanding flaws is one thing, but learning how to improve leadership abilities is another. There is no better teacher on leadership than our Savior, Jesus Christ. We sing, "I want to be like Jesus," but do we mean it? Do we really want to be a leader in Christ's church? Leadership is certainly not easy, for it is fraught with obstacles and opposition. Leaders are always under scrutiny and can hardly please everyone. Unappreciative sheep can become great thorns and can spread sarcasm and gossip with little effort. The adage that "Christians shoot their walking wounded" rings true, for sinful people do sinful things, making leaders think twice about their calling.

This book has highlighted nine symptoms of poor leadership that can cause crisis in the church. By turning our attention to Christ, who models perfectly the opposite of each of these symptoms, we will discover the antidote for the toxin of poor leadership. Jesus is first of all Lord and Savior. We are saved from our sins not by following his example but by trusting him in his death and resurrection as our Redeemer. Yet Lord and Savior are two sides of the same coin. We cannot say that Jesus is our Savior without believing that he is our Lord as well. If we say that he is Lord, that means that we are his servants.

As Lord, Jesus becomes our pattern for the Christian life—including church involvement. For leaders, he becomes the ultimate model of leadership. Jesus' life demonstrates the principles and character traits of a Christian leader. Not only did the Lord exhibit a righteous character, but he also led his flock, stood firm against his enemies, encouraged his followers, and turned bad situations into good ones.

JESUS, THE PERFECT LEADER

Jesus is the ideal leader who models nine characteristics of successful leadership. The following examples illustrate how Jesus is the positive rejoinder to every negative characteristic of poor leadership. When church leaders find themselves in a quandary and struggling with decisions, they are to refocus on Jesus, emulating his leadership and thereby avoiding the pitfalls of poor shepherding.

Making Tough Decisions

Leadership is not for sissies. It is about making tough decisions that will not please everyone. Jesus made hard decisions—ones that the members of the governing elite did not care for. In fact, as Jesus' popularity grew, they planned his demise. Knowing this, Jesus continued to make decisions that would mature his disciples and enhance the kingdom of God while at the same time causing criticism to surface from his detractors.

When a disciple asked for permission to bury his father, Jesus said, "Leave the dead to bury their own dead" (Matt. 8:22). Such a statement seems harsh, but it was instructive to all disciples. We cannot pick and choose the time of our surrender to his leading. If Jesus says, "Follow now," then we must drop all and follow him. In the instance of burying the dead, Jesus was teaching the cost of discipleship. Following him would not be easy, for followers must deny themselves and bear their crosses daily (Luke 9:23). If they do not love Jesus above father or mother or anyone else, then they are not worthy to be disciples (Luke 14:26–27). Disciples, like their Master, would have no place to call home, for they would be traveling the roads and preaching the gospel—good news for some, but an unsettling interruption for others.

Jesus was teaching his disciples that his followers would have to make tough decisions, such as leaving home and family. They would frequently have to choose between returning to the comforts of home or accompanying Jesus, which guaranteed discomfort and even pain. Leaders make the right decisions regardless of pressure to conform to the status quo and regardless of whether the outcome proves unfavorable to the majority.

Jesus also made decisions in the face of retribution. He made enemies when he said that his listeners were to do what the scribes and Pharisees instructed because they sat on the seat of Moses. His point was that, for all their orthodox belief, these religious leaders did not practice what they preached (see Matt. 23:2–4). In the face of a conspiracy to eliminate him, Jesus continued to warn the people of unrighteous leaders. Reprisals would come, but even though he knew this, it did not prevent Jesus from completing his mission of teaching truth and winning souls. At times, he would contradict the teaching of the Pharisees outright—especially on Sabbath issues. An official in the synagogue where Jesus healed a woman with a disabling spirit on the Sabbath rebuked him by reminding him that there were six days in which to work, but on the seventh, no work was to be done, which evidently included works of mercy. Jesus answered, "You hypocrites! Does not each of you on the Sabbath untie his ox or his donkey from the manger and lead it away to water it? And ought not this woman, a daughter of Abraham whom Satan bound for eighteen years, be loosed from this bond on the Sabbath day?" (Luke 13:15–16).

Jesus not only spoke of mercy, but he also preached repentance, a subject that the Pharisees did not want to hear. He denounced cities that did not repent, such as Bethsaida, Chorazin, and Capernaum (Matt. 11:20–24). These were unpopular indictments, for the ruling elite did not want to hear that they were imperfect, were teaching falsehood, and needed change. Jesus also warned the people of so-called prophets who appear as teachers of sheep but are actually ravenous wolves (Matt. 7:15). These deceptive teachers were members of the ruling class, causing their hatred of Jesus to grow even more.

The hardest decision that Christ made was probably choosing to go to Jerusalem, knowing that the Jewish leaders were plotting his death. Going to the cross was an emotional strain, for Christ asked that the cup of suffering be removed. Yet, having asked, he submitted to the Father's will and went to the cross anyway (Luke 22:42). Leaders in tune with their Savior will make the hard decisions because it is the right thing to do. They may suffer presently for their tough decisions but, in the long run, will be rewarded for their faithfulness.

A leader therefore must be clear in his decision-making. At times he must speak frankly about something although it may be unpleasant. A leader doesn't waver or bend like a reed in the wind, for such behavior causes confusion in his sheep. He therefore must be purpose driven in serving Christ by serving his sheep.

Promoting Unity

Jesus wasn't concerned about uniformity or conforming to the will of the Jewish leaders in order to preserve peace. He was about the business of unifying people under the kingdom of his Father. In his High Priestly Prayer, he asked the Father on behalf of all disciples, both present and future, to make them one, as he and the Father are one. He prayed for unity in order that the world may believe that the Father had sent him with the gospel of reconciliation. The oneness of Christians is a visible testimony of the love of the Father, which sets the tone for easier reception of the good news (see John 17:20–23).

In order for the gospel message to penetrate the world, those who carry the message must be of one heart and mind. Disciples are to give testimony of their union with Christ, and Jesus told them that their greatest witness to the world was going to be their love for one another. "By this all people will know that you are my disciples, if you have love for one another" (John 13:35). Love is a universal language that demonstrates mutual respect as well as care and compassion, which in turn attracts others to hear the message of Christ. Unity among followers of Christ is essential.

In like fashion, unity among church leaders is essential. If unified in Christ, then they will pursue peace and unity among themselves and within the congregation. Jesus and his message of reconciliation are the unifying forces of the kingdom. Peace with God, not peace in the world, is the most important message that leaders are to promote.

Crushing Idols

Jesus assailed idols, which was clearly demonstrated in his conversation with the rich young ruler (Luke 18:18–30). A young man had burst through the crowd, asking what he must do to inherit eternal life. His first words were, "Good Teacher." Jesus asked why he called him good, since only God is good. In other words, did the young man know that God was standing before him? Or was he approaching Jesus considering him as merely a rabbi, a good person, who had answers for questions about eternal life? Without waiting for an answer to his question, Jesus refreshed the man's memory about the second table of the law—man's duty to man. "Do not commit adultery, Do not murder, Do not steal, Do not bear false witness, Honor your father and mother" (Luke 18:20). Of course, the young heir said that he had done so from his youth.

Jesus then shifted to the first table of the law—man's duty to God—and tested the young man's idolatry quotient. "Sell all that you have and distribute to the poor, and you will have treasure in heaven; and come, follow me" (Luke 18:22). In other words, "You claim to uphold the commandments; let us see whether you keep the first one, which is loving God and having no idols in his place." The young ruler had inherited much and could not let his riches go. They were his idols; he preferred them to Jesus and therefore violated the first two commandments.

Good things can easily become idols if they take the place of God in our hearts. Money itself is not evil, but the love of it is (1 Tim. 6:10).

Jesus warned about covetousness and gave clear counsel that our lives do not consist in a plethora of possessions. Following this warning, he told the parable of the man who tore down his barns to build bigger ones in order to store more crops and to enjoy his retirement. Jesus called him a fool, for that very night his soul would be taken, leaving his abundance to others. The moral of the story was that laying up treasures for ourselves makes us poor toward God (see Luke 12:15–21). It allows greed to take preeminence, relegating Jesus to second, third, or fourth place in our lives. Leaders must recognize their idols, crush them, and follow Jesus without reservation. If Christ is our model of leadership, then we must remember that he is not just a good man, but is rather the God-man, who requires our devotion.

Taming the Tongue

To tame the tongue is to speak like Jesus. At times, we will speak with compassion and understanding; at other times, we will speak frankly and directly; at all times, we will not gossip or spread unfounded rumors. Jesus spoke truth in love; and leaders are to do the same. If we tell the truth, we won't worry about what we have said.

Jesus told us that we should be honest and forthright—letting our "yes" be "yes" and our "no" be "no" (Matt. 5:37). He wants leaders to tell the truth directly and succinctly—no lying, no fibs, and no half-truths. That is what he did, and that is what he expects of leaders. When he saw hypocrisy, he called it such. *Hypocrite* is a stage word from Greek drama. It means to play the part or put on a mask to misrepresent reality. Jesus is truth, and truth is reality; so Jesus would have no part in deceiving people. When Pharisees acted self-righteously, he pointed out their pretense and labeled them hypocrites (Matt. 6:1–6).

Jesus was also direct in his dealings with those who dishonored their parents. "For the sake of your tradition," he said to those accusing him of violating the laws of the Sabbath, "you refuse to help ailing parents by saying 'What you would have gained from me is given to God'" (see Matt. 15:3, 5). He called them hypocrites as well and said that they were the ones to whom Isaiah referred, who give lip service to God and who worship in vain, teaching as doctrines the commandments of men (Matt. 15:7–9).

Church leaders are to constantly examine themselves and make sure that they are not role-playing as elders, giving lip service to God. Christ will not tolerate hypocrisy in those who claim to have received a calling from him. His sheep are too important to have duplicitous elders watching over them. Leaders are to speak truth, not to spread rumors and innuendos, and they are to stop others from gossiping. In doing so, they emulate Christ, who is the Word of God (John 1:14).

Being Cloaked in Humility

Leaders are to be humble and to do nothing from selfish ambition or conceit, but should treat others as being more important than themselves and should place the interests of others above their own (Phil. 2:3–4). Their model, of course, is Christ, who "did not count equality with God a thing to be grasped, but emptied himself, by taking the form of a servant, being born in the likeness of men" (Phil. 2:6–7). If Jesus humbled himself to the point of death on a cross for the sake of ordinary people, then elders should put aside their own self-importance and become the self-effacing servants they are called to be.

Jesus was meek, which some take as weakness, a negative trait for a leader. Meekness, however, is quiet strength. It is power under control. In Matthew 11:29 (KJV), Jesus called himself "meek and lowly in heart."[1] Was the Savior a wimp? Certainly not! Was he easily managed and handled by the religious elite? Of course not! Meekness, therefore, must mean something more than a mild-mannered attitude or a quiet and unassuming personality.

A visual picture of meekness comes from horse racing. The thoroughbred that won a race was often said to be the meekest horse on the course. What did racing officials mean by this? When a racehorse was trained to become one with its rider, it was no longer unmanageable. Its strength was not lost; rather, it was harnessed and under control of the rider. The horse wasn't wild and unruly, but submissive and responsive to the touch of its master. The horse that won the race was the one that was most responsive. Meekness was power under control.

---

1. The Greek word for "meek" is *praus*, which is translated "gentle" in the ESV.

When Jesus said, "Blessed are the meek, for they shall inherit the earth" (Matt. 5:5), he was saying that those with inner strength—power under control of the Spirit—shall receive the kingdom. They are gentle, not weak; they are humble, not feeble. Good leaders are powerful because the Spirit of God controls them. They are called to a special office and are given the ability to lead the church because their authority and giftedness come from the Lord. Everything that they have was given to them, so boasting should not appear in their vocabulary or be seen in their demeanor (see 1 Cor. 4:7). A leader, therefore, should be clothed in humility as he walks in meekness.

Being an Instrument of Change

Fear of change is a symptom of poor leadership. Jesus himself is the greatest agent of change in all history. Since his appearance on earth, the world has seen the spread of good will toward humankind through the bettering of living conditions, the founding of hospitals, the care of the poor, the education of all people, and the elevation of women from being chattels to being coheirs of the kingdom.

The measurement of time itself was recalculated. Since the birth, death, and resurrection of Jesus, time has been measured as before and after Christ (BC and AD—*anno domini*, which means "in the year of our Lord"). Secularists may not like it and may attempt to gauge time as before and after the Common Era (BCE and CE), but they cannot get around the fact that a man named Jesus and his disciples turned the world upside down—a movement that is still active and growing some 2,000 years later. There is no disputing the fact that Jesus is the central figure in history and that there have been more books written about him than about any other major historical figure.

Before the advent of Christianity, many cultures practiced slavery, human sacrifice, and sexual degradation. The teaching and example of Jesus have motivated cultural change and inspired acts of compassion, generosity, and self-sacrifice that have brought benefit to people from every walk of life. Before William Carey journeyed to India with the message of the gospel, certain Hindu Brahmans and royal castes practiced *suttee*, a ritual in which a surviving widow chose to cremate herself on her husband's funeral pyre to prove her ultimate devotion. Dignity of life and promotion of liberty are Christian principles that have been adopted around the world. The positive impact of Jesus Christ cannot be overstated, for everything from education to human rights—things we cherish in our Western culture and blessings we take for granted—can be traced to the spiritual and social revolution inaugurated by Christ.

Jesus did not fear change; he caused it. His teaching astonished people, for he taught with authority and not as the scribes (Mark 1:22). Some scribes evidently made commentary on the Old Testament and entertained various views with a lack of conviction. Jesus communicated truth with love and grace. In his Sermon on the Mount, he said that he hadn't come to abolish the Law or the Prophets but to fulfill them (Matt. 5:17). Those who believed in him would understand that obedience comes as a response to grace, for those who love him would do as he commanded (John 14:15). Jesus changed how Scripture was taught, and the difference caused the powerful to hate him and the poor to love him.

As followers of Christ, Christians need not fear change, for God is actually in charge of it. God changed the world with the incarnation of Christ. It is through change that God's will is reasserted and his purposes redirected. It is through change that Christ's followers become more adaptive and more conformed to his image. Leaders will constantly be confronted with change. They cannot run from it, but are to face it and, if necessary, to lead their people through it, knowing that God is accomplishing his purpose in making them into increasingly faithful disciples.

Reconciling Relationships

Failure to be reconciled with people splits churches and widens the chasm of conflict. God the Father was about the business of reconciling the world to himself. He offered redemption to sinful and ostracized people through the death and resurrection of his Son, Jesus Christ. If Christ came to redeem reprobates and unite sinners to a Holy Father, then leaders in churches should be about the same business.

Jesus is the great Reconciler and is the model for all leaders in the church. He promoted forgiveness by encouraging his disciples to go to a brother and tell him his offense. If the brother disagreed with the rebuke, then he was to bring one or two others with him a second time to help his friend to see the error of his ways. If this did not bring the person to repentance, then the church was to bring discipline (Matt. 18:15–17). Reconciliation was not just about confronting the sin that caused fractures in relationships. Jesus also instructed people to heal relationships if they thought that a brother held something against them for whatever reason. They were to seek restoration prior to making an offering before the altar (Matt. 5:23–24). The emphasis was on the person who may have done something to offend or upset another. Since the offended person was not coming to him with his grievances, the Christian was to be proactive and to approach anyone who he thought had a complaint against him.

Leaders are to take the same approach. They should confront sin gently at first and commence church discipline only if a sinner is unrepentant. They are to go to others in the church who may have something against them and seek to heal any broken relationship. They are to encourage church members to do the same. Little jealousies can lead to bitter splits if leaders are not proactive in bringing peace and unity to their flock.

Jesus said that he did nothing on his own, but only that which conformed to the will of his Father (John 5:30). Leaders should not take matters into their own hands but should conform to the will of Christ, who is the Word of God. Since Christ came to redeem people for the sake of the Father, church leaders should have the mentality of resolving conflict redemptively and being peacemakers for the sake of Christ. The desire of those in leadership, therefore, should be to mirror Christ's desire for his church. And the desire of Jesus for his disciples is to be one, for that was his prayer to his heavenly Father.

> The glory that you have given me I have given to them, that they may be one even as we are one, I in them and you in me, that they may become perfectly one, so that the world may know that you sent me and loved them even as you loved me. (John 17:22–23)

Leaders are to be unified in shepherding the people and in ruling the church. When conflicts occur, they are to intervene quickly and try to bring harmony to the parties. The sheep need to see leaders together, building relationships and mediating differences in order to reconcile warring factions.

Being Involved with Sheep

One of the main problems with leaders, and especially pastors, is their academic exile. When leaders retreat to their studies and spend an inordinate length of time in sermon and lesson preparation, they become less involved with their sheep. Although most pastors claim to be relational, the truth of the matter is that many are task-oriented, especially when it comes to preparing sermons and/or Sunday school lessons. Preparation is imperative, but involvement with people is just as important.

Jesus both exudes truth and exemplifies the power of relationship, which is a wonderful model for pastors. Ministers are responsible for delivering truth, but in the context of relating to their congregants. Jesus poured his life into people and had an open-door policy for those who needed his attention. He took time to heal the woman with the discharge of blood while on his way to the home of Jairus, whose little girl was dying. Even though he was busy, and the crowds were pushing in from all sides, Jesus took a moment to meet a sufferer, talk to her, and heal her (Luke 8:40–48). Jesus operated out of compassion for the lost and hurting. In fact, he rebuked the Pharisees for putting heavy burdens upon people without first thinking of their well-being. He admonished the Jewish leaders for their Sabbath legalism by saying,

> I tell you, something greater than the temple is here. And if you had known what this means, "I desire mercy, and not sacrifice," you would not have condemned the guiltless. For the Son of Man is lord of the Sabbath. (Matt. 12:6–8)

Leaders are to be more concerned about the needs of people than about ritual adherence to rules and regulations, which add to people's burdens.

Preachers who exhort their congregants to holy living without balancing their teaching with grace will come across as unloving, legalistic, and out of touch with the culture. And pastors who spend more time behind their study doors than being out in the field with their sheep will be painted as pastors in ivory towers who are not relational and not faithful shepherds. Jesus is the Shepherd who proclaimed truth. Since he spent most of his time with the people, they related to him, listened to what he said, and, through grace, responded with righteous living.

Jesus traveled the country proclaiming God's truth. "When he saw the crowds, he had compassion for them, because they were harassed and helpless, like sheep without a shepherd" (Matt. 9:36). Additional shepherds were needed, and so he implored his disciples to pray for more laborers to enter the fields where the harvest of souls was plentiful (Matt. 9:37–38). The implication is that people who proclaim truth are to be where the people are. As laborers, pastors are to be in the field more than in the barn preparing sermons.

Manning Up

In England, a cross in the road in Oxford's Broad Street marks the site of the execution of Hugh Latimer and Nicolas Ridley. Queen Mary (known as "Bloody Mary") sought to reinstate the Roman Catholic faith in England, ending the teaching of Protestants. One of her first acts was to condemn the teaching of Latimer and Ridley, to arrest them, and to sentence them to death by burning. It is reputed that Latimer, to encourage the younger Ridley, whose death was slow because of green wood, said, "Be of good comfort, Mr. Ridley, and play the man: we shall this day light such a candle by God's grace in England, as I trust never shall be put out."[2]

The epitome of being a man is seen in the God-man, Jesus. If a leader is to "play the man," he is to imitate his Savior, the man above all men. Men are initiators of action, compassionate to the less fortunate, and courageous in the face of opposition. Jesus did not wait for the apostles

---

2. Quoted in John Foxe, *Foxe's Book of Martyrs: A Universal History of Christian Martyrdom; From the Birth of Our Blessed Saviour to the Latest Periods of Persecution*, vol. 2 (repr., Pittsburgh: John I. Kay & Co., 1831), xxviii.

to come to him. He went where they were, personally picking them as his disciples. While Peter, Andrew, James, and John were working in the fishing business, he approached them and said, "Follow me, and I will make you fishers of men" (Matt. 4:19). To Matthew, who was sitting in his tax office, he said, "Follow me" (see Matt. 9:9). To all his disciples, he said, "If anyone would come after me, let him deny himself and take up his cross and follow me" (Mark 8:34).

Jesus was proactive; he didn't wait for things to happen. Rather, he caused them to happen. He initiated new teaching about the kingdom of God and about his unity with the Father. When the Jews were about to stone him, he inquired, "I have shown you many good works from the Father; for which of them are you going to stone me?" The Jews replied that they were stoning him for blasphemy, for making himself God when he was a mere man (John 10:32–33). Jesus did not avoid those who sought to kill him. He continued to teach and to confront their unbelief.

Yet, as strong as he was, he had compassion on women, children, the lost, and sufferers. Out of his compassion, he healed many. To blind Bartimaeus, who cried for mercy, he asked what he should do for him. Bartimaeus replied, "Rabbi, let me recover my sight." And Jesus granted him his wish: "Go your way; your faith has made you well" (Mark 10:51–52). To the woman who had bleeding issues, he said, "Daughter, your faith has made you well; go in peace, and be healed of your disease" (Mark 5:34). Jesus had mercy even for the outcasts of society. When a leper implored him for healing, he was moved with pity, stretched out his hand, touched the leper, and made him clean again (Mark 1:40–41). He raised three people from the dead and gave them back to their families. He cried over the sinfulness of Jerusalem, the city that would have no peace and would be captured by foreign powers (see Luke 19:41–44).

Jesus as a man was courageous. He did not run from problems but faced them head-on. In the wilderness temptation, he didn't avoid Satan or cave to his feelings but parried every attack with the Word of God (Matt. 4:1–11; Luke 4:1–13). God's Word is a weapon of warfare that every leader must have in his arsenal. Jesus did not flee from those who wished his demise. Although he knew that the Jewish leaders wanted him dead, he continued to teach and to confront their misinterpretation of Scripture and their self-righteousness. He did so with understanding, at times such as when he told a scribe that he was near to the kingdom because he understood the two main commandments of loving God and loving people (Mark 12:28–34). At other times he confronted with firmness and directness, such as when he issued his seven woes to the Pharisees (Matt. 23:13–3). And, in reply to Caiaphas' question about his claim to be the Christ, with death staring at him, Jesus affirmed, "I am, and you will see the Son of Man seated at the right hand of Power, and coming with the clouds of heaven" (Mark 14:62).

A manly leader does not eschew tough situations but tackles them head-on. He calls upon his knowledge of Scripture to do the right thing and acts bravely because he has nothing to fear, for Christ is always with him. Fear, according to Rick Warren, "is a self-imposed prison that will keep you from becoming what God intends for you to be."[3] Leaders are intended to lead, for it is God's purpose for them to care for his sheep. A moment of dread and a tinge of panic, however, allow Christians to exercise courage and perseverance. The apostle Paul, after reminding us that we are heirs of Christ who walk in his Spirit, rhetorically stated, "If God is for us, who can be against us?" (Rom. 8:31). He then recited a litany of things that could never separate us from the love of Christ, including even death itself (Rom. 8:32–39). Leaders can be bold because they have nothing to lose, for Jesus has already secured the victory over death and everything else.

A leader's identity is in Christ. To be leaders, we have to know who we are and to whom we belong. Grasping this makes everything else trivial in comparison. A leader who understands his identity will "man up" in any situation and will do what Jesus has called him to do: love and protect his sheep.

LEADERS ARE FASHIONED BY GOD

God, who creates the personality of leaders, also raises them up to lead his church. There are various types of leaders, but they all have the

---

3. Rick Warren, *The Purpose Driven Life: What on Earth Am I Here For?* (Grand Rapids: Zondervan, 2012), 38.

same mission: to make disciples for Christ. When leaders are clear on this, they will not allow interruptions to occur that detract from this calling. Jesus knew where he had come from and where he was going (John 8:14). Leaders should therefore realize that they are called, with their special gifts, to serve the Lord and lead his people until they can no longer do so. In this sense, they too know where they came from and where they are going.

God has a purpose for a leader's life and ministry. If a leader does not know this, then he will not have the passion to serve the Lord's sheep. In fact, such a leader is not called to lead. Passion in a leader is a must, if people are to follow. A passionless leader is an oxymoron, for a man, if he truly loves Christ and is called to rule his church and shepherd his people, should exude energy and excitement to live for Christ.

All leaders are on earth for God's purpose, not their own. He knits each of us in our mother's womb, designing our personality and implanting the giftedness we will need to serve him and his people. This is the motivation that leaders should display. In other words, they live to please God, not themselves. Leaders will not satisfy everyone whom they serve, but they are to convince themselves that they live for an audience of one. They are to please the Father by glorifying his Son in all that they do, especially in shepherding his sheep. Opinions of others do not matter, for leaders answer to the judgment of God. Therefore, leaders are to be wary of those who cheer them and to pay little attention to those who jeer them.

Proper focus is on Christ and on Christ alone. When leaders collaborate on maintaining this vision and accomplishing the mission of making disciples, they will have followers ready to join them. And the gates of hell will not stand against men who are pushing against them with the gospel of Christ. The church needs wise and godly leadership. Without it the church will suffer, but with it there is no limit to what men and women, empowered by the Spirit of Christ, can accomplish.

Churchmen are encouraged to follow Christ more closely and to love him more deeply. May this book reinvigorate leaders to do the work that God has called them to do. Leadership is not for cowards, for it is hard work—but it is work that has untold blessings. As Christ loved us and gave himself for us—unbelievable as it seems—leaders are to lay down their lives for their sheep by selflessly serving them.

> Whatever you do, work heartily, as for the Lord and not for men, knowing that from the Lord you will receive the inheritance as your reward. You are serving the Lord Christ. (Col. 3:23–24)

Select Resources

BOOKS

Barthel, Tara Klena, and David V. Edling. *Redeeming Church Conflicts: Turning Crisis into Compassion and Care*. Grand Rapids: Baker, 2012.

Bridges, Jerry. *Trusting God: Even When Life Hurts*. Colorado Springs: NavPress, 1988.

Briner, Bob, and Ray Pritchard. *The Leadership Lessons of Jesus: A Timeless Model for Today's Leaders*. Nashville: Broadman & Holman, 2008.

Buck, Janie, and Mary Lou Davis. *Flight Path: A Biography of Frank Barker Jr*. Fearn, Ross-shire, UK: Christian Focus, 2004.

Burns, Bob, Tasha D. Chapman, and Donald C. Guthrie. *Resilient Ministry: What Pastors Told Us about Surviving and Thriving*. Downers Grove, IL: InterVarsity, 2013.

Eldredge, John. *Wild at Heart: Discovering the Secret of a Man's Soul*. Nashville: Thomas Nelson, 2001.

Grudem, Wayne. *Evangelical Feminism: A New Path to Liberalism?* Wheaton, IL: Crossway, 2006.

Laniak, Timothy S. *While Shepherds Watch Their Flocks: Rediscovering Biblical Leadership*. Matthews, NC: Shepherd Leader Publications, 2007.

Machen, J. Gresham. *Christianity and Liberalism*. Grand Rapids: Eerdmans, 1923. Reprinted 2001.

Poirier, Alfred. *The Peacemaking Pastor: A Biblical Guide to Resolving Church Conflict*. Grand Rapids: Baker, 2006.

Rainer, Thom S. *Surprising Insights from the Unchurched and Proven Ways to Reach Them*. Grand Rapids: Zondervan, 2001.

Rainer, Thom S., and Eric Geiger. *Simple Church: Returning to God's Process for Making Disciples*. Nashville: Broadman & Holman, 2006.

Reeder, Harry L, III. *From Embers to a Flame: How God Can Revitalize Your Church*. Phillipsburg, NJ: P&R Publishing, 2008.

———. *The Leadership Dynamic: A Biblical Model for Raising Effective Leaders*. Wheaton, IL: Crossway, 2008.

Sande, Ken. *The Peacemaker: A Biblical Guide to Resolving Personal Conflict*. 3rd edition. Grand Rapids: Baker, 2004.

———. *The Peacemaker Church Implementation Manual*. Billings, MT: Peacemaker Ministries, 2005.

Shelley, Marshall. *Well-Intentioned Dragons: Ministering to Problem People in the Church*. Minneapolis: Bethany House, 1994.

Spurgeon, C. H. *Cheque Book of the Bank of Faith; Daily Readings*. Fearn, Ross-shire, UK: Christian Focus Publications, 1996.

Stetzer, Ed. *Planting New Churches in a Postmodern Age*. Nashville: Broadman & Holman, 2003.

Tripp, Paul David. *Dangerous Calling: Confronting the Unique Challenges of Pastoral Ministry*. Wheaton, IL: Crossway, 2012.

———. *Instruments in the Redeemer's Hands: People in Need of Change Helping People in Need of Change*. Phillipsburg, NJ: P&R, 2002.

Walker, Williston. *John Calvin: The Organiser of Reformed Protestantism; 1509–1564*. New York: The Knickerbocker Press, 1906.

Witmer, Timothy Z. *The Shepherd Leader: Achieving Effective Shepherding in Your Church*. Phillipsburg, NJ: P&R, 2010.

ARTICLES AND WEBSITES

Ascol, Tom. "The High Calling of Women." *Tabletalk*, June 1, 2009. http://www.ligonier.org/learn/articles/high-calling-women/.

Calvin, John. *Commentary on Timothy, Titus, Philemon*. Available online at Christian Classics Ethereal Library. Last modified June 1, 2005. http://www.ccel.org/ccel/calvin/calcom43.iii.iv.iv.html.

Hadaway, C. Kirk. *FACTs on Growth*. Hartford: Hartford Institute for Religion Research, 2006. https://faithcommunitiestoday.org/sites/all/themes/factzen4/files/CongGrowth.pdf.

Keller, Tim. "Preacher-Onlys Aren't Good Preachers." *The Gospel Coalition Blog*. Oct. 19, 2009. http://blogs.thegospelcoalition.org/blogs/tgc/2009/10/19/preacher-onlys-arent-good-preachers/.

Krejcir, Richard J. "Statistics on Pastors: What Is Going on with the Pastors in America?" Into The Word. Last modified 2007. http://www.intothyword.org/apps/articles/?articleid=36562&columnid.

LaRue, John C. "Forced Exits: A Too-Common Ministry Hazard." *Your Church* (March/April 1996): 72.

Rosenthal, Shane. "The History of the Whitehorse Inn." White Horse Inn. http://www.whitehorseinn.org/resources/free-articles/253 -the-history-of-the-whitehorse-inn.

Ryken, Philip. "The Pastor-Scholar." *Tabletalk*, July 1, 2009. http://www.ligonier.org/learn/articles/pastor-scholar.

Sande, Ken. "Discover Relational Wisdom." Relational Wisdom 360. http://www.rw360.org/discover-rw.

Swindoll, Charles R. "Strengthening Your Grip on Attitudes, Part 1." Sermon, May 30, 2014. Available online at http://www.insight .org/broadcasts/player/?bid=1970.

Index of Scripture

Index of Names

Index of Subjects

Robert Stuart is pastor of shepherding and leadership at Twin Oaks Presbyterian Church in St. Louis, Missouri, and is president of Proclamation Ministries, Inc., which exists to promote the principles of the Protestant Reformation and to help churches revitalize their ministries. Bob served in the US Marine Corps, seeing combat action during the Vietnam War. His military leadership experience has been valuable in his ministry as a transitional pastor, through which he has helped churches to redeem conflict, rejuvenate ministries, and revitalize leadership.

A former lawyer and skeptic, Bob came to Christ through the witness of his wife, Deena. Married for more than forty-five years, Bob and Deena have three children and nine grandchildren. Bob is a graduate of Villanova University, The Marshall-Wythe School of Law at the College of William & Mary, and Princeton Theological Seminary. He holds the Doctor of Ministry degree from Reformed Theological Seminary in Jackson, Mississippi, and has been an adjunct professor at New Geneva Seminary in Colorado Springs, where he taught pastoral counseling and personality-based preaching. He truly believes that he, like any believer, is a "child of the living God" and a trophy of God's amazing grace.